Praise for the works (

'Rickards provides a wonderful antidote to some of the insanity too often evident around the study of monetary questions . . . A valuable contribution to our economic discourse' *Forbes*

'A bracing collection of salvos . . . Let's just hope that the next thirty years are less bleak than Mr Rickards expects' *Financial Times*

'The case for universal basic income, and similar ideas, is one of the best I have read: humane, lucid and relevant. Rickards has gone and done it again' *Wealth Briefing Asia*

'One of the scariest books I've read this year . . . Rickards's intelligent reasoning soon convinced me that we have more to fear than fear itself. The pieces, although disparate, fit together snugly, as in one of those mystery jigsaw puzzles that come with clues in lieu of cover art. The picture that emerges is dark yet comprehensive and satisfying' *Bloomberg Businessweek*

'An alarming but not alarmist book that deserves serious attention from economists and policy makers' *Kirkus Reviews*

ABOUT THE AUTHOR

James Rickards is the editor of *Strategic Intelligence*, a financial newsletter, and the *New York Times* bestselling author of *The New Great Depression* (2021), *Aftermath* (2019), *The Road to Ruin* (2016), *The New Case for Gold* (2016), *The Death of Money* (2014) and *Currency Wars* (2011). An investment advisor, lawyer, inventor and economist, Rickards has consulted for the US intelligence community, the Office of the Secretary of Defense and institutional investors. His work has been featured in the *Financial Times*, *The New York Times*, CNBC, Bloomberg, Fox and the *Wall Street Journal*. He lives in New Hampshire.

How Broken Supply Chains, Surging

Inflation and Political Instability

Will Sink the Global Economy

JAMES RICKARDS

BUSINESS

PENGUIN BUSINESS

UK | USA | Canada | Ireland | Australia
India | New Zealand | South Africa

Penguin Business is part of the Penguin Random House group of companies
whose addresses can be found at global.penguinrandomhouse.com.

First published in the United States of America by Portfolio Penguin,
an imprint of Penguin Random House LLC 2022
First published in Great Britain by Penguin Business 2022
001

Printed and bound in Great Britain by Clays Ltd, Elcograf S.p.A.

The authorized representative in the EEA is Penguin Random House Ireland,
Morrison Chambers, 32 Nassau Street, Dublin D02 YH68

A CIP catalogue record for this book is available from the British Library

ISBN: 978–0–241–58459–0

Follow us on LinkedIn: https://www.linkedin.com/company/penguin-connect/

www.greenpenguin.co.uk

FOR JAMES CLAUDE RICKARDS
A True Hero and an Inspiration

To anyone who has,
more will be given and he will grow rich;
from anyone who has not,
even what he has will be taken away.

—MATTHEW 13:12

CONTENTS

————

INTRODUCTION

———

Sometimes technology creates such a complex operation that people no longer understand the way the place works.

—REUBEN SLONE, J. PAUL DITTMANN,
JOHN T. MENTZER
The New Supply Chain Agenda (2010)[1]

There's nothing new about supply chains. They have been around as long as commerce, as long as civilization.

Off the southern coast of Turkey near a point called Uluburun lies a Bronze Age shipwreck discovered in 1982 by a sponge diver named Mehmed Çakir. Based on Çakir's descriptions of what he saw in the wreckage, including metal ingots "with ears" (recognized by experts as protrusions for ease of handling), Turkey's Museum of Nautical Archaeology in Bodrum began a series of inspections to ascertain the extent of the wreckage and the contents of the vessel. Excavation dives continued from 1984 to 1994. The vessel has been reliably dated to around 1300 BC, the Late Bronze Age. The underwater excavations have produced one of the most spectacular assemblages of Late Bronze Age artifacts ever to emerge from the Mediterranean.

Among the trade goods and works of art found in the vessel's cargo were 354 copper oxhide ingots, 121 oval copper ingots, and one ton of tin. Copper and tin were alloyed to make bronze. Other items included Canaanite jars likely made in what is present-day Israel, turquoise, lavender, and cobalt blue glass ingots, ebony from Africa, ivory tusks, tortoise shells, amber beads, gold, statues, medallions, and a scarab inscribed with the name of Nefertiti, queen of Egypt and wife of the Pharaoh Akhenaten.

The vessel also carried extensive foodstuffs, including almonds, figs, olives, and coriander. Weapons were found in the cargo. These included arrowheads, maces, daggers, axes, and four swords of varied types identified as Mycenaean, Canaanite, and possibly Italian. The vessel itself was made of Lebanese cedar.

The Uluburun vessel followed a Mediterranean trade route that relied on prevailing winds to proceed counterclockwise east along the African coast, north along the Levantine coast, and west along the coast of present-day Turkey, and into the Aegean and Ionian seas, calling at ports and palaces along the way. Apart from its sheer size and diversity, the most striking feature of the vessel's cargo is the variety of its origins and its destinations.

The scarab was bound for Egypt. The ebony and gold came from Africa. The amber came from the Baltic region. The jars likely came from the Levant. Some of the weapons came from Mycenae, present-day Greece. In effect, the Uluburun wreck was at the center of a complex supply chain stretching from modern Sudan to Sweden, and from Sicily to Syria, an area of over five million square miles. The vessel never sailed in the Baltic or the Red Sea. Goods from those regions would have had to make their way to Mediterranean ports such as Rhodes, Knossos, and Pylos, where merchants could consign them to the vessel for export or receive goods for delivery. Eventually the gold could make its way to the Baltic, and the amber would be delivered to ancient Memphis. The process was not as fast as Amazon Prime. Still, the goal of matching supply and demand was the same.

In the fourth century BC, Alexander the Great revolutionized warfare by truncating supply chains for his army. He insisted that his troops carry most of their weapons and food themselves, obviating long supply chains, carts, draft animals, and supporting personnel. This gave him unprecedented mobility, which enabled flanking maneuvers and the element of surprise. Alexander was undefeated in battle. Perhaps his tutor, Aristotle, was the real father of just-in-time inventory management.

Today's extended global supply chains (7,600 miles from Chongqing to New York) are also not new. The Silk Road, which prospered from ancient Rome to the Renaissance, ran from Chang'an (now Xi'an) to Constantinople, a distance of 4,250 miles as the crow flies. The actual overland route was longer, and as daunting as any logistics lane today. There were critical markets along the way in cities such as Samarkand and Kashgar. Goods such as silk, jade, precious stones, and spices were not carried by the same caravans from end to end. These could be off-loaded from one caravan to another in the market cities on the way. Such transfers were comparable to what's called cross-docking in today's transportation logistics. Walmart is credited with pioneering cross-docking in the retail sector in the late 1980s. Twelfth-century traders in Samarkand might dispute that claim.

Supply chains running from Egypt to Ireland, traversing the Mediterranean, were interrupted with the rise of Islam in the seventh and eighth centuries. Yet human ingenuity and a desire for trade are never completely defeated. Norsemen forged new logistics lanes that ran east through the Baltic Sea, then south along the Dnieper and Vistula rivers toward Constantinople. This route did an end run around Islamic barriers and accounts for the discovery of Roman coins in Viking graves and the rise of the blond, long-haired Varangian Guard who provided personal protection to Byzantine emperors.

The Islamic lock on Mediterranean trade was broken by the Crusades, beginning in the late eleventh century. This coincided with the rise of the Republic of Venice, which reached its peak of financial and seagoing power from the thirteenth through the seventeenth centuries. Venice and rival maritime powers in Genoa and Pisa reopened Mediterranean trade links with the Middle East that had been mostly closed for five hundred years. Today's landmark Galata Tower in Istanbul was erected by the Genoese in 1348 at the height of Italian-Byzantine commerce. Venetian trade links to the Levant were maintained even after the Holy Land Crusades ended in 1291, as Muslims and Christians found the maritime lanes too beneficial to abandon.

Supply chains have always been closely linked to military success or failure, as the example of Alexander the Great illustrates. Napoleon in Moscow and Hitler in Stalingrad suffered disastrous defeats in part because their supply chains were stretched thin. Eisenhower had success on D-Day in part because the Allies mastered the logistics and had food, water, fuel, and ammunition keeping pace with the invading troops. Chinese military threats today must be tempered by the reality that China has no oil or natural gas, and their maritime supply lines can easily be shut down.

The nineteenth-century Age of Empire mixed military and commercial motives to build some of the longest and most complex supply chains ever. Precious metals and other natural resources were extracted from Potosí to the Congo to supply manufacturing and support finance in Europe. The return trade included manufactured goods and heavy equipment used for railroads and other infrastructure. Empires were supported with military force and forms of servitude, hardly a model today. Yet they did create trade routes and supply chains on a scale never seen in world history.

The Age of Empire climaxed in the First Age of Globalization (1870–1914). There was relatively little major-power conflict from the end of the Franco-Prussian War (1870) to the outbreak of the First World War (1914). This zenith of empire coexisted with a zenith of world trade. John Maynard Keynes famously summarized the state of affairs in the summer of 1914 in his book *The Economic Consequences of the Peace* (1919):

> The inhabitant of London could order by telephone, sipping his morning tea in bed, the various products of the whole earth, in such quantity as he might see fit, and reasonably expect their early delivery upon his doorstep; he could at the same moment and by the same means adventure his wealth in the natural resources and new enterprises of any quarter of the world and share, without exertion or even trouble, in their prospective fruits and advantages; or he could decide to couple the security of his fortunes with the good faith of the townspeople of any substantial municipality in any continent that fancy or information might recommend. He could secure forthwith, if he wished it, cheap

and comfortable means of transit to any country or climate without passport or other formality, could despatch his servant to the neighboring office of a bank for such supply of precious metals as might seem convenient, and could then proceed abroad to foreign quarters, without knowledge of their religion, language, or customs, bearing coined wealth upon his person, and would consider himself greatly aggrieved and much surprised at the least interference. But, most important of all, he regarded this state of affairs as normal, certain, and permanent, except in the direction of further improvement.[2]

Foreign travel in a time of COVID is not as easy as Keynes described travel in 1914. Ease in global shopping would not be quite as convenient until the rise of Amazon in the late 1990s. In any case, the global system Keynes described came crashing down with the outbreak of the First World War.

Between 1917 and 1922, the Russian, German, Austro-Hungarian, and Ottoman empires all collapsed. The Qing Dynasty in China collapsed in 1911, although its power had waned decades earlier, under the influence of imperialism. What followed was a seventy-year period from the end of the First World War (1919) to the fall of the Berlin Wall (1989) in which world trade and global supply chains were never as extensive as those that existed in 1914.

International trade began a recovery in the 1920s, but hyperinflation in Germany, Austria, and later France combined with protracted postwar reparations difficulties to impede progress. Trade collapsed in the Great Depression of the 1930s and was disrupted again by the need for war matériel during the Second World War (1939–1945). The Bretton Woods institutions (1944) were intended to alleviate the exchange rate and reserve currency challenges of the 1920s, but progress was slow in the 1950s due to exchange controls and the costs of rebuilding industry in Germany and Japan. It was not until the U.S. Trade Expansion Act of 1962, and the Kennedy Round of the General Agreement on Tariffs and Trade (1964–1967), which cut most tariffs

on nonagricultural goods by 35 percent, that a new era of international trade expansion began. Still, the resulting trading system was
not truly global due to nonparticipation by Communist China, the
Soviet Union, and its satellites behind the Iron Curtain.

The Second Age of Globalization began with the fall of the Berlin
Wall in 1989. This was quickly followed by the collapse of the Soviet
Union in 1991 and the rise of China as a global trading power under
Deng Xiaoping. Deng's reforms began in 1979 but suffered a severe set-
back with the Tiananmen Square massacre in 1989. Deng got China's
modernization efforts back on track with his Southern Tour (1992), a
maxi-devaluation of the Chinese yuan (1994), and the reversion of
Hong Kong to China (1997). Deng died in 1997, yet his late efforts
were crowned in 2001 with China's admission to the World Trade
Organization (WTO), successor to the General Agreement on Tariffs
and Trade. Russia was belatedly admitted to the WTO in 2012.

While Russia and China were opening to trade, the West was con-
solidating its postwar progress. The formation of the European Union
(EU) in 1992, following the success of the European Economic Community (1957–1992), and the creation by the United States, Mexico,
and Canada of the North American Free Trade Agreement (NAFTA)
in 1994 were milestones in the formation of broad-based, low- or zero-
tariff trading zones. NAFTA was updated by the United States-Mexico-
Canada Agreement (USMCA), signed in 2019. The integration of Russia
and China with the EU and USMCA completed the global mosaic of
world trade. Global trade and global supply chains once again present
the scope and complexity of 1914, yet on a far larger scale.

If there's nothing new about global supply chains, why the frantic
headlines? Consumers read daily about supply chain breakdowns in
semiconductors, energy, and staples like meat, milk, and eggs. Consumers don't even have to read about it, they can see the breakdown
with their own eyes in bare supermarket shelves and queues for scarce
goods that were once stacked high. The breakdown is playing out on
a larger scale with cargo vessel traffic jams at the Port of Los Angeles

and a truck shortage that leaves containers there piled like pancakes even if they are off-loaded from the vessels.

Supply chains are not new, but the science of supply chain management is. Merchants have had to deal with uncertainty, adversity, and piracy for millennia. It is only with the rise of widespread and lightning-fast computing power, scanning, wireless communication, and sophisticated applied mathematics that merchants and manufacturers have had the tools to address the challenges of moving commodities and finished products from sources to consumers. The phrase "supply chain" was barely used before the 1980s. Today supply chain science is integral to every business process, from small retail operations to large-scale enterprise risk management. Supply chain management techniques are taught at universities, studied by experts, and made available for a fee by high-end consultants.

This applied science has led to stunning breakthroughs such as just-in-time inventory, intermodal transportation, overnight delivery, cross-docking, radio frequency identification (RFID), GPS tracking, and more. This has all been done with a single-minded focus on efficiency. Supply chain managers have ruthlessly squeezed costs and delays out of supply chains to lower costs to consumers and improve customer satisfaction. Still, this efficiency has come at a high and mostly hidden price. Eliminating redundancy reduces resilience. Stretching supply chains to reach cheap labor in China exponentially increases the risk of adverse outcomes on the way. Just-in-time inventory results in shutting down entire plants when deliveries are not just in time. Sole-supplier discounts can cause ruin when the sole supply is truncated by fire, flood, or earthquake.

These types of disruptions have been recognized and partly addressed by supply chain experts. What have not been recognized are the dynamics of complex systems. These dynamics produce emergent properties that cannot be inferred even with perfect knowledge of every factor in the system. When these properties do emerge, they quickly cascade into a succession of failures. Each system failure causes another failure in the chain. It's exactly the same process that causes an avalanche, a power grid collapse, or a tsunami. An uncontrolled cascade of failure is exactly what we see in global supply chains today.

One negative result of the global supply chain failure is inflation. Some linkages between supply chains and inflation are obvious. Mostly bare shelves should result in higher prices for what remains. Still, the inflation story is far more complicated. Beyond the supply chain disruptions, other contributing factors include money supply, asset bubbles, consumer expectations, the pandemic, and a once-in-a-century decoupling of the world's two largest economies—China and the United States. And in an ultimate irony, inflation may quickly lead to deflation as supply problems segue into lost sales, layoffs, and slow growth.

This book explores these dynamics and their complex interactions. Chapter 1 looks at the history of Supply Chain 1.0 (1989–2019), including definitions and developments in the science of supply chain management. We'll explain how the drive for efficiency has led to the frailty at the heart of the current breakdown. The supply chain failure is global and not limited to semiconductors and ships. Anything from champagne to cheesecake might be missing on the shelves. We'll look at the reasons for this. Blaming truck drivers and port operators is not good enough. Politics, the pandemic, and demographics all play a role.

In chapter 2 we'll do an even deeper dive into specific causes. Trump's trade war, robotics, green pseudoscience, real climate change caused by meridional currents, China's Zero COVID policy, vaccine mandates, and the mismatch between academic theory and real-world practice are all contributors to the supply chain breakdown. The greatest contributor to the breakdown is complexity itself. Any system that scales too far will collapse of its own weight. It's just a matter of time.

Chapter 3 introduces Supply Chain 2.0 (2020–). The prior supply chain is broken and will not return in its original form. Instead, a new supply chain paradigm will replace it. This will take ten years to build, so the current disruption will be with us for some time. The reasons Supply Chain 1.0 will not return include Chairman Xi's call for a new world order based in part on self-sufficiency in Chinese sourcing and production. The United States will support this great decoupling by onshoring production of critical goods such as pharmaceuticals, semiconductors, and electronics. The United States will also ban high-tech exports, curtail the theft of intellectual property, and outpace the Chinese in artificial intelligence (AI) and quantum computing. What's little understood by either China or the United States is that this reshuffling of the supply chain deck will result in cards scattered all over the floor due to wars, demographics, energy shortages, natural disasters, and self-inflicted fiascos such as the Glasgow Financial Alliance for Net Zero (GFANZ), an elite harebrained scheme to direct $130 trillion in assets toward the elimination of cheap, reliable oil, nuclear, and natural gas energy sources. Life will go on, supply chains will be rebuilt; they simply won't resemble the recent past.

In chapter 4 we cross the frontier from supply chains to finance and look at the current surge in inflation. The inflation is real and it's global. The question is, will it last? Short-term drivers include supply chain shortages, central bank policies, modern monetary theory, which calls for practically unlimited spending and money creation, government handouts, base effects, and asset bubbles. Still, inflation can carry the seeds of its own demise. When central banks try to control inflation, they more often crash markets and cause recessions, even depressions. Labor shortages are a statistical illusion; there are actually tens of millions of unemployed Americans not included in official unemployment numbers. This slack in the labor markets is another drag on potential price increases. We explore this anti-inflation narrative in chapter 5.

To say the world is changing fast is obvious—and an understatement. The challenge today is not the speed of change but the kind of change. When artificial or natural systems pass through what physicists call a phase transition, they do not emerge the same. Ice turns to water; water turns to vapor. Each consists of H_2O molecules, yet they are different in form, and in different states.

Supply Chain 1.0 is over. Supply Chain 2.0 has not fully emerged. Your shelves will be bare on and off for a while. The value of your money may be warped by inflation or deflation, yet greater changes are afoot. Our idea of money itself may disappear, to be replaced by a digitized simulacrum or resort to the real. This book will explore these changes in depth, look for clues to the future, and prepare you for what's next. We hope you'll find the book interesting, informative, and above all a trustworthy guide in turbulent times.

PART ONE

The Global Supply Chain

CHAPTER ONE

The Shelves Are Bare

———

One of the bedrock characteristics of disruptions is that they are almost never the result of a single failure. A large-scale disruption is usually the result of a confluence of several factors. . . . There are typically many signs that a disruption is about to take place.

—YOSSI SHEFFI
The Resilient Enterprise [1]

The Endless Supply Chain

Supply chains are not part of the economy. They are the economy. It's impossible to think of any commodity, process, or finished product that's not part of a supply chain. This precept applies to natural resources and human artifacts. It applies to objects and intangibles. It applies to goods and services. We are immersed in supply chains. The irony is that we scarcely see them.

The term "supply chain" is just a name we give to a nexus of logistics, inputs, processes, transportation, packaging, distribution, marketing, customer relations, vendor relations, and human capital that in the aggregate supports the supply and demand for every physical, digital, intellectual, or artistic artifact on the planet and in space. The supply chain is everywhere.

Supply chain management has come so far in recent decades and resulted in such efficiencies that consumers take good delivery for granted. Amazon and Walmart are leaders in the efficient delivery of high-quality, low-cost products, yet they are hardly alone. Supply chain efficiencies have trickled down to the boutique retail level, where a proprietor can go online and easily track a shipment of carved trays from Thailand arriving by container cargo on its way to a regional distribution center. When we enter her store, we expect the trays to be available. When we shop at Amazon we expect next-day delivery to our door. We don't think any of this is special. We take it for granted.

Behind the scenes from the retail buyer's perspective is not only a long, complex supply chain but an army of assembly-line workers, dockworkers, crews, drivers, warehouse managers, and other logistics experts working to keep the supply chain moving. Links in the supply chain do break, but professionals prepare for such events with backup suppliers, alternate trucking lines, safety stock (extra inventory kept in case of disruptions), and other techniques to keep goods on shelves. Most of this is invisible to consumers. That's why supply chains are not well understood.

Still, most consumers have only rudimentary notions of how supply chains work, and few understand how extensive, complex, and vulnerable they are. If you go to the store to buy a loaf of bread, you know the bread did not mystically appear on the shelf. It was delivered by a local bakery, put on the shelf by a clerk, then you purchased it, carried it home, and served it with dinner. That's a succinct description of a simple supply chain—from baker to store to home.

That description barely scratches the surface. What about the truck driver who delivered the bread from the bakery to the store? Where did the bakery get the flour, yeast, and water needed to make the bread? What about the ovens used to bake the bread? When the bread was baked it was put in clear or paper wrappers of some sort. Who made the wrappers? When we ask those questions, we move from a simple supply chain to what's called the extended supply chain. This concept includes the suppliers to the suppliers, all the way back to the source of agricultural and mineral commodities.

Even that description of an extended supply chain is somewhat simplified in terms of a complete chain. The flour used for baking came from wheat. That wheat was grown on a farm and harvested with heavy equipment. The farmer hired labor, used water and fertilizer, and sent the wheat for processing and packaging before it got to the bakery.

The manufacturer who built the baker's oven has his own supply chain of steel, tempered glass, semiconductors, electrical circuits, and other inputs needed to build ovens. The ovens are either handcrafted (engineered to order) or mass produced (made to stock) in a factory that may use either assembly lines or separate manufacturing cells to get the job done. The factory requires inputs of electricity, natural gas, heating and ventilation systems, and skilled labor to turn out the ovens.

The store that sells the bread is on the receiving end of numerous separate supply chains. It also requires electricity, natural gas, heating and ventilation systems, and skilled labor to keep the doors open and keep merchandise in stock. The store has loading docks, back rooms for inventory, forklifts, and conveyor belts to move merchandise from truck to shelf. In the case of big-box stores such as Home Depot or Walmart, the store is a warehouse. The point of big-box stores is to cram so much merchandise under one roof that the seller can eliminate actual warehouses and distribution centers, thereby lowering supply chain costs to deliver what Walmart calls "everyday low prices."

Every link in the extended supply chain requires transportation. The farmer relies on trucks or rail for deliveries of seeds, fertilizers, equipment, and other inputs. The oven manufacturer also relies on trucks or rail for deliveries of its inputs of oven components. The bakery and the store rely mainly on trucks for deliveries of their ingredients or foodstuffs, including finished loaves of bread. The consumer relies on her automobile to go to the store and return home, to solve what logistics experts call the last mile problem. These transportation modes have their own supply chains, involving truck drivers, train engineers, highways, railroads, rail spurs, and energy supplies to keep trains and vehicles moving and keep deliveries on time.

This entire network (farms, factories, bakeries, stores, trucks, railroads, and consumers) relies on energy to keep working. The energy can come from nuclear reactors, coal-fired or natural gas–fired power plants, or renewable sources such as solar modules and wind turbines fed into a grid of high-tension wires, substations, transformers, and local lines to reach the end user.

Everything described above sits somewhere in a complex supply chain needed to produce one loaf of bread. Now, take everything else in the grocery store (fruits, vegetables, meat, poultry, fish, canned goods, coffee, condiments, and so on) and imagine the supply chains needed for each one of those products. Then take all the other stores in any shopping center (home goods, clothing, pharmacy, hardware, restaurants, sporting goods) and imagine all the goods and services available from those vendors and the supply chains behind each and every product. This thought experiment is not an exaggeration. In fact, this description of an extended supply chain is a grossly simplified description of an actual supply chain. A full description of the loaf-of-bread supply chain would reach back further (where do the seeds for the wheat come from?) and branch off in tangential directions (where do the bread wrappers originate?). A full description of the loaf-of-bread supply chain would also include choice of vendor analysis, quality control tests, and bulk purchase discounts, among other decision-tree branches. A full description could easily stretch to several hundred pages. Supply chain management manuals in large corporations are that long.

Another way to understand the complexity and pervasiveness of supply chains is to put yourself at the center of your own personal supply chain. This approach was suggested by Massachusetts Institute of Technology scholar Yossi Sheffi in his book *The Resilient Enterprise*.[2] Sheffi's thought experiment goes something like this:

You wake up in the morning to the sound of an alarm clock. The clock may have been purchased at Walmart and made in China. You roll out of bed (rising from a Casper Wave mattress with individual layers made in Georgia, Belgium, Indiana, and Canada) and make some coffee (from Brazil or Costa Rica). You prepare a nice breakfast of eggs (trucked in from a local farm), toast (from a local bakery), and orange juice (moved in refrigerated railcars from Florida).

Once breakfast is done, you check your email and news (on a computer made in China and powered with processors made in Taiwan), then hop in your car (made in Tennessee by a Japanese-owned company) and do some shopping. You buy new fashions (made in Thailand and Vietnam), pick up your eyeglasses ready at the optometrist (with German lenses and Italian frames), and fill up your car with gas on the way home (with gasoline refined in Houston from oil pumped in Mexico, shipped to the refinery on tankers owned by Bermuda-based Frontline Ltd, and delivered by truck to your local gas station).

Your day goes on and so do your personal points of contact with global supply chains. You are surrounded by physical goods and services sourced from all over the world and delivered by truck, rail, or vessel to regional distribution and fulfillment centers and delivered to your local stores or to your door. You are the center of your own human supply chain.

Next we apply our extended supply chain analysis to your one-person supply chain. Your alarm clock made in China has parts from vendors all over the world (semiconductors, copper cords, plastic moldings, LED displays). Your morning coffee is made in a percolator or drip-style coffee maker manufactured from stainless steel, tempered glass, semiconductors, and other components supplied by vendors in Germany, Taiwan, and Mexico. The coffee beans were roasted abroad, packaged, and delivered by container cargo on vessels owned and operated by Maersk (Denmark), COSCO (China), or Hapag-Lloyd (Germany). The vessels themselves were built in South Korea. The automobile you take shopping relies on semiconductors from Taiwan Semiconductor Manufacturing Company (TSMC). The clothes you purchased were made from cotton grown in Egypt and fastened with buttons fabricated in Malaysia.

We can continue this analysis indefinitely. The plastic resins used in the Malaysian button factory came from a chemical firm in Germany. The fabric dyes were produced by Yamada Chemical Co. in Kyoto. That's the point. The supply chain really is endless because every output has one or more inputs, which have their own inputs all the way back to basic industries such as mining and steel. Of course, those industries have their own inputs of machinery and electricity. Making it all work is human capital, from technical expertise to manual labor. The supply chain never ends.

Scenes from a Supply Chain Debacle

A supply chain is not an object, it's a process. There's no one right way to build a supply chain—it's a matter of developing a process that meets the goals of low-cost operation and customer satisfaction. Those goals are not always complementary. At times you incur added costs in order to keep customers happy and to earn their trust and repeat business. At other times you may have to disappoint customer expectations about selection in order to achieve significant savings that satisfy a customer's desire for low prices. In those cases, sellers emphasize communications that steer expectations in the right direction. Dell Computer was widely praised for their handling of this technique. They offered limited bundles of laptop features, but they more than made up for this with quick delivery, reliability, and low prices. The customer may be at the end of the supply chain, yet they are still part of the supply chain and need to be managed like any other part.

Extended supply chains are not necessarily spread among numerous suppliers and logistics providers. In fact, one of the most extensive supply chains in history was confined to a single firm—the Ford Motor Company between 1927 and 1940. Even casual students of business history know that Henry Ford is credited with inventing assembly-line manufacturing. He took that innovation much further. Ford did not want to rely on outside suppliers if they could be avoided. He ran what is described as a vertically integrated company, beginning with the introduction of the mass-produced Model T in 1908. Ford's efforts culminated in the construction of the River Rouge Complex in Dearborn, Michigan, completed in 1928. River Rouge covered over two thousand acres and when opened was the largest industrial plant in the world.

Michael Hugos offers a succinct description of Ford's integrated production methods in his book *Essentials of Supply Chain Management*:

> In the first half of the 1900s, Ford Motor Company owned much of what it needed to feed its car factories. It owned and operated iron mines that extracted iron ore, steel mills that turned the ore into steel products, plants that made component car parts, and assembly plants that turned out finished cars. In addition, they owned farms where they grew flax to make into linen car tops and forests that they logged and sawmills where they cut the timber into lumber to make wooden car parts. Ford's famous River Rouge Plant was a monument to vertical integration—iron ore went in at one end, and cars came out at the other end. Henry Ford . . . boasted that his company could take in iron ore from the mine and put out a car 81 hours later.[3]

Of course, the vertical integration model is widely derided today. Modern supply chain managers pride themselves on outsourcing as much as possible and confining their direct processes to what are called core competencies. Still, as supply chains break down and Chinese decoupling gains momentum, the Ford model is a good reminder that complex supply chains do not necessarily require a legion of outsourced suppliers.

For an example of a twenty-first-century supply chain with far-flung suppliers, manufacturers, and distribution networks, we have this description of Whirlpool Corporation's supply chain from a consultation performed by experts Paul Dittmann and Reuben Slone:

Whirlpool made a diverse line of washers, dryers, refrigerators, dishwashers, and ovens, with manufacturing facilities in thirteen countries. It sold those appliances through big and small retailers and to construction companies and developers that build new homes. The logistics network . . . consisted of eight factory distribution centers, ten regional distribution centers, sixty local distribution centers, and nearly twenty thousand retail and contract customers. To top it off, there were several thousand SKUs. [An SKU is a stockkeeping unit, a distinct product identifiable by a scannable bar code].[4]

Of course, this description, as complicated as it sounds, can still be regarded as a simple supply chain. The extended supply chain includes sourcing for all the manufacturing inputs, as well as transportation logistics providers for deliveries from sources to manufacturers to distribution centers and finally to retail outlets.

As noted, the goals of supply chain management are to cut costs and provide customer satisfaction. These goals are usually combined under the heading of efficiency. If you can make your supply chain more efficient, savings will accrue and customer satisfaction will result from quick delivery of high-quality goods that meet expectations.

There are hundreds of ways to increase efficiency. Many of these are described in what follows. The greatest single driver of efficiency is accuracy in supply-and-demand forecasts. This sounds obvious. Don't all economic decisions boil down to supply and demand curves intersecting at a point that produces the greatest supply at the lowest price? In theory, that's true; in practice few goals are more difficult to achieve than accurate supply-and-demand forecasts.

If you know exactly what customer demand would be for particular fashions six months forward, you could organize your entire supply chain to hit that target. Orders would be placed with manufacturers for exactly the styles expected to be in demand in exactly the colors, sizes, and fabrics demanded. Transportation providers would be lined up at the factory loading docks to receive the products as they came off the production lines. Reservations for containers and passage on cargo vessels would be booked for dates that coincided with delivery by the source country trucks. Unloading in the U.S. port of entry would be conducted in a timely manner and more trucks would be waiting at the U.S. port to pick up the containers and deliver them to the distribution centers, before final distribution to retailers. The process would be seamless and highly efficient.

Conversely, if a fashion distributor knew exactly what could be supplied by factories in Asia, her supply chain could be tailored to maximize sales of those items most likely to be available. If men's hopsack-weave blazers would be more abundant than worsted-wool blazers, the distributor's marketing teams could encourage orders for the hopsack and promote sales of that particular weave. Again, the transportation logistics would be fine-tuned to move the men's blazers to retail just in time to satisfy demand generated by the preplanned promotions.

Reality bears no relationship to these ideal supply-and-demand forecasts. Supply can be highly volatile due to sourcing difficulties at the manufacturers, competing demand by other distributors, equipment failures, labor difficulties, power outages, and many other disruptions. Demand is unpredictable, especially in fashion, because tastes change, fads emerge almost overnight, and even unseasonably cold weather can cause a surge in demand for sweaters instead of short skirts.

The difficulty in predicting supply and demand is at the heart of every supply chain management technique aimed at both ends of the supply chain and all the steps in between. If a supplier might experience disruptions, you contract with two or three suppliers so you can shift orders as needed. If the Port of Los Angeles is backed up, you redirect your transportation logistics to the Port of Houston. If a trucking company experiences a strike, you can make deliveries by rail to distribution centers where different truckers can complete the journey to retail. If new fashion trends emerge, you slash prices and dump inventory on the outlets while rushing the new fashions to your premium locations by air freight. Fashionista demand will support the higher prices needed to cover increased shipping costs. The supply chain managers and their sales and distribution colleagues never rest.

Despite never-ending improvisation in the name of resilience, this is all business as usual. What global supply chains are experiencing today is not business as usual. The breakdown in the sourcing, manufacturing, and delivery of goods and services today goes far beyond anything seen in Supply Chain 1.0. Scarcity has arisen in ways not seen since the Second World War (due to rationing) or the Great Depression (due to business failures). Shelves in supermarkets and variety stores are partly stripped bare in ways never seen by most consumers in developed economies. Photos on social media and shoppers' first-hand impressions show stores that resemble those in the Third World or behind the Iron Curtain during the Cold War. When goods are available, prices are surging in a manner reminiscent of the late 1970s. This shuts many consumers out of the marketplace, not because goods aren't in stock, but because they can't afford them.

This current dysfunction in supply chains surpasses that experienced at the start of the pandemic. In 2020, stories were legion about the cleared-out paper-goods aisle at Costco. The stories were true. Shoppers hoarded toilet paper, napkins, and paper towels for reasons not entirely clear. Perhaps those were the items consumers most feared would run out. If true, then author Lionel Shriver proved highly prescient. Her 2016 novel, *The Mandibles*, portrays life following a financial collapse in the not-distant future. Her characters engage in extended discussion on just how the group gets along in a crowded house without toilet paper. Eventually the tissue issue is resolved, and responsibilities are assigned. It's unlikely most Costco shoppers read Shriver, yet her message seems to have gotten out.[5]

Notwithstanding bare paper-goods aisles, Costco and most other stores remained well stocked during the early stages of the pandemic. If stores were closed due to lockdowns, shoppers simply shifted their orders online. Amazon and Walmart were happy to oblige. Their stock prices and those of other lockdown stocks such as Netflix soared.

What you could not get in stores or theaters, could be dropped on your doorstep or streamed to your screen. Life went on.

Today is different. Most stores are open except in the more frightened quarters of New York, L.A., and Washington, D.C. The problem is that the shelves are partly bare. Online shopping does not offer the respite it did in 2020, because the online vendors from Amazon on down are encountering the same supply chain breakdown as their bricks-and-mortar peers.

Online shoppers still find friendly websites with attractive pictures of the merchandise they want. It's only when you place an order that you discover the store does not have your size, style, or color in stock. I recently tried to buy some jeans online from Brooks Brothers. I found the web page and item without difficulty, but the only waist size available was thirty inches. Sorry, my waist size is slightly larger. My online experience was no different from going to a store only to find empty shelves. If goods are stuck in containers floating off the coast of California, it doesn't matter whether you browse the aisle or go online—you're not getting those goods anytime soon.

We explain the technical reasons for the breakdown shortly, but another mode of explanation is with anecdotes. Academic economists dislike anecdote—basically storytelling—because it can be subjective and nonquantitative. The results do not fit neatly into their closed-form equations. That view is nonsense. The most complex economies are just the sum total of billions of decisions by billions of people acting individually or through agents. Every one of those decisions has a story behind it. Just getting away from your desk, going outside, traveling, and speaking with people you encounter on the way is a great way to hear the stories and understand what's happening. Here are a few of the many stories that explain the unprecedented supply chain breakdown:

As if to demonstrate that supply chain problems were not limited to semiconductors and critical drugs, the *New York Post* reported on December 18, 2021, that Christmas preparations were being hindered by a candy cane shortage. Store owner Mitchell Cohen, who runs Economy Candy, said, "We only received half of our candy cane order for the holiday season and sold out almost immediately. We currently have zero in stock."[6] While candy canes are hardly critical commodities, the reason for the shortage points to deeper problems. There have been both shortages in peppermint crops and COVID-related logistical failures. Sadly, the candy cane shortage fed into a shortage of gingerbread houses decorated with the red-and-white-striped confection.

Cream cheese is another popular food feeling the impact of supply chain disruptions. The cream cheese shortage is attributed to several factors, including a truck driver shortage, labor shortfalls in manufacturing, and increased use of cream cheese at home due to lockdowns and quarantines. As usual there are ripple effects from the initial shortage. Bagel consumption in New York was hurt by a lack of cream cheese schmears. The landmark Junior's Restaurant in Brooklyn had to pause production of its world-famous cheesecake due to the lack of cream cheese; Junior's cheesecake is made of 85 percent cream cheese.[7]

Supermarkets are scrambling to keep popular items in stock. Kellogg's reported difficulties keeping up with demand for its Pringles brand of chips. The Campbell Soup Company said it was struggling to fill orders for its Prego line of sauces. The popular Nutella brand of hazelnut cocoa spread was also in short supply on grocers' shelves. Supermarket managers described the process of keeping goods in stock as a game of Whack-a-Mole, with new shortages emerging faster than old shortages could be addressed.[8] The Nutella shortage is another example of how supply chain failures have deep roots. Nutella is made with hazelnuts. Turkey provides 70 percent of the world's hazelnut output. The currency crisis in Turkey made it almost impossible for hazelnut growers to obtain fertilizer, seeds, and other essential inputs. *The Wall Street Journal* reported, "The world is on the verge of a hazelnut shortage," in the words of Turgan Zülfikar, an expert on Turkish exports.[9] It may not be obvious why a currency crisis in Asia Minor leads to a sandwich-spread shortage in San Diego, but that's the nature of thinly stretched, complex supply chains. Disturbances in distant corners of the chain can have global ripple effects in unforeseen ways.

Revelers ringing in 2022 on New Year's Eve had to navigate a champagne shortage. Domestic sparkling wine was available in the United States, yet real champagne, including popular brands such as Veuve Clicquot and Taittinger, were hard to find in many locales.[10] The scarcity was not due entirely to a shortage of the wine itself. There were shortages of labels for the bottles, gift-box packaging, and even the wire cage that holds the cork intact on top of the bottle. The shortage is also an example of the inherent difficulties of forecasting supply and demand. Champagne consumption dropped 18 percent in 2020 compared to 2019, partly due to pandemic lockdowns. Champagne producers lowered the output cap in 2021 only to be caught off guard by surging demand. *Wine Enthusiast* magazine estimated the champagne shortage could last for years.[11] The magazine quoted Bindiya Vakil, a top supply chain expert, as follows:

> "It looks like supply chain issues will last into 2023," says Vakil. "Labor and raw material shortages, port bottlenecks and climate change are crucial components delaying the production and shipment of Champagne globally. Unfortunately, we're seeing that supply can't keep up with an increased demand for Champagne during the industry's busiest time of year."

Anecdotes are not limited to news reports and industry research. Often the best sources are those on the front lines. At dinner one evening in a local seafood restaurant, I asked our server if the restaurant was seeing supply chain problems in their operations. She said, "Yes, absolutely." I asked her to describe the problems, expecting her to name one or more food items that might be in short supply. She surprised me by saying, "We can't get the linens turned around. We're short on napkins and tablecloths all the time." I didn't explore the root of the linen delays, although labor shortages at the laundry or shortages in laundry truck driver capacity were likely explanations. The point is, you cannot turn in any direction without a direct encounter with shortages in goods and services.

Shortages are hardly confined to food and beverages. Hunters and marksmen are well familiar with an acute shortage of ammunition, including the popular 5.56mm round used in many AR-15 rifles, and popular handgun rounds such as the .357 Magnum and 10mm. These shortages are only partly due to production limitations. The main driver is a surge in demand in response to riots in U.S. cities in 2020 and sharply rising murder rates in major cities in 2021. These events lead to a spike in gun sales for self-defense. Guns are useless without ammunition, so the rise in gun purchases quickly translated into an equally steep rise in demand for ammunition. That the ammunition shortage arose due to unexpected demand rather than undersupply does not alter the fact that the supply chain failed to do its job. One consequence of the ammunition shortage is a steep increase in prices. Mark Olivia of the National Shooting Sports Foundation told reporter Matt Stoller that "5.56 ammunition for an AR-15 used to be about 33 cents a round. Now you're looking at closer to almost a dollar a round."[12] This also illustrates the tight linkages between supply chain failures and consumer inflation.

Supply chain problems extend beyond goods to include the delivery of services. I was recently in a discussion with a lawyer about some threatened litigation against a corporate consulting client domiciled in Delaware. Of course, litigation is much to be avoided, yet threats must be taken seriously. The threatening party was based in Switzerland and not necessarily conversant with the docket in Delaware. Counsel said, "If they sue, they're in for a rude awakening. The courts couldn't hear cases because of COVID, and the docket is backed up for years. They'll be lucky to get a trial before late 2023 if that's what they want." Even the legal supply chain is jammed.

Supply chain maestros Apple and Amazon reported challenges in their systems. On a quarterly earnings call on October 28, 2021, Apple said, "Supply chain disruptions are hindering iPhone and other product manufacturing and would bring increased challenges during the important holiday-shopping quarter," according to *The Wall Street Journal*. It was also reported that "Amazon posted lower than expected third-quarter sales as labor and supply chain challenges pushed costs up $2 billion and have made it harder to meet demand. The company has had to reroute products and has seen inconsistent staffing in some areas."[13] Regular Amazon users have no doubt noticed that firm overnight or two-day delivery guarantees have been replaced in some cases with uncertain delivery windows stretching over three to five days, beginning two days after the order is placed. Amazon deserves credit for being candid with customers, but the diminution in delivery deadline performance is telling.

The supply chain disruptions are not only showing up in U.S. stores and distributors. They're a global phenomenon. As part of a larger global energy shortage, Indonesia banned coal exports to China for the month of January 2022 in order to ensure domestic coal supplies during the winter. Indonesia is the top coal exporter to China, providing about 60 percent of all Chinese coal imports. China had previously cut off coal imports from Australia because of a trade war between the two nations caused by Australia's call for an independent investigation of the release of the SARS-CoV-2 virus (the cause of COVID) from China's laboratories in Wuhan. China will be able to manage the Indonesian ban and the Australian boycott by importing coal from other sources. Still, this scrambling of long-standing supply chain lanes and associated higher costs is another symptom of a global supply chain crack-up.

In December 2021, Azomures, the largest supplier of chemical fertilizers in Romania, said it would cut production in the face of higher energy costs.[14] Natural gas prices are soaring in Europe. Natural gas is one of the major inputs to nitrogen-based fertilizers. Other global fertilizer firms announced similar cutbacks including U.S.-based CF Industries, Lithuania's Achema, Norway's Yara, and the German chemical giant BASF. As the cutbacks persisted, fears grew that a fertilizer shortage for the spring planting season would adversely affect crop production in Europe, which could lead to food shortages late in 2023. Supply chain disruptions are never limited to immediate shortages but fan out into shortages in related industries and those further down the chain. This is another illustration of how shortages feed inflation and inflation expectations.

South Korea was another source of disturbance to global supply chains. On December 28, 2021, it was reported by Korea's *JoongAng Daily* that workers at CJ Logistics, a top South Korean supply chain management firm, went on strike over not receiving raises despite rising shipping costs that benefited their firm.[15] The lack of participation by CJ Logistics workers will disrupt import and export operations in South Korea. There was some chance that delivery drivers might join the strike also. Superficially a local labor dispute should not have global consequences, yet they do when supply chains are stretched super thin in the name of efficiency. Rubber bands can be stretched but eventually they do break.

On March 1, 2022, the merchant vessel *Felicity Ace* sank near the Azores as the result of a fire that began on February 17. *Felicity Ace* carried a cargo of 4,000 luxury vehicles including Porsche, Audi, Bentley, and Lamborghini models. No tears were shed for the wealthy buyers, but dealers and salespeople faced months of costly supply chain delays. On March 20, 2022, a labor dispute on The Canadian Pacific Railway involving pensions and higher pay added to the chaos as trains were halted due to a management lockout. The lockout lasted only a few days, but as with all complex systems, the effects lingered much longer. On April 4, 2022, the Maritime and Port Authority of Singapore announced it was investigating a case of thirty-four vessels receiving contaminated fuel of which fourteen vessels were severely damaged. The inspection and cleanup operations led to significant shipping delays. While these cases were manageable individually, it is precisely this accumulation of small triggers that leads to cascading collapses in densely connected systems.

Global interconnectedness was also highlighted in reports that Toyota would halt production at two of its Japanese factories due to an inability to obtain parts from Vietnamese suppliers. The Vietnamese parts manufacturers were in turn hurt by labor shortages, which were caused in part by the pandemic. The pandemic most likely started with a lethal virus that leaked from a Chinese laboratory. Eventually the Japanese car shortage due to the Vietnamese parts shortage due to the pandemic from the Chinese virus will show up in reduced supply and higher prices for Japanese car buyers. Supply chains are efficient when they work and devastating when they don't.

The impact of supply chain breakdowns is not limited to the suppliers and consumers in the supply chain itself. Bare shelves and delays affect consumer behavior more broadly. Hoarding is an obvious manifestation of this. If you encounter a bare shelf when looking for one of your favorite items in the grocery, say, Alfredo sauce, you'll be disappointed. On your next visit, you might find that Alfredo sauce is in stock even as other items are stocked out. If you normally buy one jar, you might buy three jars this time to create your own safety stock at home. You'll want to protect yourself against the item being out of stock on your next visit. That's sensible at an individual level. Yet it only takes four or five customers doing the same to deplete the item again. It's a self-fulfilling prophecy, because a future customer will find the same bare shelf sooner rather than later. This will prompt even more hoarding by more customers. Inventory that used to appear on the store shelf or in the back room is now stashed in kitchen cupboards all over town. This prompts more ordering by the store manager (and many other store managers), which just jams up the supply chain even more. There's no easy way out of this behavioral adaptation. It feeds on itself.

Another behavioral adaptation, called skimpflation, has emerged.[16] The idea is that service providers offer familiar service at consistent prices but skimp on amenities and extras in ways that amount to paying the same price for fewer goods and services. The providers skimp on service. It's like selling potato chips for the same price while reducing the package size from 12 ounces to 10 ounces. Reporter Helaine Olen describes the phenomenon:

Skimpflation is the hotel that no longer offers daily housekeeping, or the restaurant that subs a QR code for a paper menu. It's also the bank that doesn't employ enough phone operators, leaving you stuck on hold. Or it's the airline, such as American, that can't hire back workers fast enough post-covid slowdown, so a weather issue in a hub city throws the lives of thousands of people into chaos.

There are many other examples of what Olen describes. I recently stayed at a landmark hotel in New Orleans. I had to take a phone message and looked for the pen and pad set ubiquitous in better hotels. There wasn't one. I walked down to the lobby to buy a pen in the gift shop, and it was closed due to COVID. Finally, I went to the concierge in desperation to beg for a pen and she graciously offered one from her desk. I was grateful. Still, that's a lot of work for a pen that used to be free. When you get less service for the same price, that's inflation by another name.

The Biden administration claimed the supply chain crisis was over in late December 2021, as Christmas packages arrived on time. Presidential press secretary Jen Psaki crowed, "We've saved Christmas." Biden himself said, "Earlier this fall, we heard a lot of dire warnings about supply chain problems leading to a crisis around the holidays. So we acted . . . and the much-predicted crisis didn't occur. Packages are moving, gifts are being delivered, shelves are not empty."[17]

This was mostly nonsense. Shelves were empty. It's true that packages from UPS, FedEx, and Amazon Prime were mostly delivered on time. That's because Americans ordered early after hearing about the supply chain crunch in October. It's also because distributors could use up their safety stock to fulfill demand. That works once, but when the safety inventory is gone, any failure in the supply chain quickly becomes visible. It's also the case that on-time deliveries are self-selected, because if vendors show that goods are unavailable or unlikely to be delivered on time customers don't order them in the first place. If you order only what can be delivered, then it should come as no surprise when delivery is made. This ignores all the desired goods that were never ordered. Biden and Psaki misinterpreted the signals.[18]

As if to emphasize that supply chain shortages were getting worse, not better, one of the most acute and threatening conditions emerged in April 2022—a shortage of baby formula. More than a mere inconvenience, this was potentially damaging to the health of millions of infants and a source of anxiety to parents and caregivers. Baby formula is not generic. The numerous types are carefully formulated to provide nutrition to infants subject to allergies, adverse respiratory reactions, and other conditions caused by cow's milk and other substitutes. Breastfeeding was not an option for many and not ideal for some infants. The formula shortage was recognized by mothers as early as the fall of 2021; of course, government officials who caused the shortage were the last to know.

As with most government fiascos there were many points of failure. Abbott Laboratories provides about 42 percent of the U.S. supply of baby formula, including popular brands such as Similac and Alimentum, through a single facility in Sturgis, Michigan. The Food and Drug Administration (FDA) prompted the shutdown of the Abbott plant in February 2022 by issuing a warning letter connecting recent infant deaths to conditions at the Abbott plant. After extensive investigation, no linkage between the deaths and the plant was shown. Still, the supply chain damage was done. Other suppliers including Nestlé, Reckitt, and Perrigo were not able to make up the missing output.

This initial blunder by the FDA was amplified by the U.S. Department of Agriculture (USDA), which administers the Special Supplemental Nutrition Program for Women, Infants, and Children (WIC). The WIC program covers half the U.S. formula market and its rules require each state to have a sole supplier of formula. Mothers are prohibited from buying a different brand if the sole supplier's brand is sold out. Wealthier mothers who could afford it switched brands, but poorer mothers were put to the choice of not feeding their infants or buying formula they could not afford without WIC benefits. As with any shortage, hoarding arose. Soon, no one could find formula with or without benefits.

After a public outcry, President Biden invoked the Defense Production Act, a Cold War statute intended for national security, to commandeer civilian aircraft to fly needed ingredients from overseas despite the fact that there was no evidence of a shortage of ingredients. The bottlenecks were in the plants and the logistics lanes, not ingredient supplies. As with most things Biden, the Defense Production Act announcements were all for show and did nothing to solve the problem.

In a bizarre fillip to both supply chain breakdowns and food shortages, the United States was beset by a wave of fires and explosions at food processing plants around the country in early 2022. A Shearer's Foods potato chip processing plant in Hermiston, Oregon, suffered an explosion and fire on February 22, 2022. Company officials estimated it would take up to eighteen months to rebuild the facility. On April 13, 2022, a small plane crashed into the Gem State potato processing plant in Heyburn, Idaho. Also on April 13, the Taylor Farms food plant in Salinas, California, was disabled by a four-alarm fire. On April 21, another small plane crashed and exploded at a General Mills factory in Covington, Georgia. Other explosions and fires occurred at food processors in both San Antonio and El Paso, Texas. Over a dozen fires and explosions at food processors were reported in a one-month period from late March to late April. There was no evidence of conspiracy or intent in this wave of food plant accidents. Still, the coincidence was striking, and the detrimental impact on food supply chains was undeniable.

The Heart of the Matter

There are endless examples and anecdotes attesting to the extent of the supply chain crisis. Still, two sectors stand out as more critical than the rest because they affect so many other supply chains. These sectors are semiconductors and automobiles. We'll consider these in detail before reviewing supply chain diagnostics and a list of contributing causes of the global supply chain breakdown.

Semiconductors are miniaturized integrated circuits called chips, consisting of billions of transistors, capacitors, and resistors layered on silicon. Semiconductors are more than just inputs to other devices. They are the heart, brains, and lungs of most physical and digital systems we use. Computers and smartphones are the most obvious uses for semiconductors, but they barely scratch the surface of the totality of uses. Your washing machine, dryer, and dishwasher all have embedded chips that regulate temperatures, cycles, and timing. The same is true for your coffee maker, refrigerator, home alarm system, treadmill, and thermostat. Above all, your automobile will not operate without signals and sensors controlled with semiconductors. Industrial equipment and robotics are run by semiconductors. These applications and many more are lumped under the heading Internet of Things, or IoT. These devices don't only interact with you as you use them, they communicate with the manufacturers of the devices. That's why you routinely receive emails or texts asking if you need printer ink, an oil change, or a new water filter. The device already knows the answer and is prompting you to act. In a more sinister trend, these devices can talk to each other. A group of Alexa listening devices in a neighborhood can communicate with each other about what are deemed to be irregular goings-on. We're one short step away from Alexa calling the cops—or maybe the FBI.

Semiconductors are not just ubiquitous; they comprise a huge part of the global economy. Over 22 percent of global GDP consists of activities that are part of the digital economy enabled by semiconductors. Semiconductors are the fourth most-traded product in the world. Chips used in smartphones and computers embed design features, including central processing units and image-processing cores. Smartphones, personal computers, servers, and storage comprise 60 percent of the total market for semiconductor applications. That leaves 40 percent used in industrial electronics, consumer electronics, automotive, and wireless infrastructure applications. We live in smart homes and cook in smart kitchens. A typical car has over fourteen hundred semiconductors that process information on every system from seat-belt warning lights to RPMs. Your car is a computer on wheels. Semiconductors are like air—they're everywhere and you can't get by without them.

This means the global supply chain is coterminous with global semiconductor supply. Even soft goods like textiles and organic produce are made and transported with equipment using semiconductors. Unfortunately, the global semiconductor industry is highly concentrated at the source. Over 60 percent of global semiconductor manufacturing revenue in 2020 was attributable to one country—Taiwan. Over 54 percent of that global revenue was attributable to a single company—Taiwan Semiconductor Manufacturing Company. The only other country with a more than 10 percent share of global semiconductor manufacturing revenue is South Korea, at 18 percent; almost all of that share is attributable to Samsung. The importance of TSMC and Samsung is not limited to their market share, because they produce almost 100 percent of the most advanced chips (now 5 nanometers, soon to be 3 nanometers). Communist China is a relatively small player (about 5 percent of global output) and has almost no capacity in the most advanced chips. This type of highly concentrated sourcing for any manufacturing input is the opposite of what supply chain risk managers recommend. Diversity in sourcing provides resilience in the event of disruption. Heavy concentration is the reality.

A price is now being paid for this concentration in the form of supply chain bottlenecks. On October 28, 2021, *The Wall Street Journal* reported:[19]

> The global semiconductor shortage is worsening, with wait times lengthening, buyers hoarding products and the potential end looking less likely to materialize by next year. Demand didn't moderate as expected. Supply routes got clogged. Unpredictable production hiccups slammed factories already running at full capacity.
>
> What's left is widespread confusion for manufacturers and buyers alike. Some buyers trying to place new orders are getting delivery dates in 2024, said Ian Walker, operations director

at electronic-components distributor Princeps Electronics Ltd., which helps companies find chips.

"It really feels as if we are running out," Mr. Walker said.

There's more to this bottleneck than delays by semiconductor fabricators. The fabs themselves are encountering difficulties sourcing their own inputs, including substrates, a resin panel with thin copper wiring that connects chips to circuit boards, and even the silicon dioxide found in silica gravel needed to make pure silicon used in chips. It can take up to two years to build a new substrate factory. Delays in the substrate supply are expected to last until 2023 or later. Other delays were caused by bad weather and related energy shortages in Texas that caused fab shutdowns, and by pandemic-related fab closures in Malaysia. Even when the chips are made, they run into other supply chain bottlenecks affecting deliveries of all kinds, including global shipping delays. In these conditions, end users resort to overordering and hoarding, which makes the situation even worse. This is another example of the fact that it's rarely one event that causes a complex system breakdown: it's often a confluence of events—in this case inputs, weather, shipping, and the pandemic.

The impact of the semiconductor shortage appeared immediately as an automobile shortage. The pandemic caused an exodus from large cities like New York and Los Angeles to suburbs and rural areas. This caused a spike in demand for new cars, as those accustomed to mass transit or walking around urban centers took to the roads. Auto manufacturers such as GM and Ford could not keep up with demand for new cars because of the shortage of semiconductors, which are the brains of a twenty-first-century vehicle. Even the cars produced could not easily make their way to dealers because of short staffing on the railroads and a shortage of truck drivers to make deliveries. The dealers themselves could not fully service the customers because of lockdowns and absenteeism due to COVID. The supply chain was snarled from semiconductors to auto plants to transportation logistics to customer service. Once again, the supply chain distress fed directly into inflation as prices of used cars also skyrocketed. Those cars may have been used but at least you could buy one at a price. For those needing autos they were the only game in town.

These constraints are not easy to alleviate. Observers look at the trucker shortage and say, "Just hire more drivers!" Yet drivers are not eager to sign up for what many perceive to be dead-end jobs (partly due to the advent of robotics and driverless vehicles), and fleet operators are not eager to hire more drivers if it means laying them off in six months if the bottlenecks abate. Of course, that approach more or less guarantees the bottlenecks won't abate.

Reporter Peter S. Goodman describes what life is like these days for a truck driver at a dispatch center servicing the auto industry:[20]

Dave Pinegar has already been on the road for three hours, having driven here from his home in Wichita, Kan., nearly 200 miles to the southwest.

"The early bird gets the worm, man," he says.

He scrolls through the options. A run to Broken Arrow, Okla., would earn him $452, while a longer journey to Malvern, Ark., would bring $717. The longest route—a 641-mile trip to Batavia, Ohio—would pay $929, but would keep him away from his wife and two daughters for at least one night.

He selects a trip back to Wichita, which pays only $299. Absent any drama, he will be home by midday. Mr. Pinegar's cargo illustrates the complexities of the supply chain.

First, he will stop at a dealership in Emporia, Kan., dropping off three Chevy Trailblazer S.U.V.s built at a factory in South Korea. Then, he will continue to Wichita bearing two Chevy Malibus from the Fairfax plant, and a pair of Cadillacs—a CT5 sedan made in Lansing, Mich., and an Escalade S.U.V. produced near Fort Worth, Texas. Finally, there is a blue Chevy Silverado pickup truck built in Mexico. . . .

Sometimes, he confronts angry dealers, steaming over how long it has taken for the cars to arrive. But in recent months, as the chip shortage has turned cars into precious commodities, he is frequently greeted by applause, and even people videotaping him as he unloads.

"I feel like I'm Santa Claus," he says.

Out in the yard just after 6 a.m., as the first glimmers of light seep through a leaden sky, Mr. Pinegar begins driving his assigned vehicles up the ramp of his trailer like a circus trick. Then he rolls through the gates and disappears down the interstate.

If anything goes awry out there, the margin for error has shrunk.

The same dynamics playing out in semiconductors and trucking are appearing in textiles, aircraft maintenance, mining, and many other sectors. These supply chains have their individual bottlenecks, but they affect each other when one output is the input for another process, or one transportation link is the lane for diverse products. This interdependence is the essence of complex dynamic systems such as supply chains.

Why Can't We Fix the Supply Chain?

Since supply chain science has come so far, and the problems in the supply chain are identifiable, why can't they be fixed? If ports are backlogged, why not keep ports open longer? If there's a truck driver shortage, why not hire more drivers? If there's an energy shortage in certain locales, why not increase energy supplies with fracking and natural gas? The same simple logic can be applied to a long list of supply chain constraints. Problems won't be solved overnight, yet with persistence and patience the supply chain can be mended and sooner rather than later return to the relatively smooth operation it exhibited prior to 2019. Isn't it just a matter of allocating resources to known problems and giving the remediation process some time?

The answer is no. When complex dynamic systems break down,

they cannot be put back together. The collapse needs time to play out; the larger the scale of the system the longer this process takes. Once the collapse has led to a simplified state space, the system can be rebuilt along new lines. The collapse and rebuilding marks the phase transition from Supply Chain 1.0 (1989–2019) to Supply Chain 2.0 (2020–). The new supply chain will bear little resemblance to the one it replaces. The rebuilding process will take at least five years. The supply chain will be unreliable in the meantime. There is no alternative but autarchy.

In chapter 2 we'll explore supply chain science and examine the role of complexity in the current breakdown. In chapter 3 we'll look at the geopolitical and economic impediments to building a new supply chain, which will drive the rebuilding in new directions with different lanes. For the remainder of this chapter, we'll call the roll of reasons for the current breakdown. This list will make it evident why the current supply chain cannot be rebuilt and why the shortages consumers are experiencing will persist.

The most popular narrative is that goods are in short supply because container cargo vessels were backed up at the Port of Los Angeles and could not off-load their cargoes. The Port of Los Angeles is the largest port in the United States and one of the largest single supply chain bottlenecks in the world. The backlog in Los Angeles led easily to assumptions that the port operators were not working hard enough or that truck drivers were not getting the job done in terms of moving the containers off the docks once they were unloaded from the vessels. Whether you blamed the shippers or the truckers or both, it seemed the villains were easily identified. From there it was just a matter of ordering everyone to work longer and harder to break the logjam. Problem solved.

Other than some superficial burnish, this narrative is almost entirely false. Here's the real story. The cargo container vessels are backed up at the Ports of Los Angeles and Long Beach and other major maritime destinations. Still, the reason has nothing to do with how long the port is open each day or how many people are working to unload the vessels. It's simply a matter of capacity in both the unloading and the storage of containers. In November 2021, as the supply chain crisis was worsening, there were 540,000 shipping containers waiting to unload at the Port of Los Angeles. The daily unloading capacity is 18,000 containers. That's true no matter how long the port stays in operation each day. If no new containers arrived, it would take thirty days to unload the backlog. But containers were arriving at a tempo of 29,000 per day. This means that far from being reduced, the backlog was increasing by 11,000 containers per day. Absent some increase in the infrastructure of the port, a multiyear project if it was even possible, or a diminution in the number of new containers arriving—unlikely given overordering by those already suffering shortages—the simple math says the backlog will never be cleared. It's not a question of policy or hard work; it's just a question of capacity and math. The situation is nonsustainable. Shippers will stop directing vessels to the Port of Los Angeles or simply stop shipping entirely if they cannot unload in a timely way. Of course, redirecting container traffic to other ports such as Savannah or Houston simply moves the problem elsewhere and causes backlogs at those ports. The entire scenario of port delays and rerouting is aggravated by the aging of the global shipping fleet. New vessels take three to four years to build, including design time, so there will be no early relief for the breakdowns and retirements occurring among currently operating vessels.

There's more to the port backlog than mere delay. Leaving containers on vessels anchored offshore is extremely costly. The vessels themselves are effectively out of service until they can be unloaded. This imposes huge costs, called demurrage, on shippers and vessel operators. Goods onboard may be unwanted or go out of fashion due to delays. Who wants to buy Christmas gifts six months after Christmas? Also, goods in transit are a form of inventory for the importers. Every dollar of inventory is one less dollar in cash and imposes huge financing and opportunity costs on the importer. Both exporters and importers lose when goods are stuck in transit.

Experts estimate up to $90 billion in trade could be delayed each month. That figure only accounts for the gross value of goods delayed in transit. It does not account for inventory financing costs, impaired customer relations, lost jobs as parts of the supply chain go under-utilized due to delays in upstream parts, and the costs of spoilage, obsolescence, and receiving out-of-season deliveries. To suggest that the global economy could be looking at annual losses of $1 trillion or more due to the supply chain breakdown in major ports is not a stretch.

Still, the situation is worse than those numbers reveal. Even if new containers stopped arriving, the port could not unload the backlogged containers because there's no place to put them. Ports have large parking-lot-type spaces adjacent to the cranes that unload the containers. The containers are stacked in those lots awaiting trucks or trains to remove them. The containers can only be stacked six high for safety reasons. The lots are now stacked that high and densely arranged so the trucks and lifts can barely find and remove the containers as needed. The trucks are not arriving fast enough. When they do, they often have to wait outside the port facility gates for their turn to pick up their designated containers. Sometimes the wait stretches for days, and truckers give up and go home, and the shipper has to start the process over. Sometimes the trucks enter the facility only to find their intended cargo container is at the bottom of a six-stack, and it takes hours to remove the top five layers so the target cargo can be loaded on the truck.

To make matters worse, cargo thefts are spiking. Stacked-up containers, some with luxury goods and expensive high-end semiconductors, create an inviting opportunity for organized crime. Cargo thefts in California rose 42 percent in the third quarter of 2021 compared to the prior year. Stolen goods will never be delivered, except on the black market. In addition to container thefts, Los Angeles faces a wave of train robberies, in the form of freight trains that had either stopped on main lines or were on rail sidings being looted. The robberies began on a large scale in the fall of 2021 and continued to grow in early 2022. KTLA in Los Angeles reported: "Thousands of Amazon and UPS packages in transit to people across the country were recently found rifled through and abandoned on the side of the train tracks in Los Angeles. . . . Littering the side of the tracks were packages addressed to recipients from Seattle to Las Vegas and other places around the country."[21] No effort is being made to either clear the looting debris or complete disrupted deliveries. The rail lines are covered in trash. The proximate cause of looting is the abdication of law enforcement and prosecution duties in Los Angeles. Regardless of cause, it's one more nail in the coffin of efficient supply chains.

Before examining the trucking situation at the ports, it's important to look at the Biden administration's approach to the port backlog. What is the administration doing about port delays? They're making it worse.

The administration first ordered the Port of Los Angeles to stay open twenty-four hours per day and work three shifts to ease the backlog. As noted, working longer was never the problem. The port can't unload the vessels because there's no place to put the containers. The piers and storage yards are full. Containers are stacked to the sky. Working longer hours achieves nothing when there's no place to put the cargo.

The next administration move was even more misguided. They imposed a penalty on containers that remain on the docks for more than six days. But shippers were never dilatory. No one wants the containers moved faster than the shippers. Movement is a physical impossibility when trucks can't get to the containers. The World Shipping Council noted, "The fee is on the ocean carrier, but the control over when the cargo is to be picked up sits with the cargo recipient. Having the ocean carrier pay more does nothing to encourage the cargo interest to pick up the cargo." The penalty does not speed up the transportation process, but it does increase the cost of goods, which makes inflation worse and can drive some retailers out of business. A real supply chain crisis with unavoidable delays and added penalty costs is a bad combination for the economy.

The Biden administration's next move bordered on fraud. Secretary of Labor Marty Walsh and the executive director of the Port of

Los Angeles, Gene Seroka, held a press conference at the port on November 30, 2021. At that press conference, Walsh touted improved cooperation between unions and shippers at the port, and Seroka said, "Since we instituted a penalty for long-aging containers, the number of ships at anchor has decreased by more than forty percent over a four-week period." This led to a number of follow-on stories saying the supply chain crisis was over and delays would be resolved in time for Christmas.

The story was essentially false. The 40 percent decline cited by Seroka was based on a report by FreightWaves, a trade publication, that the logjam of ships had dropped from eighty-six to sixty-one between November 16 and November 23, 2021. That's a 30 percent decline. Other counts showed the numbers dropping from eighty-four vessels to forty-four vessels, a 47 percent decline. The percentages varied depending on the day you took the measurements.

The reality was that the backlog of vessels increased 27 percent. The number of vessels waiting to unload had grown from seventy-five ships on October 25, 2021 (the day penalties were announced) to ninety-six ships on November 29, 2021 (the day before the press conference). The discrepancy between the claimed backlog and the actual backlog was due to the fact that the reporting services had changed the definition of what it meant to be waiting to unload. The new definition reported by Walsh and Seroka was limited to the queue in what's called the Safety and Air Quality Area (SAQA), which extends 150 miles west of Los Angeles and 50 miles to the north and south.

To avoid fines, the vessels simply moved outside the SAQA. Using GPS and the Pacific Maritime Monitoring System (PacMMS), the Marine Exchange of Southern California determined that the total number of vessels in the queue for the Port of Los Angeles had actually increased to a then all-time record of ninety-six ships. The ships in the queue for Los Angeles simply moved down the coast to Mexico's Baja Peninsula or were even backed up in Taiwan and Japan waiting for the chance to deliver in Los Angeles. Some vessels were closer to L.A. yet waited farther out to sea, outside the SAQA. What had been a backlog in Los Angeles had now become a trans-Pacific traffic jam.

This turn of events is a lesson in the law of unintended consequences. Biden's regulatory solution only made things worse and spread out the problem. It's also a lesson in how complex supply chain logistics are. Glib headlines about an easing in the backlog of unloaded ships are not only wrong but give a false sense of accomplishment to government bureaucrats. Analysts of the situation need to rely on logistics experts and not government officials if they want to understand what's happening.

Independent of these port constraints, there is a shortage of trucks and truckers. Again, the reasons are complex and have to do with logistics rather than the willingness of truckers to show up and do their jobs. Intermodal transportation means that containers can be unloaded from ships and attached directly to a specially designed chassis to be pulled away by a truck. On arrival at a distribution center, the container is removed from the chassis and either stored in a warehouse or placed on another chassis for a final destination, an example of cross-docking.

Problems arose during the pandemic lockdowns when Americans splurged on goods available online rather than services such as travel, leisure, and restaurants. Imports of goods greatly exceeded exports, and warehouses became jammed. Trucks could not unload at the distribution centers and simply remained parked. The container on the chassis became a temporary warehouse on wheels. This meant chassis were not returned to the ports, and there weren't enough available to continue removing containers from the port parking lots. The backup then rippled across the supply chain to ships at sea and across the Pacific to loaded vessels in Yokohama and Shanghai that did not embark because there was nowhere to unload. The initial problem was not a shortage of trucks and drivers. It was a shortage of intermodal chassis.

As 2021 progressed, the supply chain crisis grew worse, and a shortage of truck drivers did emerge. There were several reasons for this.

The first was that the supply chain crisis meant longer hauls with more stops for drivers who were available. This made the work more dangerous and less attractive and caused many drivers just to sit out the crisis or retire early. The second problem was the pandemic. Drivers became infected by the coronavirus just like everyone else and had to take time off the job to quarantine and recover. Vaccine requirements and documentation made the truckers' task harder or even impossible at locations or firms where the jab was required. Crossing the border into Canada meant dealing with vaccine requirements that were even more strict.

So-called experts said the driver shortage could be resolved by recruiting younger drivers with attractive pay and benefit packages. It's true that driver pay has been skyrocketing (another contributor to inflation in goods prices). Yet younger people have more sense than the experts. For years, they've heard about the rise of robotics and the coming of self-driving vehicles. Elon Musk's Tesla Semi truck with autopilot is the avatar for this future. The Semi can be preordered now for a twenty-thousand-dollar reservation fee. What future does a young driver have in a world of self-driving trucks? The answer is none. The young drivers are not signing up. The older drivers are retiring. The prime-age drivers are burned out or recuperating from COVID. There is a serious shortage of drivers. This won't change soon.

The litany of other contributors to the supply chain fiasco is a long one. Pointless vaccine mandates have driven not only truckers but many other participants in the supply chain out of the workforce. The omicron variant of the SARS-CoV-2 virus proved the vaccines do not stop infection or spread of the virus (although there was ample proof of this before omicron; the medical evidence was simply squashed by the government and social media and ignored by legacy media). Still, ostracizing the unvaxxed became Washington's favorite sport, with serious damage to the ability of workers in warehouses, distribution centers, retail outlets, and transportation logistics to do their jobs or even keep their jobs. The sad irony of punishing the unvaxxed to the detriment of the supply chain is that many of the containers stuck offshore contain N95 masks, test kits, protective gear, and pharmaceuticals needed to fight the virus.

As if the impact of SARS-CoV-2 were not bad enough, outbreaks of two strains of avian flu, labeled H3N8 and H5N1, were reported in April 2022. The first known case of transmission to humans of the H3N8 strain was reported in Henan province, China, on April 5, and the first known case of H5N1 in humans was reported in Colorado on April 20. While the risk to humans is regarded as slight, the impact on poultry and eggs in the United States, Canada, and China was enormous. By May 9, 2022, the U.S. Department of Agriculture reported that over thirty-seven million poultry in thirty-four states had died from the bird flu. These losses contributed to the runaway inflation in the prices of poultry and eggs impacting the United States in 2022.

The weather hasn't helped. Winter in the southern hemisphere from July to September 2021 saw record cold spells and an unusually large snowfall that diminished coffee and soybean crops in Brazil and slowed economic activity from Australia to South Africa. This was followed by extreme cold in the northern hemisphere in January 2022, which trapped vessels in ice on the Northern Sea Route in Russia. Frozen seas are not unusual in Arctic waters, but the ice came earlier and thicker than usual and stranded over twenty vessels on the East Siberian Sea, including three ships carrying iron ore from Canada to China and two oil tankers.

Weather was also a problem in the northeast United States in January 2022, as extreme cold combined with labor shortages and high transportation costs contributed to bare shelves in East Coast supermarkets. Periodic snow and ice storms, such as the January 3, 2022, blizzard that paralyzed Virginia and disabled a fifty-mile stretch of Interstate 95, and a nor'easter two weeks later played havoc with supply chain logistics. The *New York Post* reported, "Grocery stores and other retailers face a 12 percent out-of-stock level on many household staples compared to 7–10 percent in regular times."[22] Bad weather is not unusual, yet when it comes on top of an already frail and failing supply chain it can have a multiplier effect that makes the delays worse and recoveries more difficult.

The labor shortage emerging in the United States and other developed economies is another headwind to efficient operation of supply chains. The best evidence is that there is no shortage of potential labor. There are over ten million prime-working-age Americans who are sitting outside the labor force, not technically counted as unemployed by the government (because they are not actively seeking work) but entirely capable of working. Yet there is an actual labor shortage considering that those not counted in the labor force show no signs of returning and those in the labor force are quitting jobs at historic rates. Some of this is attributable to government benefits that subsidize non-work, and some to weak revenues and low margins that prevent employers from paying a market-clearing wage. Pandemic illness and fear of contracting COVID have contributed to low labor-force participation also. This phenomenon predates the recent acute stage of supply chain disruption. Still, it is a major contributor to the current shortage in logistics and service workers such as restaurant servers, retail clerks, drivers, and hospital staff. It's one more example of a trend that does not trace to the supply chain breakdown but does exacerbate it.

Nothing occurs in the supply chain without energy inputs. Whether it consists of bunkers for cargo vessels, diesel for truckers, electricity for lights and conveyors in warehouses, or heat for retail outlets, the entire supply chain, from commodity sources to customer satisfaction, is bathed in energy from oil, natural gas, coal, wind, solar, or uranium. Each of these energy sources is the end product of its own supply chain of mines, reactors, power plants, and hydroelectric dams that are as vulnerable to disruption as the linkages that bring you fresh bread or milk.

An adverse barrage of energy policies from the Biden administration in 2021, including closing the Keystone XL Pipeline, bans on new oil and gas leasing on federal lands, limits on fracking, and other constraints, hindered oil and gas output and moved the United States from being a net exporter as it was during the Trump administration to a net importer position. Corporate do-gooders like Larry Fink of the gigantic BlackRock asset management firm cooperated in board-room coups at ExxonMobil and other firms that pushed those com-panies away from core competencies in oil and gas toward ephemera like wind turbines and solar, which are intermittent sources and have no capacity either to maintain baseloads on power grids or to scale as needed to keep up with rising global energy demand.

The combination of supply chain–induced energy shortages and shortsighted public policy meant that energy inputs needed to main-tain manufacturing and transportation were failing. This played out from closed factories in Manchuria to shuttered assembly lines in Mu-nich. A feedback loop in which less energy meant less manufacturing, and reduced transportation, which in turn hindered energy output, took hold. Available energy supplies were diverted to civilian popula-tions at the expense of industry. Supply chains suffered even more.

In an effort to bring more quantitative rigor to the flood of anec-dotal evidence about supply chain failure, the Federal Reserve Bank of New York announced the creation of the Global Supply Chain Pres-sure Index (GSCPI) on January 4, 2022. While the index is new, the data behind the index has been reported for decades so the creators were able to carry their calculations back to 1996 for comparison pur-poses. The GSCPI is measured in standard deviations from a long-term average value. In statistics, one standard deviation accounts for 68 percent of all events. Two standard deviations covers 95 percent. Three standard deviations covers 99.7 percent.

As might have been expected, the index was between –1 and +1 with few exceptions from 1996 to February 2020. None of the excep-tions exceeded –2 or +2 standard deviations. In December 2021, the GSCPI hit 4.45 standard deviations, an extreme measurement consis-tent with events that occur once every four hundred years. The index fell slightly until March 2022 before rising again in April partly due to COVID lockdowns in China and the spreading effects of the war in Ukraine. While useful, the GSPCI is far from comprehensive in terms of the factors it considers. Still, it does provide empirical evidence that the world is in uncharted waters when it comes to supply chain dysfunction.

The supply chain breakdown is well under way. It's unclear if it can be arrested quickly or at all. Consumers should expect worse effects in the months ahead. How much worse remains to be seen.

This completes our overview of what's happening in the global supply chain. In chapter 2 we look behind the scenes to understand why.

CHAPTER TWO

Who Broke
the Supply Chain?

---

*Supply chains are becoming noticeably more complex than
they previously were. Companies now deal with multiple tiers
of suppliers, outsourced service providers, and distribution-
channel partners. This complexity has evolved in response to
changes in the way products are sold, increased customer service expectations, and the need to respond quickly to new
market demands.*

—MICHAEL HUGOS
Essentials of Supply Chain Management (2018)[1]

Prelude to a Meltdown

The best description of how complex systems break down was written
by Ernest Hemingway in *The Sun Also Rises*, when war veteran Bill
Campbell asks the constantly drunk Mike Campbell how he went
bankrupt. Mike replies, "Two ways. Gradually, then suddenly." Supply chains break down the same way; gradually at first, climaxed by a
sudden catastrophic collapse.

We see the sudden phase now, although it has room to play out.
We're at the midpoint of Hemingway's description, dangerously close
to events that could rival the oil embargo of the 1970s or the collapse of world trade in the 1930s in their global impact. Before we consider the scope of this sudden phase, it's instructive to go back to the

gradual stage. The supply chain crisis was impossible to ignore in late 2021; bare shelves told consumers all they needed to know. Still, it didn't start then. We can be highly specific on the date. The supply chain breakdown began on January 23, 2017. That was Donald Trump's third day in office as president. He signed an executive order that day officially withdrawing the United States from the Trans-Pacific Partnership multilateral trade agreement. The trade wars had begun. The supply chain would become its biggest victim. Of course, this action should have come as no surprise. Trump had criticized numerous trade deals, including the Trans-Pacific Partnership (TPP), for years during his candidacy and threatened to renegotiate or tear up most of them. Now he was president, and the threats were put into action.

From there, the trade war tempo picked up considerably. On March 1, 2017, Robert Lighthizer, the U.S. trade representative, revealed the 2017 Trade Policy Agenda for the Trump administration. This included protecting national security, protecting intellectual property rights, expanding exports, and enforcing existing laws and treaties. This policy platform led to formal reviews as a prelude to specific trade-related actions to come. On January 22, 2018, just one year after his inauguration, Trump imposed tariffs of 30 percent to 50 percent on washing machines and solar panels. These tariffs applied to all imports of those items regardless of source, but it was clearly aimed at China, which was the major exporter of both items to the United States. Trump relied on Section 301 of the Trade Act of 1974, which permits trade sanctions on trading partners who engage in unjustifiable or unreasonable practices that burden U.S. commerce. This was quickly followed by 25 percent tariffs on steel and 10 percent tariffs on aluminum imports into the United States, which were imposed on March 1, 2018, under Section 232 of the Trade Expansion Act of 1962, which allows tariffs designed to protect national security. On March 22, 2018, Trump used Section 301 to impose tariffs on $50 billion of Chinese imports in retaliation for theft of U.S. intellectual property. The Dow Jones Industrial Average fell 724 points in response. By using both Section 301 and Section 232, Trump showed he was willing to use the entire arsenal of statutory tools to defend U.S. commercial and geopolitical interests.

The global reaction was swift. On April 2, 2018, China implemented a 15 percent tariff on 120 U.S. products, including fruit, wine, and pork. On April 9, 2018, the Chinese filed a complaint against the United States in the World Trade Organization concerning the steel and aluminum tariffs. The EU followed suit on June 1, 2018. Canada joined in the retaliation by imposing tariffs on U.S. exports including whisky, yogurt, and sleeping bags on July 1, 2018. On August 1, 2019, Trump imposed a 10 percent tariff on an additional $300 billion of Chinese goods not covered by prior tariffs. The Chinese imposed further retaliatory tariffs on U.S. exports on August 23, 2019. Trump shot back by increasing the rates from 25 percent to 30 percent on $250 billion of previously taxed Chinese goods. Trump tweeted, "We don't need China and, frankly, would be far better off without them." The Dow Jones Industrial Average fell about 600 points that day. The trade war escalated further from there.

The next several years were marked by tariffs, retaliation, exemptions, selective relief, and heated rhetoric as the trade accusations and trade restrictions went back and forth. In the end, many of the tariffs were rescinded or reduced, while certain trading partners received exemptions. Significant tariffs remain in place, though, especially those affecting trade between the United States and China. For all of Joe Biden's criticism of Trump, the Biden administration has not rolled back most of the Trump tariffs. Trump did achieve important new trade deals as a result of his hard-line policies, including the revision of NAFTA called the United States-Mexico-Canada Agreement and a bilateral treaty with South Korea, the United States-Korea Free Trade Agreement (KORUS FTA). On February 14, 2020, the United States and China reached the Economic and Trade Agreement Between the Government of the United States of America and the Government of the People's Republic of China: Phase One. The Phase One deal was more of an armistice than a peace treaty. China agreed to increase purchases of certain U.S. exports. In exchange, the United States stopped the escalation of tariffs on Chinese goods. Following the Phase One deal, the world became consumed with the pandemic caused by the Wuhan virus (SARS-CoV-2), and there was little additional action on the trade-war front. For the time being, the shooting stopped, but the war was not over.

As the trade war progressed from 2018 to 2020, global supply chains became scrambled. Many of the tariffs imposed had notice periods or comment periods by statute or treaty provision that delayed their effect for thirty to ninety days after they were announced. This gave importers time to flood the lanes with particular items before the tariffs applied. They did. This was the beginning of the supply chain fiasco that's now visible to all.

This phenomenon was tracked by maritime cargo expert Lori Ann LaRocco in her book, *Trade War: Containers Don't Lie, Navigating the Bluster.*[2] LaRocco's main insight is that politicians and the media might bloviate about the pros and cons of trade wars, but real shipping data by cargo, destination, and date could be used to track what importers and exporters were actually doing, despite political claims. LaRocco shows an excellent command of this data and combines it with interviews of shippers, industry experts, and port officials. The analytic benefit of LaRocco's book is that it was written before the pandemic. That's important because it's too easy to blame the supply chain breakdown on the impact of COVID. Certainly, the virus played a role in how systems have broken down since 2020, but it's far from the only reason. LaRocco's analysis is like a controlled experiment in how supply chains were performing independently of the pandemic. The answer is: not well. The roots of the crisis go back to 2017 and have only gotten worse since.

Some commodities traders could see the sanctions coming and began to stockpile metals, such as aluminum, as early as 2016. The aluminum hoard held by megatrader Castleton Commodities International near New Orleans was so large it could be seen from space. Some cargo vessels diverted from Gulf ports such as Houston to ports in New England to beat the deadline on tariffs. Other vessels with aluminum arrived in Los Angeles from Australia, since Australia was exempted from the first round of aluminum tariffs. Canada canceled shipments from aluminum smelters in Quebec to the United States due to tariffs and began shipping their products to Europe. This tariff-related improvisation on the part of importers and exporters not only affected port capacity due to changed destinations, it also jammed up trucking capacity and warehouse space as importers stockpiled goods ahead of tariffs. Increased inventory levels also increased costs to buyers, but those costs were still less than the tariffs. The backlogs and price increases that came into full view in 2021 had begun.

The biggest impact of the trade war was in the agricultural sector, especially on soybeans. Prior to 2018 the United States was the world's biggest soybean producer; China was the world's biggest buyer, and Brazil was the world's biggest exporter. China's trump card in the trade wars was to cancel new purchases of soybeans from the United States and shift their buying to Brazil. American soybean exports to China dropped by 50 percent in 2018 compared to 2017. Brazilian soybean exports to China increased by 15 percent in the first eight months of 2018 compared to the year before. When the source of soybeans shifts on this scale, the selected maritime carriers, ports of embarkation, and destinations shift also. Established supply chain operators were playing poker, and it seemed every card was a joker. China quickly extended its ban on U.S. agricultural imports to include dairy, pork, and feed grains. Other U.S. exports smacked with tariffs included lentils, chickpeas, cherries, and even lobsters. American producers who lost sales to China scrambled to find new customers in countries such as the Netherlands, France, Vietnam, Spain, and Taiwan. These efforts were successful, albeit at distressed prices. Importantly, once old trading relationships are destroyed and new ones established, the import/export traffic does not easily revert to the prior patterns if trade disputes are resolved. Market participants prefer long-term relationships whenever possible, which means the new patterns will persist indefinitely. Again, our primary focus on the trade wars is not as much about the costs of tariffs and lost sales (although that is enormous) as it is on the stress placed on supply chain logistics. That legacy is still with us and growing more tangled by the day. LaRocco reports the following conversation with Gene Seroka, of the Port of Los Angeles, on the topic of increasing shipments to beat tariff deadlines called front-loading:

> On an average day before the trade war began, the Port of Los Angeles processed 10 vessels; the Port of Long Beach processed eight. "For argument's sake, the front-loading increased that number of vessels to 14 and 10," said Seroka. "We also worked through the largest exchange value ever. Each ship got bigger. We were doing more boxes on and off. The average time those ships were in port depended on their size, and they were there anywhere between three and five days." A normal stay for a vessel before the trade war was two to three days. . . .
>
> "There was so much cargo coming in," Seroka continued. "Although we did a good job working on the water side, you started to see longer dwell times at the terminal because of the longer truck wait times, and then longer street dwell times because those containers were on chassis not being moved. Truck chassis became mini-warehouses." . . . Containers were stored on truck chassis because there was a lack of space at area warehouses as a result of the dramatic increase in containers.[3]

All the elements of the 2021 supply chain crisis—increased vessels, more cargo, longer unloading times, truck delays, and shortages of chassis—are contained in this 2019 interview. This makes it clear that the supply chain breakdown began in 2018 as a result of the trade war and was independent of COVID. It's also a good example of the fact that crises seldom emerge full blown but are preceded by warning signs that mostly go ignored. As Hemingway wrote, crises emerge "gradually, then suddenly."

The Quest for Efficiency

While the 2018 trade war is the proximate cause of today's supply chain crisis, the roots go back even further to the rise of supply chain science in the 1990s. The study of supply chains may involve dozens of critical nodes involving hundreds of suppliers, transporters, and distributors, and thousands of separate components in each product, but the entire effort comes down to one metric—efficiency. The word "efficiency" is synonymous with cost in this context. If you can make a process more efficient, it will cost less, which means you can charge lower prices to customers or increase profit margins or both. This goal of efficiency has driven the supply chain management process for over thirty years.

If you have five suppliers in China and you reduce that number to three by scoring each supplier on quality and reliability, the result can be more efficient in terms of purchase orders and supply forecasting. If you have seven maritime cargo lines and you reduce those shippers to four, the result can be more efficient in terms of price concessions in exchange for greater volumes and more long-term commitments. If your imports were entering through three ports and you reduce the number of receiving ports to two, that can be more efficient in terms of directing your trucking providers to fewer pickup points. Efficiencies can also be achieved by reducing the number of trucking firms you use and concentrating deliveries so you have full truckload (FTL) instead of more expensive less-than-truckload (LTL) shipments. Electronic load boards (a digital system for matching shippers and truckers through a reverse auction) also create efficiencies in terms of faster pickups and lower prices. Shippers also use sophisticated warehouse management systems (WMS) to monitor load tracking and cross-docking and to facilitate picking of items in a warehouse when distribution is needed. These systems and many more are designed to allow supply chains to function smoothly even when breakdowns occur.

Take the simple example of the loaf of bread in the bakery section of your grocery store discussed in chapter 1. What could cause the bread supply chain to fail? The list of discrete points of failure is long. The farm producing the wheat might suffer a drought or lose its water allocation, causing the wheat crop to be delayed or to fail entirely. There might be a shortage of truckers to make timely deliveries to the wheat processor, the oven factory, or the bakery. The baker might suffer labor shortages. Unionized workers in the grocery store might go on strike, causing trucks to be backed up on the loading dock or shelves to remain unstocked. The power grid might fail, stopping all the processes in the chain at once. Baked bread might go stale before it can be delivered. The consumer might fear going outside because of the pandemic, leaving bread piled up on the shelves. Or all of the above. This list of potential breakdowns and bottlenecks is simplified compared to actual extended supply chains. The point is to illustrate how complex supply chains really are and how vulnerable they are to breakdowns.

These supply chain links and bottleneck examples are purely domestic. We've described local farms, factories, bakeries, and stores. Consider that very few supply chains are entirely local. CEOs, logistics engineers, consultants, and politicians have spent the past thirty years stretching supply chains into global systems. We've heard discussion of globalization since the early 1990s. What one may not have realized until now is that the process being globalized was the supply chain.

You know your iPhone comes from China. Did you know that the specialized glass used in the iPhone comes from South Korea? Did you know that the semiconductors in the iPhone come from Taiwan? That the intellectual property and design of the iPhone is from California? The iPhone includes flash storage from Japan, gyroscopes from Germany, audio amplifiers, battery chargers, display port multiplexers, batteries, cameras, and hundreds of other advanced parts. In total, Apple works with suppliers in forty-three countries on six continents to source the materials and parts that go into an iPhone. Of course, every supplier in the Apple supply chain has its own supply chain of sources and processes. Again, supply chains are immensely complex.

Once the global perspective is added, we have to expand our transportation options from trucks and trains to include ships and planes. That means ports and airports are additional links in the chain. Those facilities have their own links and inputs, including cranes, containers, port authorities, air traffic controllers, pilots, captains, and the vessels themselves. And to our list of trucks, trains, ships, and planes we can add pipelines that transport liquids such as petroleum, gasoline, and natural gas. Every process and every node in these global supply chains is under continual scrutiny by experts to wring a bit more efficiency from the node.

Adam Smith wrote extensively about supply chains in his 1776 book *The Wealth of Nations*. He did this to illustrate economic gains from productivity achieved through a division of labor and free markets. Still, the modern science of supply chain management did not begin until the 1980s. That's when the rise of globalization and the expansion of computing power combined to make supply chains more complex while offering tools to deal with the complexity.

Supply chains can be thought of as a bundle of costs that manufacturers bear in order to realize revenues and profits once the costs are netted against the revenues. These costs include sourcing inputs, transportation, manufacturing processes, quality control, labor, equipment, distribution, inventory, and associated legal, administrative, and insurance expenses. Those cost centers are all links in the supply chain. There are limits to what producers can charge for their products based on consumer preferences and competition. Given those limits, the most direct way to increase profits is to reduce costs. Supply chain management takes aim at those costs by creating options, sharing information, eliminating redundancies, encouraging cooperation among supply chain participants, and other innovations. These efficiency techniques are numerous and go by many names. Here's a summary of some of the most widely used techniques:

Lean: This is the technique developed by Toyota in the early 1980s and now almost universally adopted. It is sometimes referred to as the Toyota Production System, or TPS. The idea is to run a supply chain with the least amount of time, effort, and money necessary. Specific innovations that have emerged from Lean are just-in-time inventory, and the idea of minimizing shipping costs by colocating related functions. Lean aims to reduce motion, reduce waiting time, and reduce inventory at every step of the production process. It also seeks to eliminate overprocessing (taking steps that do not add value) and defects (in part by tapping into the skills and creativity of rank-and-file employees).

Six Sigma: This is a statistical methodology designed to minimize variation in production processes. The idea is to have a smooth process that reduces product defects to the sixth sigma (6σ). Statistically this translates into 3.4 defects out of one million events. Six Sigma is implemented through a five-step process described as: define, measure, analyze, improve, and control. Since this is a process of continuous improvement, it is sometimes combined with Lean into a program called Lean Six Sigma.

Theory of Constraints: This methodology begins with the assumption that every supply chain process is constrained by the slowest step in the chain. If an assembly line requires a thousand tires per day to produce vehicles at maximum capacity, and the warehouse can only supply eight hundred tires per day, then the car assembly line must slow down to a point 20 percent below capacity because of the tire delivery constraint. Once these bottlenecks are identified, available resources should be used to fix the bottleneck in order to make the entire supply chain run more smoothly and increase output to capacity. Yet the Theory of Constraints teaches that the process of improvement is never done. Once a constraint is removed, another constraint is revealed somewhere else in the chain. That second constraint was, in effect, hiding behind the first constraint. Now the hidden constraint becomes the limit on the entire supply chain and must be eliminated in turn. The process never ends, because each success reveals a new constraint somewhere along the chain. By this process, the Theory of Constraints segues into the process of Continuous Improvement, another part of supply chain management culture.

RACI Matrix: This is a supply chain management technique used to improve teamwork in solving problems. RACI stands for Responsible, Accountable, Consult and Inform. It is intended to let every member of a team know what they are responsible for doing, establish benchmarks to hold team members accountable for performing their tasks, encourage consultation among team members to ensure that efforts are coordinated, and inform team members that specific tasks have been accomplished or are ongoing.

DIRECT Model: This is a technique used by leaders in supply chain management improvement projects. It's another acronym that requires managers to: Define the objective, Investigate the options, Resolve on a course of action, Execute a plan, Change the system, and Transition people to new roles once a project is completed. It's a classic business-management technique applied to the unique challenges facing supply chain managers.

SCOR Model: This is another management tool for those involved in supply chain optimization. SCOR stands for Supply Chain Operations Reference. It's a framework for mapping supply chain improvement processes and evaluating results. The high-level elements of an efficient supply chain are defined as: plan, source, make, deliver, return, and enable. These concepts involve planning the supply chain itself, sourcing inputs and raw materials, making the product in as efficient a manner as possible, delivering finished products with optimized transportation lanes, allowing for the return of defective products or disposal of any waste, and enabling people with the right skills to carry out these tasks.

Looking over these techniques and tools one is not surprised to learn there are hundreds of additional supply chain management techniques. Without getting into great depth, some of these other techniques are called:

Master Scheduling: This is a technique that combines information from transportation logistics and manufacturing processes (the master production schedule) and demand estimates (the master demand schedule) to ensure the tempo of inputs and deliveries is synchronized to allow maximum output with minimal inventories.

Demand Planning: This takes into account expected demand, some inventory for the unexpected (safety stock), and just-in-time deliveries to meet demand with minimal inventories.

Total Quality Management: Product defects are bad for consumer satisfaction and costly to repair or replace. Total quality management aims to minimize defects to improve the brand and reduce costs.

Continuous Improvement: This is a management philosophy that says the job of supply chain management in all its aspects is never done. As soon as bottlenecks are relieved or improvements accomplished, the management should return immediately to the task of finding additional means of improvement.

Warehouse Management: This is mainly a process of identification and automation designed to make it easy to store goods in warehouses and to pick them out as needed for delivery; QR codes, UPC codes, radio frequency identification (RFID), GPS locators, and robots are all tools of modern warehouse management. Decisions are also made about whether warehouse management is done in-house or outsourced to expert warehouse operators.

Materials Requirement Planning (MRP): This technique focuses on inputs rather than outputs. Before goods can be manufactured, all the component parts and materials must be delivered to the manufacturing site. MRP managers use a bill of materials (BOM) and purchase orders (POs), and combine them with transportation logistics and tracking technology to ensure that all inputs required for production are delivered to the right locations in a timely way.

Cross-Docking: This is the technique perfected by Walmart in which goods delivered to a distribution center by truck are moved to another truck for final delivery to a store. The goods never enter the warehouse and are never included in distribution center inventory. It's as if the goods were shipped directly from the cargo ports to the individual stores; the distribution center is just a place to change trucks, not a place to stack inventory. This process saves time and money and lowers costs to the consumer.

Vendor-Managed Inventory: This technique puts the supplier in charge of the buyer's inventory. Instead of monitoring inventory and entering purchase orders, the buyer simply tells the seller to ship whatever is needed when it's needed in accordance with demand estimates and past practice. This eliminates buyer purchase orders and lowers overall costs.

There are many more techniques.

All these supply chain management models have one goal in common: to reduce costs. And these supply chain tools have been greatly enhanced by computers, algorithms, and artificial intelligence. A company receiving inputs from ten countries entering through four U.S. ports, being distributed to ten warehouses via seven major trucking companies, has 2,800 possible transportation lanes. Computers can be used to optimize these lanes in ways that reduce the actual routes to perhaps forty that make the most sense in terms of time and money. The manufacturer selects from among these forty options while using the computer to update the optimization software with new inputs and continually searching for the best routes.

This brings us to the second hurdle in supply chain management—energy. It may appear that energy is plentiful on a global basis notwithstanding higher energy prices. How can energy be blamed for the supply chain breakdown?

All systems run on some form of energy. It can take the form of electrical energy from nuclear power plants, hydroelectric generators in dams, natural gas plants, coal-fired plants, or renewable sources such as wind and solar. Energy can also be provided in the form of human labor, which is fueled by food. Money is a form of energy. It takes energy to produce profits in the form of money. The money is a store of value, which can be used in the future to release energy through the purchase of electricity, buying inputs, or paying wages. Money is like a battery for storing energy between the input and output stages in the supply chain.

Complex dynamic systems such as the supply chain run on energy. The problem is that the energy inputs rise in a superlinear fashion relative to the scale of the system. In plain English, this means if you double the systemic scale, you may increase the needed energy (electricity, money, or labor) by a factor of five. If you double it again, you increase the energy inputs by a factor of five again. After doubling systemic scale twice, the system is four times larger, but energy inputs are twenty-five times larger. When the profits from increasing the scale of the system are high and energy costs are low, these lopsided ratios of scaling functions may still be profitable on net. Yet when profits start to shrink (because of competition from disruptive technologies) and energy prices start to rise (because of government regulation and inflation), the impact of energy input costs on a highly leveraged supply chain network becomes a constraint on the operation of the system as a whole.

The rising cost of energy inputs is exacerbated by outright energy shortages, as are now emerging in China and Germany. China has coal shortages; coal accounts for over 50 percent of China's electricity-generating capacity. Germany has natural gas shortages, which have grown worse since Russia invaded Ukraine and the United States imposed sanctions on Russia. These energy shortages are slowing output in China and Germany right now. Both are export powerhouses.

Energy issues weaken supply chains in one of two ways. Outright energy shortages as are arising in China and Germany slow production as plants close down temporarily and as energy is diverted to consumers and population centers to allow lights, home heating, cooking, and local transportation. Even where energy is available, higher costs offset supply chain efficiencies and result in higher costs to consumers or lower margins for producers, or both.

If efficiency in the form of lower costs is the goal of all supply chain management, why does efficiency actually weaken supply chains and lead to breakdowns? The answer is cost reductions have hidden costs. When you increase the length of supply chains to reach lower labor costs in Asia, you also increase the number of things that can go wrong along the way. When you reduce your trucking providers to the two who offer the lowest rates, you increase your vulnerability if one of those two suffers a strike or is disrupted by a natural disaster. If you route all your inbound cargo to the Port of Los Angeles (instead of Houston, New York, or Savannah) in order to be close to your distribution center, your goods will be stranded when the Port of Los Angeles becomes a global bottleneck. Put differently, the hidden cost of efficiency is vulnerability. It might be more costly in the short run to use multiple ports of entry, multiple trucking companies, and widely separated distribution centers. Yet those redundancies will produce great savings in terms of keeping manufacturing processes running and avoiding lost sales if one of those ports, truckers, or distribution centers is disrupted by pandemic, weather, natural disaster, or power outage.

The best way to think of how the added costs of redundancy can produce savings is to think of it as insurance. When you buy insurance you hope you never need it. When you pay your insurance premium you consider it money well spent even though it has no immediate return. When you have an insurance claim you receive great value. The insurance can save you from financial ruin, even though the premium is a short-run cost. Redundancy or resilience built into supply chains operates the same way. It has short-term costs (like an insurance premium), yet it can save your business from ruin.

These trade-offs between short-term costs and long-term gains, and between redundancy and efficiency, present paradoxes that are characteristic of all complex dynamic systems. The global supply chain is one of the most complex systems ever created. To understand the breakdown of supply chains we must understand complexity.

Complex Systems Always Fail . . . (Unless They Descale)

Why do ski patrols on high mountains use dynamite to cause controlled avalanches? The reason is if they don't, they will have uncontrolled avalanches at times and in places that threaten lives and destroy property. It's impossible to predict the exact time and place of an uncontrolled avalanche. Yet you can predict with near complete certainty that an avalanche of some magnitude will occur in certain conditions. You just don't know when. A controlled avalanche is a way to remove the uncertainty, descale the system, and avoid loss. You're using dynamite to blow up a system for the good of those around it. That's an apt description of complex dynamics. It's not a metaphor; an unstable snowpack on a steep mountain actually is a complex system. So is the supply chain.

Analysts looking for the cause of the supply chain breakdown are chasing shadows. When complex systems collapse there is no single cause. Put differently, the cause is the scale of the system itself; complex systems collapse of their own weight and an inability to receive needed energy inputs. Observers blame truckers, port congestion, labor shortages, the pandemic, weather, power outages, and more. The fact is, these are all symptoms of overall breakdown or discrete breakdowns in parallel complex systems. The problem with the supply chain is . . . the supply chain. It's too big, too frail, too stretched, and utterly dependent on inputs in the form of cooperation, information, and human capital. When the inputs fail (as they inevitably do) the system fails. You don't blame an avalanche on the last snowflake; you blame the unstable system.

Complexity is not the same as complication. A Swiss watch is complicated. Still, an experienced craftsman can take it apart, clean the parts, replace some, put it back together, and the watch works fine. Complexity is more like a fine white wine. You can catch the bouquet and taste the apples, lemons, butter, and other flavors in the finished product. But you can't take it apart and put it back together. The taste and bouquet are what physicists call emergent properties in a complex system. The finished wine is greater than the sum of its parts. It's also vulnerable. Leave the bottle open long enough and it turns acidic. Global supply chains are approaching the acidic phase.

A supply chain has all the components that make up a complex system. The first is a set of diverse components called autonomous agents. These agents take actions and make decisions on their own that collectively allow the supply chain to function. The second component is connectedness. Diverse agents must interact with each other to form a complex system. When one considers how shippers, distributors, and retailers all interact, a supply chain qualifies as densely connected. The third component is interdependence. This means that what one agent does affects what others do. The effects work in both directions. In supply chains, if a warehouse is full, the owner's marketing department may launch a sale. If a warehouse is empty, the purchasing department may double their orders. Again, interdependence is at the heart of supply chain dynamics. The fourth component is adaptation. This means more than just change; it implies learning. When a port is consistently congested, you learn to direct orders to a different port, and so on.

Here's a summary of how diversity, connectedness, interdependence, and adaptation blend to form a complex system:

To understand how a complex system operates, it is necessary to think about the strength of each of these four elements. Imagine each one has a dial that can be turned from settings of zero to ten. At a setting of one, the system is uninteresting. It will have elements of complexity, yet nothing much is going on. Diversity is low, connectedness and interdependence are weak, and there is almost no learning or adaptation taking place. At a setting of ten, the system is chaotic. Agents receive too much information from too many sources and are stymied in their decision making by conflicting and overwhelming signals. . . .

Where complexity is most intriguing is in what Scott Page of the University of Michigan calls the "interesting in-between." This means the dials are set somewhere between three and seven, with each dial different from the others. This allows a good flow of information, interaction, and learning among diverse agents, but not so much that the system becomes chaotic. This is the heart of complexity—a system that continuously produces surprising results without breaking down.[4]

Simply put, the never-ending quest for efficiency in supply chains has moved the dials close to ten. The result is chaos and breakdown.

There are three other features of complex systems that have applicability to supply chains. The first was discovered by Edward Lorenz, the founder of modern complexity theory. Complex systems have existed since the Big Bang 13.8 billion years ago. The formation of the universe was the mother of all complex dynamic systems. It was not until the invention of computers and mathematical algorithms to model complex dynamics that complexity science took shape.

In 1961, Edward Lorenz was conducting mathematical simulations of weather patterns on a Royal McBee LGP-30 computer, primitive by today's standards but suitable for his calculations. He ran a simulation and read the results on a paper printout. He decided to run the same simulation (a standard scientific technique) and entered output data from his printout to begin the process. He went out to lunch, returned, and was completely surprised when the results of the second trial were radically different from those of the first. They should have been the same.

On examination, Lorenz determined that his input on the first trial was expressed to six decimal places, but the computer had truncated the printout to three decimal places. His data point 0.506127 had been rounded to 0.506. In most experiments a change of 1/10,000 in an input would be immaterial, yet in this case it produced enormous changes in the results. From this, Lorenz correctly inferred that certain systems exhibit complex dynamics in which even minor perturbations at the start of a process can lead to end results that range from equilibrium to total collapse.[5] Lorenz summarized his findings by writing, "Prediction of the sufficiently distant future is impossible by any method, unless the present conditions are known exactly. In view of the inevitable inaccuracy and incompleteness of weather observations, precise very-long-range forecasting would seem to be non-existent." What Lorenz applied to weather applies to all complex dynamics.

The second feature of complex systems relevant for our purposes was discovered by the astrophysicist Eric J. Chaisson. Here's a summary of his theory:

> Chaisson posits that the universe is best understood as the constant flow of energy between radiation and matter. The flow dynamics create more energy than is needed in the conversion, providing "free energy" to support complexity. Chaisson's contribution was to define complexity empirically as a ratio of free energy flow to density in a system. Stated simply, the more complex a system is, the more energy it needs to maintain its size and space. . . .
>
> It is well understood that the sun uses far more energy than a human brain. Yet the sun is vastly more massive than a brain. When these differences in mass are taken into account, it turns out that the brain uses 75,000 times as much energy as the sun, measured in Chaisson's standard units. Chaisson has also identified one entity vastly more complex than the human brain: society itself in its civilized form. . . . Chaisson's key finding is that civilization, adjusted for density, uses 250,000 times the energy used by the sun and one million times the energy used by the Milky Way.[6]

To the extent that supply chains dominate the global economy, and the economy is a proxy for civilization, Chaisson's energy-density equations apply perfectly to the global supply chain. The more complex, that is dense, the supply chain system, the more energy (including energy in the form of human capital) is required exponentially to keep the system from collapse.

The third feature of complex systems was contributed by anthropologist and historian Joseph A. Tainter in his seminal work, *The Collapse of Complex Societies*.[7] Tainter studied the collapse of twenty-seven separate civilizations over forty-five hundred years. He considered well-known cases such as the collapse of the Roman Empire and little-known cases, including the Kachin civilization of highland Burma. He noted that historians have assigned specific causes to each collapse, including drought, earthquake, barbarian invasion, plague, and other calamities. His insight was that the collapsed civilizations had suffered these disasters many times before. Rome was invaded by Celtic tribes led by the warlord Brennus in 387 BC, eight centuries before Attila the Hun invaded northern Italy in 452 AD. Brennus violently pillaged Rome and killed most members of the Roman Senate. Still, Rome recovered. It never fully recovered from Attila's attack.

Using this and many other examples, Tainter concluded that the collapse of a complex system is not explained by a specific cause such as a barbarian attack but by the response function of the civilization under attack. Societies that succumbed to invasion, plague, or drought had overcome those threats many times before. In the end, society fell because it was no longer motivated to recover. Whether it was taxation, corruption, decadence, or weak leadership, the members of society did not rally or rebuild. They just let it happen and migrated or lived in simplified conditions.

These three insights into complex systems—small changes produce large results, energy inputs grow exponentially with scale, and system participants cease being robust to change—explain the ongoing collapse of the supply chain. Perturbations are ubiquitous, systemic scale is too large, and key political participants no longer care or at least they no longer share the goals of supply chain advocates. The drive for efficiency has been displaced by a drive for self-sufficiency. This is a profound political shift. Supply chain managers are the first to feel its effects yet seem to be among the last to comprehend the changing political winds.

It Gets Worse from Here

The breakdown of global supply chains is a massive real-time case study in the failure of complex systems. The core problem is that supply chain experts have spent the last thirty years making supply chains more efficient. Supply chains impose costs on business. Efficiency amounts to cutting costs. Cutting costs increases profits. The supply chain revolution since the early 1990s has been about cost reduction, which gets passed to consumers in the form of lower prices. This efficiency revolution has flown directly into the eye of the complexity storm. Increased scale, increased participation, greater diversity, more linkages, and more interconnectedness in supply chains are a recipe for systemic collapse. In the end, the system lacked both robustness (the ability to withstand shocks) and resilience (the ability to bend and recover). Now the shocks have broken the system, only to reveal that resilience was mostly an illusion. Conditional correlation has led to simultaneous ruptures in widely separated parts of the chain. A badly broken vase cannot be reassembled. You must buy a new one. A new supply chain, Supply Chain 2.0, is the only solution.

For decades we've heard about trade deals such as NAFTA (1994) and China's admission to the World Trade Organization (2001). Tariffs were also cut on a bilateral basis even when multilateral agreements were not in play. Larger trade deals have been implemented recently, including a revised TPP (2018). Historic predecessors included the European Free Trade Agreement (EFTA) and the European Union (EU). All these agreements and treaties were done under the banner of free trade, a mostly mythical concept favored by academics. In the real world, trade is a rigged game of subsidies, nontariff barriers, national champions, cheap labor, and comparative advantage pulled from thin air through mobile capital. Free trade sounds like a high-minded purpose, yet the not-so-hidden agenda was to expand supply chains without tariffs so that cheap labor could connect with rich consumers. The supply chain revolution involved more than cheap labor, mostly in Asia. It also involved scarce commodities from Africa, high technology from Taiwan, financial capital from the United States, and high value-added human capital from Europe, Canada, and the United States, among other sources.

Supply chain managers and consultants became experts at optimizing the links and cutting costs. A more distant source might be more efficient than a local source because of cheap labor. Expensive air transport might be more efficient than ships for high-demand lightweight products since the goods would spend less time in inventory. Long-term purchase agreements were more efficient than one-time purchases because of lower unit costs. Conversely, short-term purchase agreements might be more efficient because they allowed for substitutions of certain components. There was no single right answer. There was only a relentless search for optimized, that is, cheaper, supply chains.

The touchstone of these efforts was the idea of just-in-time inventory. If you are installing seats on an automobile assembly line, it is ideal if those seats arrive at the plant the same morning as the installation. That minimizes storage and inventory costs. The same is true for every part installed on the assembly line. The logistics behind this are daunting but can be managed with state-of-the-art software. All these efforts are fine as far as they go. The costs savings are real. The supply chains are global. The capacity of this system to keep a lid on costs is demonstrable.

There's only one problem. The system is extremely frail. One missed delivery can result in an entire assembly line shutting down. One delayed vessel can result in empty shelves. One power outage can result in a transportation breakdown. In a nutshell, that's what happened to the global supply chain. There's a lack of redundancy. The system is not robust to shocks. The shocks have occurred nevertheless (pandemic, trade wars, decoupling, bank collateral shortages, and more), and the system has commenced a collapse.

The failures have cascaded. Delays in receiving commodity inputs in China have resulted in manufacturing delays for exports. Energy shortages in China have resulted in further disruption of steel production, mining, transportation, and other basic industries. Port delays in Los Angeles have resulted in component and finished goods delayed in the United States. Semiconductor shortages have halted production of electronics, appliances, automobiles, and other consumer durables that rely on automated applications—the Internet of Things. Everyone is blaming everyone else. Ships that can't unload at ports blame the truckers who are supposed to remove the containers already ashore. Truckers blame state regulators who make them wait in line for days to pick up containers only to tell them to come back tomorrow. Retailers blame distributors. Customers blame retailers. They're all right. Still, they're all missing the point. These complaints are symptoms, not causes. The supply chain breakdown is not located at one bottleneck. It's up and down the supply chain at all levels, from component suppliers to manufacturers to transportation providers to customers.

Using Lorenz's discovery that small changes in input result in dramatic outcomes, Daniel Stanton, one of the world's leading authorities on supply chain management, describes a classic supply chain phenomenon called the Bullwhip Effect:

> A customer comes in to buy a widget, which turns out to be the last widget in the store, so the store needs to order more inventory from its wholesaler. But the wholesaler doesn't sell individual widgets; it sells widgets in cases of 100 units. Now the store has to buy a full case—100 widgets—even though it sold only one. If that case was the last one in the warehouse, the wholesaler will replenish its inventory by ordering more widgets from the factory. The factory, however, sells widgets in batches of 100 cases, so the wholesaler has to buy 100 cases of 100 widgets each.

The wholesaler just bought 10,000 widgets even though it sold only 100.

How many widgets did the factory sell? 10,000. How many did the wholesaler sell? 100. And how many did the customer buy? Yep: 1. A small demand signal at the end of the supply chain became amplified at every step, creating a Bullwhip Effect on inventory. The store may never sell another widget, so it would still be stuck with 100 widgets in inventory. . . . All that extra inventory costs money for everyone in the supply chain without adding any value.[8]

Of course, there are remedies for the Bullwhip Effect. Factories and wholesalers can sell in smaller batches. All parties in the supply chain can do better forecasting so they can place orders before inventory runs so low. The store, the wholesaler, and the factory can improve communications to help do a better job of managing inventories. Still, the Bullwhip Effect is real. The point of describing it is not to critique supply chain participants but to illustrate the acute sensitivity of global supply chains to the most minute perturbations.

Another case study that illustrates the complexity of supply chains is aircraft operation, particularly avionics, the electronic brains of modern aircraft. When you peek into a passenger jet cockpit while disembarking, the lights, switches, and dials you see are the output and interface of avionics. The backstory on avionics disruption is not just about input and transportation delays; it reveals the dark side of vaccine mandates and deception by government and the airline industry.

The story begins with a December 31, 2021, letter from U.S. Transportation Secretary Pete Buttigieg and Federal Aviation Administrator Steve Dickson calling upon Verizon and AT&T to delay the rollout of 5G wireless communication services.[9] That coauthorship is unusual on its face since neither the DOT nor the FAA is typically involved with mobile phone operators; that's the jurisdiction of the FCC. The letter spells out the connection. New 5G wireless service could interfere with avionics and pose a risk to airline safety. Buttigieg and

Dickson claimed aircraft could suffer "widespread and unacceptable disruption," and landings might be diverted from airports deemed unsafe from the 5G interference. The letter went on to say these diversions could cause "ripple effects throughout the U.S. air transportation system." The government's concern involved radar altimeters that pilots rely upon for safe landings in bad weather or low-visibility conditions. The letter asked for a two-week delay from January 5, 2022, to enable the aviation industry to designate airports "where a buffer zone would permit flights to continue safely." However, the delay could continue indefinitely for what Buttigieg and Dickson called "priority airports." Initially AT&T and Verizon refused the FAA's request, but the next day they reversed their positions and agreed to the delay. Perhaps most surprising was the urgent, last-minute nature of this request. Radar altimeters were developed in the 1930s using technology first identified by Bell Labs in the 1910s; 5G technology was introduced in 2016 and started widespread deployment in 2019. Why was the danger of interference between the two technologies only coming to a head in early 2022?

The answer brings us back to the supply chain fiasco. In fact, there are straightforward changes that can be made to radar altimeters to make them safe to use even in proximity to 5G transmission towers. The difficulty is that the engineers who work on avionics are badly backlogged. The avionics industry is clustered around the Wichita, Kansas, area for historic and logistical reasons. Many work for Textron Inc. or Spirit AeroSystems. This is not uncommon. Computer developers are clustered in Silicon Valley and medical research is clustered near Raleigh, North Carolina. In any field, the best want to be around the best. Avionics engineers are typically in their forties or fifties and are predominately white males. That's a group with a low rate of COVID vaccinations—closer to 50 percent versus the national average of 80 percent.[10] They are overwhelmingly federal contractors because they work on military as well as civilian aircraft. As such, they are covered by President Biden's executive order issued on September 9, 2021, requiring vaccination and other COVID safety protocols.

Biden said, "If you want to work with the federal government and do business with us, get vaccinated. . . . If you want to do business with the federal government, vaccinate your workforce."[11] It's the case that many of the engineers are not vaccinated. As a result, they are leaving their jobs, being fired, or starting new firms outside the reach of Biden's vaccine mandate. This vaccine exodus—the foreseeable result of Biden's policies—contributes directly to the supply chain slowdown in radar altimeter fine-tuning. This has led to a delay in the 5G rollout. That's how supply chains work or in this case don't work.

A pilot correspondent informs me as follows with regard to landing without a radar altimeter:

> There is only one known visual technique for making a landing that doesn't damage anything. That is to be able to focus on the horizon in the last 3–5 seconds before touchdown. If the visibility does not permit doing that, and you have to look at a negative elevation angle in those last few seconds, it is literally impossible to make a smooth landing because you cannot judge your pitch angle by eye.
>
> With enough practice, a pilot can learn at least not to wreck the aircraft on touchdown in low visibility using only visual cues, but that isn't exactly an endorsement. Normally, the radar altimeter tells the pilot when to flare (it's a matter of preference; most will start the flare when the radar altimeter announces "10," meaning 10 feet above the runway).
>
> We already know what will happen next: The chief pilots in the major airlines will require that the radar altimeters be "placarded off" (for most aircraft models, that means pulling the circuit breaker on the radar altimeter) because it can no longer be trusted. . . . Chief pilots aren't going to want their pilots flying precision approaches to minimums without a radar altimeter; at least until they have accumulated several more hours of practice and recurrent proficiency in landing in bad weather with only visual cues.

It's unlikely the White House understands this. They know how to issue orders and buy time, but they don't know how to connect the dots between vaccine mandates, federal contractors, air safety, the 5G rollout, and crash landings. Many flight cancellations announced by American Airlines, Delta, United, and Southwest during the holiday season in 2021 blamed on "bad weather" were actually related to this radar altimeter bottleneck. The bad weather connection simply meant the planes could not land safely without the altimeter calibrations. And those were not being done because the federal contractor work-force were not on the job due to ineffective vaccine mandates. In the end, the 5G rollout went forward in late January with AT&T and Verizon agreeing to delay installation in close proximity to certain airports. This buys time but does not address the issue for the long term. Expect the flight cancellations to continue. It really is all connected.

The Biden administration was not alone in implementing policies seemingly intentionally designed to destroy supply chains. Canada's government led by Prime Minister Justin Trudeau imposed a requirement that unvaccinated truck drivers returning to Canada from the United States face lengthy quarantines upon reentry. This despite the fact that vaccines don't stop infections or spread of the SARS-CoV-2 virus, and drivers work alone so they can't infect anyone anyway. Most of the Canadian population live within one hundred miles of the U.S.-Canada border. The USMCA makes north-south traffic across the border more important than east-west traffic across Canada. The mandate was devastating to U.S.-Canada supply chains and to the well-being of truckers caught in the crossfire. In late January 2022, thousands of Canadian truckers joined the Freedom Convoy protest traveling from British Columbia to Ottawa along Highway 1 and other routes. On the truckers' arrival on January 29, the capital was effectively shut down. Prime Minister Trudeau went into hiding but not before disparaging the truckers as a "fringe minority." In fact, the trucker protest drew widespread backing across Canada and the United States. Prominent voices from Elon Musk to Tucker Carlson expressed support for the trucker protest. Politics aside, tying up thousands of trucks in the convoy and Ottawa protest was one more blow to supply chain efficiency.

The supply chain difficulties will certainly grow worse. Even more troubling is the fact that the remedies will take years and sometimes decades to implement. The reasons for this have to do with long lead times in onshoring. For example, the United States can cut its dependence on Asian semiconductor imports by building its own semiconductor fabrication plants. The problem is that these plants take from three to five years to build, and the cost is enormous.

There are other impediments to supply chain recovery that are not directly related to particular supply chains that nonetheless hurt the process of adaptation and substitution. There's already a labor shortage in America. The causes are complicated. There's no literal shortage of potential workers, but many workers prefer to stay home because of some combination of government benefits, childcare responsibilities, or inadequate pay offered by employers (who can't afford to pay more themselves because they'll go out of business). A lot of this labor shortage centers on lower-wage jobs such as waiters, store clerks, fast-food staff, and office assistants. Still, there will be a labor shortage coming soon in more high-skilled areas such as engineers, pilots, machinists, and medical personnel. This high-skilled shortage will not be due to low pay, but to a combination of vaccine mandates and pandemic burnout.

Biden's policy response to the supply chain background was misguided and mostly for show. In recent remarks, Biden made muddled references to decades-old shortages of Cabbage Patch Kids and Beanie Babies (which were driven by excess demand, not failed supply). Such remarks only increased doubts about Biden's mental competence. Biden's press secretary, Jen Psaki, mocked what she called "the tragedy of the treadmill that's delayed," betraying an elite sensibility at a time when some Americans could not buy milk or eggs. Biden's Chief of Staff Ron Klain endorsed a statement that referred to inflation and supply chain disruption as "high-class problems," another tone-deaf dismissal of issues confronting everyday Americans.

On December 22, 2021, Biden held a meeting with senior executives from FedEx, GAP, and several large logistics providers to discuss the status of the supply chain. This followed an earlier meeting at the White House on November 29, 2021, attended by CEOs of Walmart, Etsy, Samsung, Kroger, Best Buy, and CVS. Both meetings produced platitudes and little else. Biden said, "Shelves are not empty." In fact, many were. Biden did announce a release of fifty million barrels of oil from the Strategic Petroleum Reserve, which is trivial considering that the United States consumes almost twenty million barrels per day. Biden also touted $4 billion of infrastructure improvements at U.S. ports starting in February 2022, led by the U.S. Army Corps of Engineers. That's laudable, but those projects will take five to ten years to complete. These meetings were for public consumption and offered nothing of substance to alleviate the current crisis.

Biden also indulged in finger-pointing, which is more a matter of shifting blame than solving problems. The president accused meatpackers of price gouging despite clear evidence that meat prices were going up because of inflation in input costs for labor, feed, fertilizer, and transportation. Prices for nitrogen fertilizer needed to grow feed for livestock rose 210 percent in the year ending September 2021. Biden also threatened antitrust action against big meatpackers despite evidence of healthy competition among the "big four" (Tyson, Cargill, JBS, and National Beef) and ample output from smaller packers with niches in local markets or all-natural products. Increased regulation for meatpackers will simply drive prices higher and slow the supply chain even more. An investigation by the Federal Trade Commission announced on November 30, 2021, targeted Amazon, Walmart, Procter & Gamble, and six other major retailers with claims of anticompetitive practices. This was another government action just for show. In fact, Amazon and Walmart are among those with the most efficient supply chains that have suffered fewer disruptions than many other distributors. The Biden administration's response to the supply chain breakdown should be understood as a public relations ploy at best and a contributor to further breakdown at worst.

President Biden ordered that all federal contractors must be fully vaccinated by December 8, 2021. That's in addition to federal workers and the military, who are already subject to vaccine mandates and have no choice. This federal contractor mandate is different from the OSHA vaccine mandate that applies to all employers with one hundred or more employees. The OSHA mandate was stopped by the U.S. Supreme Court on January 13, 2022. The federal contractor mandate was stopped by several U.S. circuit courts of appeals in early 2022, although further appeals are pending. Still, extensive damage was done before the courts clarified that these mandates were illegal. Many workers quit their jobs in the face of mandates, as private-sector employers mimicked the mandates, to the detriment of their workers. The vaccination rate among federal contractors is lower than that of the country as a whole. The national vaccination rate is approaching 80 percent, while the federal contractor rate is closer to 70 percent, and even lower in some specialties such as avionics. These workers know the vaccine is available, understand the risks (both ways because of side effects), and have chosen not to be vaccinated. It's almost impossible to change their minds at this point. The Biden administration is not backing off the mandates and is exploring new ways, including executive orders, to achieve the same results. The federal contractor workforce is huge, in the tens of millions. The U.S. economy is already weak. The supply chain is already in disarray. Any mass termination of skilled workers will put the economy into a recession. Some analysts have even suggested the global supply chain is being sabotaged by major participants such as China in order to hurt Western economies for geopolitical reasons. It's difficult to tell if the supply chain is being intentionally sabotaged or whether it's just collapsing under its own weight. Possibly both.

It's also the case that each participant in the supply chain achieves its own efficiencies, yet no one is looking at the global system in terms of aggregate resilience. It is possible that one or more parties chose to disrupt the system intentionally without realizing how vulnerable the entire system really was. Some combination of intentional acts and unintended consequences is a staple of history, including the out-break of World War I. The point is that once the implosion begins, there's no way to stop it until you have devolved to a simpler yet al-most unrecognizable state. For these and other reasons, the supply chain crisis will grow worse from here and persist for years to come.

No Way Home

There is no easy solution to the supply chain breakdown. Complex systems collapse in cascading fashion. Each problem leads to a larger problem downstream. The ripple effects fan out and cannot be reversed. The river doesn't run backward. Efforts to solve particular problems by hoarding, overordering, or seeking new sources of supply only make the situation worse. Those remedies come at the expense of someone else in another supply chain. It's a negative-sum game. The overall situation grows more dire even if Band-Aids provide temporary relief to some.

If you expand your perspective to extended supply chains, you're still missing the whole picture. The global supply chain is a system of systems. Each separate supply chain system is complex, and the sys-tem of systems is immeasurably more complex. Trying to model this complexity requires processing power greater than the entire compu-tational capacity of the planet. We call this system of systems the meta supply chain.

Increasing output does not help when the transportation lanes are blocked. Marshaling more transportation lanes doesn't help when the warehouses are full. Getting deliveries to manufacturing centers doesn't help when other critical deliveries are late. Profits are eaten alive by higher energy costs, higher labor costs, higher inventory costs, and lost sales.

It is U.S. government policy to try to increase oil and natural gas prices in order to enhance the attractiveness of wind and solar energy. These Green New Deal policies will fail. While wind and solar have a place, such intermittent energy sources cannot maintain the baseload levels needed to run a modern power grid and cannot scale fast enough to meet rising energy demands. Meanwhile, higher costs for gasoline, jet fuel, diesel, and natural gas will exacerbate existing problems in the supply chain.

As noted, collapse is unidirectional. Once water goes over the waterfall, you cannot push it back up the falls. The meta supply chain will have to find a new level. It will be slower and more costly yet perhaps more resilient to adversity and more robust to future failure. The biggest loser will be China, because it is a source of many inputs in the broken supply chain that will be abandoned. The biggest winner will be the United States because it has the greatest capacity to onshore critical links and source replacements for lost capacity elsewhere. Still, reconfiguring the meta supply chain will take five to ten years to accomplish. In the meantime, investors should expect empty shelves, higher costs, and slower growth in the companies most affected.

CHAPTER THREE

Why Shortages Will Persist

———

Neither the benefits nor the ravages of globalization come about by themselves; someone has to decide to source products from overseas rather than the supplier next door, to shift production offshore rather than keep the local factory open, or to move capital into tax havens rather than invest it at home. . . . It is largely the production, sourcing, and investment decisions of multinational corporations that drive the process of economic globalization.

—ANTHEA ROBERTS AND NICOLAS LAMP
Six Faces of Globalization (2021)[1]

Supply Chain 2.0

In chapter 1 we considered specific ways in which global supply chains are breaking down. In chapter 2 we examined the causes of the breakdown, including trade wars, the relentless drive for efficiency, and the inherent delicacy of complex dynamic systems scaled beyond viable bounds. In this chapter we explore why supply chains built from 1989 to 2019 are broken beyond repair and need to be rebuilt around shorter lanes, onshore production, and decoupling from Communist China. This reconstruction marks the transition from Supply Chain 1.0 to Supply Chain 2.0. It will not be easy and will not be fast. Still, it will be necessary to get the most out of global trade among democracies without empowering dictators or worse.

The predicates for inability to revive the failing supply chain structure are ongoing trade wars, logistics bottlenecks, the pandemic and failed public policy response, the energy crisis, and climate alarmism. It's not enough to blame truckers, ports, and labor shortages. Those situations are symptoms, not causes. Just as there is a meta supply chain, there are meta causes of supply chain breakdown. Two causes stand out above all—decoupling from Communist China, and efforts by Russia to force a new security order in Europe. We will consider each of these predicates with expanded analysis of imperatives in China and Russia. When finished, the reader will have no doubt about the inevitability of changes coming to supply chain science and systems.

Trade, Trucks, and Tariffs

The trade wars begun by President Trump are far from over. They are getting worse. The Biden administration has not reduced the tariffs on China that Trump imposed despite frequent criticism of Trump's trade policies. In fact, Biden has imposed new tariffs, including a May 2021 tariff of 221 percent on chassis imported from China.[2] The chassis shortage in the United States is one contributor to supply chain bottlenecks at U.S. ports. The tariff has raised the price of chassis from about twelve thousand dollars to almost forty thousand dollars, making their purchase noneconomic for most U.S. shippers. The wait time for truckers at Southern California ports has increased from forty minutes to seven hours. The wait time also adds to fuel costs. The tariff may help U.S. chassis manufacturers in the coming years and may increase employment in chassis manufacturing. That's in the future. For now, the chassis shortage and port bottlenecks just get worse.

China has not lived up to its Phase One commitments to increase purchases of U.S. goods and services by $200 billion in 2020 and 2021, in accordance with the trade agreement between the United States and China that went into effect on February 14, 2020. That agreement called for $80.1 billion in agricultural purchases; actual purchases through December 2021 were $56.3 billion, 30 percent below target. Manufactured goods imports were $137 billion compared to a target of $234.4 billion, a 41.5 percent shortfall. Energy imports were $28.6 billion versus a target of $66 billion, a 57 percent shortfall. In February 2022, the final tally on Phase One was in. Chinese purchases of U.S. goods did not even reach the predeal levels, let alone achieve the increases promised. Capital Economics reported, "China made none of the additional purchases it committed to under the Phase One trade deal. The Biden administration isn't pleased but doesn't have good options to force China to do more."[3] The Phase One agreements were a complete failure. No work is currently under way on a Phase Two. The 2020 trade agreement intended to end the 2018–2019 trade war is a dead letter.

A new dispute between China and Australia emerged in 2020. From 2009 to 2019 Australian exports to China tripled. China was by far Australia's largest trading partner. Australia provided about half the iron ore needed to feed China's steel industry and to support China's construction boom. Australia also provided substantial portions of China's total imports of coal, natural gas, and agricultural produce. Hard currency remittances by Chinese students working in Australia were an important source of foreign exchange for China.[4] These growing and mutually beneficial trading relations abruptly collapsed in April 2020 when Australia called for an independent international inquiry into the origins of the SARS-CoV-2 virus that causes COVID. Despite compelling evidence that the virus leaked from the Wuhan Institute of Virology in China's Hubei province, Australia reserved judgment and simply called for a fair inquiry.

Beijing retaliated by calling Australia's suggestion a witch hunt. One week later, China's ambassador to Australia, Chen Jingye, demanded consumer boycotts by Chinese of certain Australian imports, including wine. In May 2020, China imposed massive duties on Australian barley, which effectively priced Australia out of the Chinese market. In the following months, China imposed additional duties on Australian beef, wine, wheat, wool, sugar, copper, and timber. Chinese energy producers were told to stop buying Australian coal and to halt spot purchases of Australian liquid natural gas. Canberra was uncowed.

The Australian government did not back down from its call for an inquiry into the origins of the virus. After the initial shock of the boycotts and tariffs, Australia smoothly found other foreign markets for its much-needed coal and LNG exports, as well as its food and mining output. This is an example of trade diversion, similar to what U.S. soybean exporters did after Chinese boycotts in 2018. As one market closes, another buyer emerges as long as the goods are needed anywhere in the world. Analyst Jeffrey Wilson of the Perth USAsia Centre suggests that the Australia-China 2020 trade dispute makes a real-world case study in how decoupling from China might actually work. The bad news for China is that it seems to work quite well.

A smaller but still significant trade war broke out in 2021 between China and Lithuania, an EU member nation. In August 2021, the Republic of China opened a representative office in Vilnius, the capital of Lithuania, using the name "Taiwanese" instead of the less provocative "Taipei." In December 2021, Lithuania reported that all imports to China from Lithuania had been halted, and China had reprogrammed its computers to delist Lithuania as a country of origin for imports. The dispute quickly escalated, with the EU filing a complaint in the World Trade Organization alleging illegal discrimination under WTO rules. EU Executive Vice President Valdia Dombrovskis said, "[China's] measures are a threat to the integrity of the EU single market. They affect intra-EU trade and EU supply chains. And they have a negative impact on EU industry."[5] This dispute is another example of China's bullying tactics in using world trade to achieve political goals. It also illustrates how a seemingly minor dispute over the name on a rep office can escalate into a proceeding between two of the largest political and economic actors in the world—China and the EU.

On January 3, 2022, EU sanctions against Chinese officials having to do with human rights abuses in Xinjiang aimed at Uyghurs and other religious groups were extended until December 8, 2022. This decision came after the European Parliament suspended implementation of the EU-China Comprehensive Agreement on Investment (CAI) in May 2021. The CAI was agreed to in December 2020 after seven years of negotiations, yet implementation will likely be delayed at least until 2023 because of the EU sanctions on China and Chinese retaliation. Unlike matters involving tariffs and quotas, human rights sanctions leave little room for compromise.

On November 5, 2021, China's Taiwan Affairs Office (TAO) announced that any individuals supporting Taiwanese independence will be considered criminally liable for life, and companies supporting such individuals will be barred from conducting business in China. This holding has more to do with political interference by China in Taiwanese elections than direct trade. Still, it is one more impediment to commercial relations between Taiwan and China and another headwind to the efficient functioning of supply chains. Steps toward a Chinese invasion of Taiwan, as the Russian invasion of Ukraine shows, will trigger a tsunami of trade sanctions in both directions between the West and the invaders, which are explored in detail below. Other trade and investment disputes, some large, some small, are emerging daily. Far from winding down, the trade wars and strategic sanctions are on the rise.

Trade wars and tariffs are not the only elements disrupting supply chains. Regulation plays a role, with no relief in sight. The backup in Southern California ports is due at least in part to environmental regulations and labor policies. The expansion of warehouses and distribution centers in California has led to a backlash against associated noise and traffic. In turn, this led to overregulation. Certain localities have limited the hours when trucks can deliver to retailers. The state of California has limited the hours per day that diesel-powered equipment can operate and required that forklifts and facility trucks be electric, with onsite charging stations mandatory. Other requirements imposed by California for new warehouses include green construction standards and reduced CO_2 emissions on construction equipment. The South Coast Air Quality Management District has mandated that three thousand warehouses under its jurisdiction take steps such as installing solar panels and using electric vans for deliveries.[6] It's not clear how easily the solar panel mandate can be implemented when the United States is imposing high tariffs on solar panels. One can debate the requirements, although many make no sense. What is not debatable is that these requirements snarl supply chains and are not going away.

California also enacted a law in 2019 called AB5 as a sop to the International Brotherhood of Teamsters. The law reclassified many truckers as employees rather than independent contractors. This opened the door to union organizing efforts since unions were not able to organize independent contractors under the National Labor Relations Act. It also limited truckers' ability to work flexible hours and drive for multiple trucking firms. This limited flexibility increased costs because of mandatory overtime pay and reduced truckers' ability to respond flexibly to increased demand in certain lanes. AB5 also reduced the supply of truckers, as some simply quit the occupation because of red tape and reduced pay. Again, the point is not to debate the merits but to illustrate how ever-increasing regulation makes supply chains more dysfunctional.

The American Trucking Associations estimates that there is currently a shortage of eighty thousand drivers.[7] It's expected this shortage will double by 2030. Among factors affecting the truck driver shortage and making it worse include the prospect of self-driving robotic vehicles. What young prospective driver wants to embark on a career that may be obsolete in a few years? Long hours and time away from home have also taken a toll. These are traditional stresses in truck driving, but the isolation and vaccine requirements stemming from the pandemic have amplified the stress. The demographic skew of drivers, many in their fifties and sixties, leaves them more vulnerable to COVID, a good example of an emergent property of complex systems where two factors (age and COVID) interact in deleterious ways. At the other end of the age spectrum, truck drivers have to be twenty-one years old or older to obtain commercial driving licenses. The eighteen- to twenty-year-old window for the non–college bound is when many individuals make initial career choices. If you can't be a truck driver, you'll do something else and perhaps never revisit trucking as a choice. A new pilot program has begun to permit eighteen-year-olds to intern as drivers. That's fine, but it will take years to have a material impact, and there are legitimate safety concerns with under-twenty-one-year-old drivers in the world of big rigs. Meanwhile, drivers are aging out of the occupation at an accelerating rate. Leaving port facilities open longer as Biden mandated does no good when trucks don't show up due to driver shortages.

Another difficulty is truckers are usually paid by the mile. They are not paid for the first two hours of waiting time at pickup locations. As waiting times increase, driver pay declines, since the mileage-based pay is spread over more hours on the job. *The New York Times* reported these remarks by Bob Costello, chief economist at the American Trucking Associations: "If we don't fix this driver shortage, I think going into some of these stores and seeing some of the shelves with nothing on it could be our future."[8]

Beyond logistics issues involving trucks, chassis, and labor, there are strategic concerns that will impede supply chains. China is home to major port facilities including Ningbo near Shanghai and is the home country to COSCO Shipping, one of the largest marine transportation and ship chartering companies in the world, with over 1,310 vessels in its fleet. With these maritime logistical operations under its direct or indirect control, China has access to sophisticated cargo-data systems including Logink, a global logistics data platform. Access to such maritime information systems has raised concerns in both the U.S. national security community and the maritime industry that China could exploit the data for commercial advantage or military advantage in the event of embargoes, blockades, or interdiction of strategically important cargoes. If the United States were to attempt to cut off oil supplies to China, knowledge of the exact locations, vessels, and cargoes among oil shipments could enable China to swap cargoes or reroute vessels in a manner designed to defeat the embargo. In the commercial context, China's superior access to maritime information could facilitate its Belt and Road Initiative, or BRI, which includes a string of ports from Sri Lanka to Piraeus intended to facilitate Chinese exports and imports. Inna Kuznetsova, an expert in shipping data, said, "In logistics today, the flow of information is as important as the flow of money or goods."[9] China's potential misuse of critical logistics information will curb otherwise cooperative efforts to improve information sharing.

Every expert on supply chain management emphasizes the importance of information sharing, automation, and cooperation among participants in the logistics chain. In business, it's customary to closely hold data, customer lists, and shipping information. Such trade secrets offer competitive advantage. In supply chain management, the opposite can be true. The more information participants are willing to share, the more efficiently supply chains can operate. If retailers know a surge in products is arriving at distribution centers, they can plan sales and promotions to help move the merchandise. If shipping agents know that a client's factory output is expanding and more containers will soon be under way, they can select less congested shipping lanes to expedite delivery. These efficiencies and many others require data sharing with third parties, including potential competitors. This necessitates a cultural adjustment away from traditional business practices. Once logistics data is widely available, it can be automated and applied in ways that benefit everyone and minimize costs. That's the goal.

Reality is quite different, even after decades of improvement. Data is still withheld for traditional reasons despite potential gains from sharing. Some of this is because smaller supply chain participants are not acquainted with the benefits of cooperation or do not see how theoretical benefits accrue to them. Other participants simply do not have the resources to roll out the large logistics teams needed to realize benefits. Some data withholding is due to classic free riding behavior, where participants reap gains from others sharing data but do not do so themselves. Still, the difficulties are mostly due to inertia. Old habits die hard. Kendra Phillips, chief technology officer of Ryder, said, "What outsiders have difficulty understanding is how paper-based the supply chain really is."[10] Paper orders, phone calls, and hand-delivered bills of lading are still common. Not only are these processes not automated, they consume time when participants take steps to enter the manual data into systems that are. You cannot easily digitize a paper bill of lading on the spot. It's just paper.

Trucks and containers are critical links in supply chains, yet they rely on their own supply chains. Truck replacement parts are in short supply. Traffic delays are growing worse because of antiquated highway infrastructure. A J.B. Hunt Whitepaper estimates that traffic delays are equivalent to a 17 percent reduction in trucking capacity. Maritime expert John Monroe said, "A lot of companies will abandon their containers," because the price of fines and recovery is greater than the cost of the container. Actual implementation of automation, digitization, and optimization in transportation logistics lags far behind what academics recommend and envision. Experts agree on potential solutions. Still, the reality of segmentation, autonomy, lack of trust, money, time, and hurdles like traffic, downtime, and degraded infrastructure is real and growing worse. These problems are persistent and feed on themselves. None will be solved soon.

Pandemics and Public Health

The ongoing pandemic has impeded the efficient operation of global supply chains. The ruinous public policy response made the impact of the pandemic exponentially worse. Supply chains would have broken down with or without the pandemic. The pandemic would have been devastating with or without a supply chain breakdown. The combination of the two amplifies the damage of each. This ensures the damage will be long lasting.

Pandemic-related deaths have depleted the labor force, although economic effects were manageable since fatalities were heavily weighted to those over sixty-five years old. Of greater impact was the quarantine required of those of prime working age who contracted the virus and recovered. The typical two-week home quarantine meant that truckers couldn't haul loads, forklift drivers couldn't pick pallets, and crane operators couldn't off-load vessels. At the same time, consumers were stuck at home ordering goods online instead of spending money on services such as movies, restaurants, concerts, and sporting events. The result was a surge of imported goods and a simultaneous shortage of logistics personnel—a recipe for bottlenecks. The omicron variant that surged through global populations in December 2021 and January 2022 produced milder cases and fewer fatalities as a percentage of total cases than earlier strains, but the impact of self-quarantines was more severe. Even mild cases meant staying home, and that added to the acute labor shortages. Humans are not ancillary to supply chains, they are critical components.

These rolling and unpredictable labor shortages were enough to disrupt supply chains on their own. Still, that was not the worst impact of the pandemic. Much greater damage was done by the public health response, which was misguided at best and intentionally misleading at worst. Here are the baseline facts for evaluating public health policy during the pandemic:

- Vaccines do not stop infections and do not stop the spread of the virus. They are somewhat effective at reducing symptoms and acute cases in vulnerable populations for a few months after injection. So-called breakthrough infections among the vaccinated are just infections. There is no breakthrough because there is no protection against infection to begin with. This became abundantly clear during the December 2021 omicron wave when millions of double-vaxxed and boosted people became infected, although the evidence that vaccines didn't stop infection was available long before. There is emerging evidence that third and fourth shots, so-called boosters, effectively train the virus to avoid the genetic manipulation of mRNA vaccines and make the vaccinated more vulnerable to infection than the unvaccinated.
- Masks don't stop the spread of the virus. The SARS-CoV-2 virus is about 1/5000 the size of the weave in a typical mask. The virus

passes easily through the mask. Leave aside the fact that people don't wear the masks correctly. Masks do cause users to inhale recirculated CO_2, which causes lethargy and dizziness. Forcing children to wear masks is a kind of child abuse.

- Lockdowns don't work to stop the spread of respiratory viruses, a point made in a 2006 paper coauthored by Dr. D. A. Henderson, winner of the Presidential Medal of Freedom for his lead role in eradicating smallpox, and former dean of the Bloomberg School of Public Health of Johns Hopkins University.[11] Lockdowns create incubators in closed quarters with adults coming and going and spreading the virus. The safest conditions are to be outside with no mask getting exercise, sunshine, and fresh air. Children are scarcely affected by the disease and would have been much safer in school than stuck at home.

Based on this evidence and more, the best public health response to the pandemic would have been to have vaccines available for the most vulnerable, no vaccine mandates, no mask mandates, no lockdowns, voluntary quarantine for those who tested positive, no school closures, and no documentation requirements. The actual public policy response was the opposite in every respect. Mandates were imposed by politicians with no scientific training and public health bureaucrats with no clinical experience. It will be looked back upon as one of the greatest public policy blunders in history. The impact on supply chain operation was catastrophic.

Apart from labor shortages due to cases of COVID, the supply chain was impeded by vaccination mandates. Participants in U.S. transportation and warehouse logistics tended to have lower vaccination rates than the overall population. Many were terminated from their jobs or subjected to onerous testing requirements. This had no medical benefit for logistics teams, since the vaccines don't stop infection. Terminations did reduce operational capacity and tempo. Retail outlet closures caused inventory buildups in distribution centers, since expected sales never occurred. Warehouse vaccine mandates degraded operators' ability to pick and ship packages because unvaccinated employees could not work. Vaccine requirements among restaurant staff caused worker shortages, which slowed service and dissuaded customers from going to restaurants at all. Unnecessary school closings forced many parents to miss work in order to care for school-aged children. Crew quarantines in certain ports caused shipping lines to reroute vessels to friendlier destinations. Vaccine mandates, always pointless, vitiated human capital needed to operate supply chains at every stage.

Vaccine mandate mania reached its height on November 29, 2021, when popular business news host Jim Cramer said on CNBC, "How do we save lives and get business back and put dinner on the table? Simple: the federal government needs to require vaccines. It's time to admit we have to go to war against COVID. Require vaccinations universally. And have the military run it."[12] Cramer's ignorance of the role of vaccines is stunning. They don't stop infection or spread as the omicron variant showed soon after his remarks. His recommendation was both illegal and unconstitutional, as courts consistently held when similar mandates were tested in court. And his suggestion of mandatory injections of unwilling subjects by uniformed military is familiar to students of fascist regimes where government and big business hold hands to suppress free choice. Still, Cramer's rank fear was shared by CEOs, who threatened their employees and customers with similar mandates. Many supply chain workers simply stayed home, retired early, or otherwise quit the labor force. Shipping delays spread, and in-store service declined in a predictable manner.

The apogee of the anti-vax movement among truckers came on January 29, 2022, when over fifty thousand trucks in multiple convoys, including one stretching forty-five miles at times, converged on Ottawa to protest overreaching vaccine mandates from the government of Justin Trudeau. In bitterly cold weather, the Freedom Convoy surrounded Parliament Hill and paralyzed central Ottawa. Trudeau had already fled his home in a self-imposed quarantine resulting from exposure to a COVID sufferer a few days earlier. Another serious blow to the supply chain arose on February 7, 2022, when Canadian truckers blocked the Ambassador Bridge between Detroit, Michigan, and Windsor, Ontario. Almost 30 percent of U.S.-Canada trade passes over that bridge; it is the most heavily trafficked land crossing between the two countries. Omar Alghabra, the Canadian transport minister, said, "I've already heard from automakers and food grocers. This is really a serious cause for concern."[13] Ford and Honda began production shutdowns.

The Canadian protest endgame emerged as a real-time exercise in neo-fascist control of money. Prime Minister Trudeau used the Royal Canadian Mounted Police to trample protesters, smash truck windows, and arrest peaceful protesters, who were held without bail. His deputy prime minister, Chrystia Freeland, obtained hacked donor lists from a crowdfunding website supporting the truckers and moved quickly to freeze bank accounts and seize crypto wallets of truckers and their donors. Freeland's actions, a preview of events to come, are in keeping with the tenets of the Great Reset initiative advocated by the World Economic Forum, where she serves as trustee.

The truckers' protests spread to other U.S.-Canada border crossings and threatened fertilizer supplies to Western farmers. Similar protests arose around the world, including in France and Australia. Those living in fear of the virus à la Cramer disparaged the protesters. Whatever the politics and science, these protests contributed further to the disintegration of supply chains. The thousands of trucks involved could have delivered goods instead of fighting the mindless mandates.

A special kind of COVID mindlessness has emerged in Communist China. Chairman Xi is pursuing a Zero COVID policy. This is impossible to do. It's something like a zero-cold policy. People get colds and they always will. Still, ideologues don't flinch at impossible policies since there's no accountability for the damage they cause. Careers of Communist Party officials could be derailed or enhanced depending on how the outbreaks were handled. As the name implies, China had zero tolerance for any COVID outbreak of any magnitude. A single case resulted in a massive track-and-trace effort and quarantine of the infected individual and anyone who had come in recent contact with that person. Multiple cases caused entire parts of cities to be locked down and thousands of individuals to be forcibly relocated to quarantine camps located outside the city limits. Small outbreaks resulted in entire cities being locked down, all transportation links severed, and massive testing regimes imposed until zero cases were detected. One toddler in Ruili on China's border with Myanmar received over a hundred swab tests.[14] On October 31, 2021, tens of thousands of visitors were locked inside Disneyland in Shanghai after one person tested positive. Exactly that type of lockdown on a much larger scale happened in January 2022 in Xi'an in central China, a city of over 1.5 million residents and a major manufacturing center. In April 2022, China locked down all of Shanghai, a city of twenty-six million people, after an outbreak of the highly contagious omicron variant of the SARS-CoV-2 virus. Lockdown conditions in Shanghai were so extreme that workers in an Apple factory rioted in protest on May 5, 2022. By mid-May, the outbreak had spread to Beijing, a city of twenty-two million people, and selective lockdowns began there also.

On December 13, 2021, China closed dozens of manufacturing plants in the city of Shaoxing based on 173 reported cases of COVID. Most such cases were mild and nonfatal. Shaoxing is next to the port city of Ningbo, which is the world's third-largest port based on container volume. More than fifty thousand people in the Shaoxing-Ningbo area were placed under quarantine. Similar mass lockdowns and factory shutdowns occurred in Zhejiang province, a major manufacturing and logistics hub. The combination of manufacturing shutdowns and disruptions in port operations in Ningbo sent ripples throughout the global supply chain. Inside the containers waiting to be shipped from Ningbo were parts needed to meet downstream supply chain requirements at manufacturers, retailers, and distributors around the world. It is estimated that the Ningbo lockdown delayed over $4 billion in trade, including over $235 billion in semiconductor shipments.

China also imposed strict quarantine rules on foreign crews aboard vessels arriving in China. The crews cannot disembark and are locked down on their vessels. The stress on crews, who often spend six months on board and need some shore time for rest and recreation, is such that cargo-ship operators are now planning routes that avoid China. For good measure, Hong Kong announced on January 5, 2022, that it banned all flights from the United States, the UK, Australia, France, Canada, India, Pakistan, and the Philippines. When the so-called factory of the world shuts down willy-nilly, the impact on global supply chains is clear.

Zero COVID comes on top of unmistakable signs that Xi Jinping is decoupling China from global supply chains independently from pandemic policies. Xi has attacked China's publicly owned social media and big-tech firms on content and as potential political rivals. Jack Ma, the multibillionaire founder of tech giant Alibaba, has disappeared from public sight and remains under de facto house arrest. In February 2020, the initial public offering of Alibaba affiliate Ant Group was canceled. Chinese ride-hailing firm Didi, similar to Uber, was put under investigation by Chinese regulators, and its apps were ordered removed by China's Cyberspace Administration. On December 3, 2021, Didi announced it would delist from the New York Stock Exchange and relist on the Hong Kong Stock Exchange. While Pony Ma, founder of another Chinese tech giant, Tencent, has toed the party line, his firm has come under attack for its gaming business. Stock losses cost Pony Ma almost $14 billion. These are just a few examples of an all-out assault by the Communist Party of China on wealthy entrepreneurs and their megacompanies. This trend is a far cry from naive Western notions that the Chinese will be "just like us." China is not so much ending supply chains as it is creating new lanes controlled by the Chinese government. Existing supply chains will wither as Western firms onshore manufacturing, and China migrates to Chinese-controlled channels.

SOLD OUT

China's Zero COVID approach will fail. The Chinese vaccines don't work against the omicron variant, and the Chinese population has had no opportunity to gain herd immunity or natural antibodies because of Zero COVID protocols. The virus goes where it wants. Omicron is highly contagious. When a mass outbreak finally occurs, the impact on China and its economy will be devastating, made worse by futile efforts to maintain Zero COVID. Factories, ports, and entire cities will be shut down and transportation will grind to a halt. Hospitals will be overwhelmed while millions will get no care at all. Critical care centers will be superspreader sites. The impact on global supply chains will be more severe than anything seen so far.

Green Energy, Green Money

In another example of otherwise uncorrelated factors converging to produce unforeseen outcomes, long-standing climate alarm has impacted supply chains in costly ways. This is another drag on efficiency that will not fade soon. Before detailing the impact of climate alarm on supply chain management, it's useful to review the history of unfounded climate claims.

The climate is changing as it has for billions of years. Climate change is one of the most complex phenomena ever addressed by science, and perhaps the most difficult to model. The nature and causes of climate change are a worthy challenge for the best scientists using the most sophisticated tools available. Unfortunately, the study of climate change has been co-opted by pseudoscientists using flawed models, selected data, and hyperbolic claims echoed by ill-informed media and politicians with hidden agendas. Among the best-known boosters of climate alarm are Gillian Tett at the *Financial Times* and BlackRock's Larry Fink. Fortunately, there are rigorous scientists using hard data and robust models to address the phenomenon. This group includes Michael Shellenberger, Steven E. Koonin, Bjorn Lomborg, Bruce C. Bunker, M. J. Sanger, and many more.

These sober voices mostly agree that slight global warming is detectable but it's not a crisis and will not become a crisis in the foreseeable future. They concur that it's unclear whether CO_2 emissions are the main cause of warming even if they are a contributing cause. They point to other causes, including solar cycles, ocean salinity, ocean currents like El Niño and La Niña, cloud cover, aerosols, volcanoes, agricultural practices, and natural methane release. There are also numerous official reports that reach the same conclusion, although you may have to scan the footnotes to discover that; official reports produce scary headlines heavily diluted by detailed content. The single most important contribution of real scientists is to demonstrate how badly flawed the models used by the climate alarmists are.

A climate model divides the surface of the planet into a grid with squares of about 360 square miles each over land surfaces, and 36 square miles each over the oceans. That's about 101 million squares. Each square is extrapolated into a stack about 30 miles high to the outer edge of the stratosphere. All weather occurs in this zone, with most weather occurring within 10 miles of the earth's surface, in the troposphere. The vertical stacks are sliced horizontally into thin layers like pancakes, and each layer is analyzed separately for climate conditions in that slice, and the impact of such conditions on adjacent pancakes in adjacent stacks, and so on. One has to model this activity to a first approximation before getting to recursive functions.

If each pancake is one-mile thick, that comes to 3.03 billion pancakes. Analyzing one pancake is tricky. Analyzing 3.03 billion pancakes is mind-boggling. Analyzing the interaction of each of the 3.03 billion pancakes with each of the other 3.03 billion pancakes, even allowing for attenuated interaction at a distance, is a superlinear function that borders on the impossible in terms of computational complexity. One scientist estimates that if we had supercomputers one thousand times faster than today's computers the run time on the problem described above would be several months.[15] Climatology is complexity theory par excellence.

So how do scientists actually work with models that cannot be run with today's computers? They make assumptions. Lots of assumptions.

This process begins with a recognition that there are no direct observations of most of the atmospheric slices. We have satellites and weather stations recording temperature and precipitation, but those inputs include only a small fraction of the surface areas and heights described.

The point is that climate models are so complex and so sensitive to assumptions that scientists can get almost any result they want by tweaking inputs and running multiple scenarios. It also means the outputs are mostly worthless because of unfounded assumptions, computational complexity, and flawed model design. Most climate models are so deficient they can't even simulate the past based on known data let alone forecast the future. If a model of your own design can't backtest correctly, why should it be relied on to forecast? Yet these models are routinely touted as showing an "existential threat to mankind."

Let's begin an overview of the climate alarmist position by considering a few of their claims in the light of real science:

Surging sea levels will inundate the coasts. This is false. Sea levels have risen at the same pace for one hundred years, unaffected by climate change or human activity. The rate of increase is about seven inches per one hundred years. That's barely enough to get your feet wet in 2121 if it persists, which it may not.

Hurricanes are becoming more powerful and more frequent. This is false. The 2014 U.S. National Climate Assessment said, "There has been no significant trend in the global number of tropical cyclones nor has there been any trend identified in the number of U.S. land-falling hurricanes." There is evidence that property damage from hurricanes is increasing. Does this mean hurricanes are getting stronger? Not at all. It just means that rich owners with subsidized insurance are building mansions on sandbars where they don't belong. That's not climate change. It's stupidity.

Tornadoes are more powerful and more frequent. This is false. National Oceanic and Atmospheric Administration (NOAA) records from 1954 to 2014 show the number of tornadoes in the

United States of EF1 or greater (EF is the Enhanced Fujita Scale of tornado strength) is fairly consistent at about four hundred (with occasional spikes in 1973, 1982, 2008, and 2011). The number of tornadoes in the United States of EF3 or greater has been steady at around forty (with spikes in 1957, 1965, 1973, and 2011). No correlation has been shown between tornado strength and CO_2 emissions.

Snowstorms are becoming more frequent with greater accumulation of snow. This is false. Snowstorms are highly localized so, of course, measurements vary, with some locations getting more snow, some less. A chart of annual snowfall in Washington, D.C., from 1889 to 2018 shows the annual snowfall in inches has been trending downward for the entire 130-year period. If climate change has any impact at all, it is causing less snow. And there is no correlation between any climate change and an increase in CO_2 emissions.

Wildfires are destroying larger areas more frequently than ever before. This is false. Satellite data from NASA reveals that the global area burned annually by fires from 1998 to 2015 has declined by about 25 percent.

Similar data exists for ice sheets, droughts, floods, and other weather-related outcomes. In short, none of the extreme outcomes that the climate alarmists shout about are true. And there is no conclusive evidence that any extreme weather when it does occur is caused by human activity or CO_2 emissions.

It is true that CO_2 emissions are increasing. It's also true that scientists have detected a slight trend toward global warming. There is no clear evidence that human-caused CO_2 emissions are the principal source of global warming, although emissions could be a contributing factor along with sunspot cycles, ocean currents, and other natural causes that are difficult to measure. What is clear is that global warming, if any, is proceeding slowly; there is no looming catastrophe.

Despite climate alarmist claims, renewable energy sources are on the rise. Solar power is efficient and can make a valuable contribution to reducing CO_2 and CH_4 (methane) emissions. It is useful in remote locations and for powering single buildings or complexes where the photovoltaic system with batteries is in close proximity to the facility. Yet when used at scale, solar power is an inefficient contributor to the power grid. Solar has a use-it-or-lose-it dynamic that is unavailing in darkness or bad weather. When the solar field is producing electricity, it may not match the grid needs at the time. Huge amounts of land are needed to build large-scale fields. Batteries are a solution to unreliability, but they create their own problems in terms of expense, maintenance, and space. Also, the manufacture and disposal of batteries with poisonous chemicals and metals creates environmental problems at odds with the problems it is intended to solve. Solar has its place, but the contribution is marginal. It cannot replace carbon-based fuels.

Wind turbines are less efficient than solar panels and are not practical in terms of a robust replacement for oil and gas. Wind turbines are capable of generating significant amounts of energy without CO_2 and CH_4 emissions in their operation. Of course, this ignores the enormous amount of carbon-based energy used in the manufacture, transportation, and installation of turbines. Still, wind turbines today generate over 650 gigawatts of power, and 60 GW are being added each year (1 gigawatt = 1 billion watts). It takes 3.125 million solar panels (3' x 5' each) to generate 1 GW. A single wind turbine using the latest technology with a height of about three hundred feet can produce 3,000kW (1 kW = 1,000 watts). To that extent, wind turbines are an efficient substitute or alternative to photovoltaic systems in terms of the amount of space utilized relative to electrical output. Despite that efficiency, wind turbines are subject to the same problems as solar panel systems. They produce power on an intermittent basis. For solar power, that means when the sun is shining. For wind power, that means when the wind is blowing. While engineers will search for optimal locations, it's the case that the wind doesn't blow at all times even in the windiest corridors. This leaves wind power in the use-it-or-lose-it category also. Wind power can feed the grid, but it cannot be relied upon by the grid operators. Power cannot be stored without expensive batteries, which are impractical on a large scale.

Electric vehicles, or EVs, are not an efficient solution to carbon emissions either for two reasons. The first is that the EVs need to be charged with electricity from the grid, which is still powered by oil, natural gas, and coal. In fact, China has the largest potential market for EVs, and over 50 percent of China's domestic energy comes from coal-fired plants. The supposedly clean EV is just a battery-powered intermediary for coal-generated electricity. The other problem is the same issue we have encountered with solar power and wind turbines—batteries. Unless you are feeding the grid on an intermittent and un-reliable basis, wind and solar depend on batteries.

If neither the renewable sources such as wind and solar nor the EV is a complete answer to the issue of carbon emissions, why do global elites insist on a radical overhaul of the existing energy system? What accounts for the climate hysteria of the political and media elites de-spite the lack of scientific evidence for human-caused global warming? Some of those repeating outrageous claims are doing just that—repeating things they've heard from other media or political leaders without independent inquiry or investigation. Unfortunately, the pub-lic relies on media elites and political leaders for their information. As decades roll by and scare stories are discredited time and again, pub-lic skepticism will rise, and the alarmists will lose credibility. The danger is that alarmists may pass legislation, limit choices, and im-pose costs in the name of climate change before the public catches on to the scam. At that point, the economic damage becomes semiper-manent even if alarmism fades.

Some scientists who espouse alarmist positions on climate change are in line for large research grants from activist foundations and NGOs. Executives who take alarmist positions may find their stock prices boosted by institutions making ESG-style investments (for en-vironment, social, and governance criteria). Wealth advisers who promote ESG funds profit from management fees and performance fees as the money rolls into those investment schemes. Academics who caution that the climate threat is overblown may be denied tenure or publication and be subject to cancel culture disparagement. Media anchors who promote climate alarmism can improve ratings. Websites that feature climate catastrophe stories get clicks. Politicians can get votes by appearing to "do something" about a supposed existential threat.

Financial elites claim the climate is a threat as a basis for garnering power. A powerful echo chamber of academics, wealth managers, bankers, regulators, celebrities, politicians, and CEOs who talk up climate threats has emerged. They create feedback loops in which media attention justifies bank regulation, which supports green investing, which supports research grants, and so on, until the world is thoroughly convinced that a climate catastrophe is real. It's not real, but the narrative thrives.

One of the most potentially damaging developments is the creation of the Glasgow Financial Alliance for Net Zero, an elite group using climate alarm as a Trojan horse to pursue global financial control. The head of GFANZ is Mark Carney, previously the head of three central banks—Canada, UK, and the Bank for International Settlements— and de facto leader of the global financial elite. His cochair is Michael Bloomberg, multibillionaire of the eponymous information network and prominent climate alarmist. The principals list includes the usual suspects: Brian Moynihan, CEO of Bank of America; Larry Fink, CEO of BlackRock; Jane Fraser, CEO of Citi; Nili Gilbert, board member of the David Rockefeller Fund; and their ilk. The complete membership controls over $130 trillion in assets. GFANZ's convening power was the United Nations.

GFANZ plans to pressure central banks and bank regulators to issue rules that will steer asset allocations and bank lending away from oil and natural gas providers and ancillary businesses such as pipeline and crude oil shipping toward unreliable energy sources such as wind turbines, solar modules, and batteries built from poisonous chemicals. The real purpose of these efforts is centralized control of global finance by an elite group. Climate alarm is a convenient platform. What better way to impose global control than to rely on a global catastrophe, even an invented one? GFANZ is just the beginning of a series of steps to employ unified financial control to squash dissenting voices and push unpopular agendas such as gun control, population control, world money, and world taxation. These efforts will fail, as they always do, but not without damage in the meantime. Predictable results include higher energy prices, energy shortages, disruptions in transportation logistics, and tax burdens imposed on reliable sources of oil and natural gas. Again, efficient supply chains will be the primary victim. Consumers will bear the costs.

In light of unsettled real science, what conclusions can be drawn? The following appear:

1. The climate is changing. It always has and always will. There's plenty of room to disagree with the climate alarmists without falling into the trap of being a "climate-change denier." Yes, climate changes, yet it's a slow process and quite complex. What's needed is observation and experimentation, not hysteria.

2. Carbon emissions are increasing. These emissions consist mainly but not exclusively of carbon dioxide (CO_2) and methane (CH_4). The quantity is small relative to the composition of the atmosphere; nitrogen (N) and oxygen (O) together make up 99 percent of the atmosphere; argon (Ar) makes up over half the remaining 1 percent, but the reflective heat-trapping qualities of carbon dioxide and methane are significant. CO_2 alone accounts for 7 percent of the atmosphere's heat-trapping capacity. The CO_2 concentration increased from 280 parts per million (ppm) in 1750 to 410 ppm today. Still, most of that increase occurred before significant consumption of oil and gas, and most of the increase is from natural causes. So, humans are contributing to carbon emissions, but they are not the sole source, and the impact on total warming is unclear.

3. Sea levels are rising. This is true, but they have been rising for one hundred years at about the same pace and there's no evidence for the impact of global warming on sea levels. The current pace is about seven inches per century. That's far from an existential threat and, no, cities will not be underwater.

4. Solar modules and wind turbines can contribute renewable energy to the grid to reduce carbon emissions. Yet they are not a substitute for oil and gas. They are intermittent sources and therefore unreliable. Battery storage is too expensive and causes its own increase in the use of poisonous chemicals. Even as solar and wind capacity increases, global demand for energy will increase faster. EVs have limited range, and charge with electricity provided by oil, gas, and coal, and therefore do not reduce overall emissions.

Far from the hysterical claims of climate alarmists, the prospect for climate change is straightforward. Climate change will continue despite efforts to reduce emissions. Wind and solar power will grow, yet they will not replace oil and gas. The more extreme remedies of the climate alarmists such as global carbon taxes, caps on carbon emissions, and a ban on oil and gas exploration and development will fail because they lack popular support and are unnecessary according to the best available science.

Shutting down the Keystone XL Pipeline project is high-profile political theater, but it won't change anything. Alberta tar sands oil will still arrive in the United States. It's just that it will come by rail instead of pipeline. Rail transportation is dirtier than pipeline transportation; the alarmists don't care—they just want the show of shutting down a pipeline. So, there will be costs imposed and inefficiencies locked in because of political posturing.

In the end, CO_2 emissions will continue to rise but at a slower rate. Sea levels will rise for reasons unrelated to emissions, but at such a slow rate not to be noticeable. Average global temperatures may rise slightly for reasons that science does not fully understand. This will have almost no economic costs and may create economic benefits as certain regions become more productive in terms of agricultural output due to longer, warmer growing seasons. Hurricanes, tornadoes, wildfires, and droughts will continue as they have in the past, unaffected by climate change or even global warming. Life will go on. Energy demands will increase as developed economies continue to grow in order to support aging populations. Developing economy energy demands will grow even faster to support a youth cohort looking for at least a middle-income lifestyle. Oil and gas are not going away. They are too important, have too many embedded structural advantages, and have huge economies of scale. Once politicians and the media become more aware of the real science of climate change and distance themselves from climate alarmists, the oil and gas industries will regain their footing. While climate alarm may fade, the damage to supply chains will not.

Geoeconomics and the Supply Chain

In considering supply chain disruptions coming from China and Russia, it's helpful to perceive these situations through the lens of geoeconomics, a portmanteau from the words "geopolitics" and "economics." There's nothing new about combining those two disciplines. Wars are geopolitical and are often won through industrial capacity and supply chains, which are primarily economic. The UK won the Napoleonic Wars in part because of its ability to impose a commercial blockade on continental Europe through the Royal Navy. The Japanese attack on Pearl Harbor was triggered in part by Franklin D. Roosevelt freezing Japanese bank accounts and imposing an oil embargo in the months before the Japanese attack. Economics and global strategy have always been entwined.

What is new is the idea that economics is not just an adjunct of geopolitics; it is the main event. This does not mean that warfare is over or that military prowess does not count. It means the major powers in a globalized age will base their calculations on economic gain and loss and will use supply chains and productive capacity not as ancillary tools but as primary weapons.

This change was described at the beginning of the new age of globalization by strategic thinker Edward N. Luttwak in a seminal article, "From Geopolitics to Geo-Economics: Logic of Conflict, Grammar of Commerce."[16] Luttwak asserted that the end of the Cold War and the start of globalization meant armed conflict was too costly and uncertain for great powers. Economic interests would now be the arena for great-power conflict. Luttwak wrote, "The waning of the Cold War is steadily reducing the importance of military power in world affairs. . . . The deference that armed strength could evoke in the dealings of governments over all matters—notably including economic questions—has greatly declined and seems set to decline further. Everyone, it appears, now agrees that the methods of commerce are displacing military methods—with disposable capital in lieu of firepower, civilian innovation in lieu of military-technical advance, and market penetration in lieu of garrisons and bases."

To be clear, Luttwak's analysis principally applied to great powers including the United States, China, Russia, Japan, and EU members. Luttwak recognized that middle powers such as Israel, Iran, Iraq, Pakistan, North Korea, and some others might still find warfare beneficial. He did not rule out the fact that great powers might be engaged in wars involving these middle powers, such as the U.S. interventions in Iraq and Afghanistan, and Russia's invasion of Ukraine. His point was not that war was obsolete, only that it would not involve direct confrontation between great powers.

Geoeconomics—great-power competition using economics as a goal and a weapon—is an excellent tool for analyzing the breakdown of global supply chains and their likely replacements. For example, if the United States and Russia directly fight each other in Eastern Europe, that would mark a breakdown in the Luttwak thesis. Conversely, if the U.S.-Russia standoff unfolds through channels involving global payments and flows of natural gas and energy supplies, it validates

Luttwak. This provides a useful frame for analysts trying to understand the current supply chain crisis and what comes next.

We'll begin consideration of the current and future fate of supply chains by focusing on the most critical link in the chain—China.

China: Canceled

China is on both the sending and receiving ends of global supply chains. Many of the finished goods it sends around the world come from assembling inputs that it imports from elsewhere. China's significance in global commerce is due to its unique role as both the destination for natural resource inputs and the source of manufactured goods. China has earned its nickname: factory to the world.

This role was achieved by design. Beginning with Deng Xiaoping's opening to the world in 1979, renewed by his 1992 Southern Tour in the wake of the 1989 Tiananmen Square massacre, China sought direct foreign investment, foreign technology, and jobs for the hundreds of millions of Chinese moving from rural areas to cities in search of higher incomes and better lives. This opening by China was welcomed by Western leaders. From the advent of globalization in 1989 until the 2008 global financial crisis, liberals in the West adhered to the idea that economic growth in China would lead to political liberalization. In a nutshell, liberals believed that with enough time and enough prosperity China would become "just like us." In the meantime, the economic gains from globalization and global supply chains would accrue to Western consumers and investors. It would be a global win-win.

This elite plan for the gradual liberalization of China was the driving force behind China's admission to the World Trade Organization in 2001, and the inclusion of the Chinese yuan in the International Monetary Fund's world money basket called the Special Drawing Right (SDR) in 2016 alongside the dollar, euro, yen, and pounds sterling. China did not technically qualify for WTO or SDR status, yet it was being ushered into these exclusive clubs with a view that China would soon conform to what are known as the rules of the game.

This view was amplified by the huge numbers of Chinese students attending top U.S. universities. The belief was that Chinese students attending Harvard, MIT, and the University of Chicago, among other schools, would return to China, assume leadership roles, and implement policies similar to those promoted by thought leaders in the United States who had attended the same schools. Realist observers never put much stock in this view. They insisted that Communism was a pervasive ideology, the Chinese Communist Party maintained rigid control, and any dissenting views would eventually be crushed. China would take the economic gains (and stolen intellectual property) from interaction with the West but would otherwise stay on the Communist road.

The realist view was always correct, yet it took the liberals thirty years to see reality. The awakening of the liberal glitterati to the reality of Communist China—including slavery, genocide, concentration camps, thought control, organ harvesting, arbitrary arrest, and torture— is now in full swing. Detailed policy responses vary, yet Democrats and Republicans are united in the view that China is an adversary if not an outright enemy and needs to be confronted on both economic and humanitarian grounds.

The second major recent development affecting global supply chains is the rise of Xi Jinping. After the chaos of Mao Zedong and the rejection of Maoism by Deng Xiaoping, China settled into a calm and orderly governance process. The key was consensus. There would be a leader, but the leader would build consensus inside the Politburo, continue the economic growth started under Deng Xiaoping, and avoid high-profile blunders and confrontations. Each leader would serve two consecutive five-year terms, with the successor clearly identified during the second term so there would be an uneventful transition. This pattern was followed by Jiang Zemin (1993–2003), by Hu Jintao (2003–2013), and initially by Xi Jinping (2013–).

Now, Xi Jinping has broken the mold. Through a series of Party Congresses and other forums, he has elevated himself to a place comparable to Mao Zedong in the pantheon of the Communist Party, enshrined "Xi Jinping Thought on Socialism with Chinese Characteristics for a New Era," and made it clear that he will remain in office beyond the customary expiration of his term in 2023. In effect, Xi is president for life, and the new Mao.

This change in leadership and governance has resulted in profound changes in policy. Xi actively attacks big tech and media firms inside China. He has pushed to delist Chinese companies from NASDAQ and the NYSE and move those listings to the Hong Kong stock exchange. He has crushed the last traces of democratic process and free speech in Hong Kong. Most dangerously, he has threatened to take Taiwan by force.

To put Chinese geoeconomic threats in perspective, it's essential to have a gauge of just how critical China is to global supply chains. The impact of China's role goes far beyond delivery and pricing of needed inputs and manufactured goods. China's role as supplier of commodities, components, and finished goods has strategic implications for the national security of its trading partners.

A recent monograph entitled "Breaking the China Supply Chain: How the 'Five Eyes' Can Decouple from Strategic Dependency" presents a rigorous quantitative summary of the degree of dependence on China by leading developed economies.[17] Five Eyes is the name of an intelligence-sharing collective that includes Australia, Canada, New Zealand, the United States, and the UK. This intelligence aspect has been broadened to cover strategic concerns, including supply chain vulnerabilities. The Five Eyes report defines strategic dependence as "a level of reliance on imports from another country that gives the exporting country the ability to significantly impact the overall domestic availability of that imported good." The test of whether an importing nation is strategically dependent is based on whether more than 50 percent of its imports of a category of goods come from China, whether the nation is a net importer of those goods, and whether China has a greater than 30 percent global market share in those goods. If the answer to all three questions is yes, then your country is strategically dependent on China. The same analysis can be applied at the industry and sector levels using the UN's Harmonized System of categorization for traded goods.

The Five Eyes study considered 5,910 categories of goods under the Harmonized System. The results showed strategic dependence by number of categories as follows: Australia, 595; Canada, 367; New Zealand, 513; the UK, 229; and the United States, 414. It is likely that similar analysis applied to other major developed economies in the EU and Japan would show similar levels of dependency. The study was further broken down to include only those categories of goods that fell into what the Five Eyes consider the Critical 11 industries of the ongoing Fourth Industrial Revolution. The Critical 11 are: communications, energy, health care, transportation, water, banking, critical manufacturing, emergency services, food, government facilities, and information technology. In Critical 11 industries, strategic dependence on Chinese goods among the 5,910 categories studied appeared as follows: Australia, 167; Canada, 83; New Zealand, 144; the UK, 57; and the United States, 114. This is a shocking level of dependence by the West on imports from China that could, if interrupted, shut down critical infrastructure and needed services in developed economies.

Finally, the Five Eyes report looked at what it called the Future 9. These are sectors that will dominate future economic growth and technological superiority. Staying ahead of China in future technologies will be more important than staying even in existing technologies, from a national security perspective. The Future 9 are: artificial intelligence, robotics, computer hardware, cryptography, materials and manufacturing science, nanotechnologies, networking and data communications, quantum technology, and synthetic biology. The results showed strategic dependence by the Five Eyes on Chinese exports of goods from the Future 9 sectors as follows: Australia, 35; Canada, 25; New Zealand, 35; the UK, 12; and the United States, 25. Again, a strikingly high level of dependence on Chinese goods is at the center of the struggle for global hegemony.

Strategic dependence varies by types of goods and the particular Chinese trading partner selected. Australia relies on China for 69 percent of its penicillin and almost 100 percent of its manganese used in medicine and as a metallic alloy. New Zealand relies on China for 100 percent of its aspirin and 96 percent of its penicillin. Canada imports 77 percent of its magnesium used in specialized steel, electronics, and nanotechnology applications from China. Canada also imports 71 percent of its shipping containers, 87 percent of its laptops, and 58 percent of its vitamin C from China. The United States is no less dependent. Chinese exports account for 51 percent of lithium-ion batteries, 68 percent of certain rare-earth metals, 93 percent of laptops, and 52 percent of penicillin in the United States. The UK is only slightly less dependent, with 68 percent of its laptops and 61 percent of its mobile phones coming from China.

These figures only scratch the surface of Chinese dominance of strategically important inputs to the global supply chain. China controls 39.67 percent of the global market for lithium-ion batteries used in numerous devices from smartphones to electric vehicles. China also accounts for 68.75 percent of global laptop exports and 62.33 percent of the global market for vitamin C, which has health benefits and is an ingredient in food preservation. China controls 80 percent of global production of magnesium. Similar dominant market shares of global output appear in a long list of critical commodities, foodstuffs, and manufactured products.

This litany of Chinese export dominance and developed economy dependence on key products seems to position China for the regional hegemony and global superpower status it seeks. Western analysts are counting down until Chinese GDP surpasses U.S. GDP to make China the world's largest economy. China already has the world's largest population, the world's second-largest economy, and the world's fourth-largest nuclear arsenal. Does the future belong to China? Actually, no. China is moving quickly toward a world historic economic and demographic collapse. And that is the single most important reason that global supply chains will collapse alongside. The supply chains will be rebuilt, but they will bear little resemblance to Supply Chain 1.0 that has prevailed since 1989.

The reasons for China's coming collapse are well known if mostly ignored by the media. Of these, the most important reason is China's looming demographic disaster. The key metric in demographics is 2.1 as a measure of children per couple. This is called the replacement rate: the number of children each couple must have on average to maintain a given population at a constant level.

A birthrate of 1.8 is below the replacement rate of 2.1. This means your population is declining. It may be aging also, as the existing population lives longer and new births neither replace the dying nor lower the median age. A birthrate of 4.1 is well above the replacement rate. This means your population is expanding and your median age falls even as individuals live longer. The replacement rate of 2.1 is the dividing line between population growth and decline.

Why isn't the replacement rate 2.0? If two people have two children, doesn't that maintain the population at a constant level? The answer is no, because of infant mortality and other premature deaths. If a couple has two children and one dies before reaching adulthood, then only one child can contribute to future population growth as an adult. A birthrate of 2.1 makes up for this factor and contributes two adult children per two adult parents. Obviously, no one has 2.1 children. The replacement rate is an average. If five couples have three children each and two other couples have one child each, the average of the seven couples is 2.43 per couple, comfortably above the replacement rate of 2.1.

Demographics are not merely one among many factors affecting economic growth; demographics are the dominant factor by a wide margin. Other factors that affect economies include interest rates, exchange rates, inflation, deflation, central bank policy, geopolitics, consumer expectations, and many more. Still, none of these are as important as demographics, because demographics are about people and economies are nothing more than the sum total of the actions of people in those economies.

China's population is 1.4 billion people, about 17 percent of the world's population. According to World Bank statistics, China's birthrate is 1.7, well below replacement rate. China's situation is likely far worse than this high-level data suggests. There is some evidence that China's birthrate figures are overstated for political reasons, and the actual birthrate is close to 1.1 or lower. That will produce a shocking rate of population decline and economic decline. On January 17, 2022, China announced that its birthrate in 2021 had declined for the fifth straight year. *The New York Times* reported, "China is facing a demographic crisis that is beyond the imagination of the Chinese authorities and the international community."[18]

The simplest way to describe the impact of demographics on GDP is with the equation L x h = GDP. In this equation, L is labor productivity and h is the total hours worked. You multiply hours worked by productivity and the result is total output, or GDP. If a population is shrinking on the one hand and aging on the other, it's axiomatic that fewer hours will be worked and each hour will be less productive on average because considerable resources will be devoted to the care of the aged, which does not lend itself to productivity gains.

Today, more than 160 million Chinese are sixty years old or older. By 2040, the over-sixty cohort will be in excess of 250 million people, with many in their eighties and nineties. Aging is highly correlated with dementia, Alzheimer's disease, and Parkinson's disease. Hundreds of millions of prime-working-age Chinese will be needed to provide eldercare. Giving a dementia patient a bath is a worthy occupation, but bathing has not changed in seven thousand years of civilization. The last productivity gains in bathing were the introduction of indoor plumbing and hot water between 1870 and 1930. The demographics of smaller populations and aging mean slower growth in productivity and ultimately declining GDP. This hasn't happened on a large scale since the Thirty Years' War (1616–1648), and before that the Black Death of the 1350s.

China's one-child policy from 1980 to 2019 led to between 30 million and 60 million cases of sex-selective abortions, or female infanticide—baby girls were drowned in a bucket of water kept next to the delivery bed. The normal sexual skew is 105 boys to 100 girls.

China has been producing 120 boys to 100 girls by killing girls. This means future reproductive potential is even lower than the low birthrate implies because of excess males who cannot have babies. Researchers Darrell Bricker and John Ibbitson summarize the Chinese case as follows:

> The Chinese population will fall to around 754 million by 2100, a quarter billion people below the UN's medium estimate, and an astonishing 630 million fewer people than are alive in China today. China's population could decline by almost half in this century. And even that is not the lowest-case scenario. If . . . Lutz's Rapid Development Model . . . turns out to be accurate, the population could collapse to between 612 and 643 million. Several hundred million people could disappear from the face of the earth.[19]

This has implications far beyond economic growth and world trade. A collapse of this magnitude would result in a crisis of political legitimacy and could presage the collapse of the Communist Party of China. Bricker and Ibbitson conclude: "China appears to be on the verge of a deliberate, controlled, massive collapse of its population. Nothing like this has ever occurred."[20]

Declining population and lower productivity are only the beginning of challenges faced by China. In the late 1990s, China expanded a social welfare system that provides a modest pension and health insurance. Researcher Thomas J. Duesterberg reports that "in 2020, some 456 million people were covered by the employer-based urban plan and another 542 million by the supplementary urban and rural plan. This still leaves hundreds of millions not receiving pension support. . . . Data show that revenues for both plans were roughly 10 percent below outlays in 2020 and required government subsidies. . . . A study in 2019 concluded that the state pension fund would 'run dry by 2035' due to the decline of the workforce."[21] Efforts were announced in July 2022 to extend benefits coverage to "flexible workers" (mostly rural migrants without needed documentation). Despite such efforts, China's pension plans offer spotty coverage, suffer negative cash flow, and will be broke in thirteen years without more government support.

China has shocking income inequality. The World Bank estimates the top 10 percent of earners in China captured more than 40 percent of total income in 2018. China's Gini coefficient (a measure of income inequality) rose from 0.33 in 1990 to 0.53 in 2013 according to IMF figures. China suffers income distribution problems based on geography too, with workers in coastal and north-central China earning more than 2.5 times the income of those in rural regions.

China suffers extreme environmental degradation. Foreign policy scholars Hal Brands and Michael Beckley report that "China is running out of resources. Half of its rivers has disappeared, and pollution has left 60 percent of its groundwater—by the government's own admission—'unfit for human contact.' Breakneck development has made it the world's largest net energy importer. Food security is deteriorating; China has destroyed 40 percent of its farmland through overuse and become the world's largest importer of agricultural products."[22]

China is utterly dependent on the rest of the world for energy. China is the world's largest coal producer and generates about 58 percent of its electricity from burning coal. Despite China's production, it still imports 300 million tons per year mainly from Australia and Indonesia. China also imports over 10 million barrels per day of oil, roughly equal to the total daily production of Saudi Arabia. China's natural gas imports were over 1.5 trillion cubic feet in 2020 and are rising at a rapid pace. China is currently negotiating long-term take-or-pay liquid natural gas purchase agreements with Qatar.

Other factors hindering Chinese growth and its ability to feed global supply chains are excessive debt, shadow banking, asset bubbles, real estate speculation, and overinvestment in nonproductive infrastructure, including ghost cities, and white elephant public facilities such as train stations and airports. As much as 20 percent of China's reported GDP growth in the past fifteen years has been wasted on excessive construction that can never pay its way.

The biggest headwind to Chinese growth is the radical pivot of Chinese Communist Party leader Xi Jinping from the expansionary policies of Deng Xiaoping to the hard-line policies of Mao Zedong. There are two views on why this happened. The first is the realist view that Xi is a true ideologue, and there is nothing surprising about his efforts to arrest successful oligarchs, handicap big tech in China, favor state-owned enterprises (SOEs), and force publicly held Chinese companies to delist in New York and move their listings to Hong Kong. Chinese Communists have a long history of liberalizing economic and social policies as a way to encourage liberal voices, only to cut off those voices through arrest, torture, and execution once they are exposed. This trend toward totalitarian methods has also been used to crush dissent in Hong Kong, in violation of the Sino-British Joint Declaration of 1984, meant to ensure Hong Kong's autonomy until 2047. Xi Jinping has endorsed an approach to the West called wolf warrior diplomacy, which relies on insults, name-calling, and threats. Xi's approach is widely ridiculed among seasoned diplomats. It does nothing to advance China's case among global elites.

The second view, expounded by liberals, is that Xi intended to continue Deng's policies but simply failed at every turn. As explained by analyst Daniel H. Rosen, efforts by the People's Bank of China in 2013 to reduce short-term funding supporting asset bubbles ended in a 10 percent stock market minicrash.[23] The PBOC backed off and the bubbles resumed. Xi's efforts in 2013 to allow the Chinese to invest overseas led to a $1 trillion collapse in China's reserve position and the imposition of capital controls. This taxonomy of attempted easing and repeated failure continued through stock market crashes and a major yuan devaluation in 2015. The latest fiasco is the collapse of Evergrande, the world's largest property developer and mortgage lender, in 2021. These cumulative failures resulted in a drying up of direct foreign investment, as Western investors lost trust in China's ability to grow. In Rosen's telling, Xi's retreat into hard-line Communism was not by design. It was the last resort of a leader on the brink of political failure. The Communist Party can at least protect the interests of its members even if it cannot help the citizens or the economy.

For purposes of our global supply chain analysis, this debate between realists and liberals doesn't matter. Both sides agree that Xi Jinping is now squashing the most innovative companies in China and promoting inefficient but malleable SOEs. That approach will buy time but will kill growth and the innovation needed to support global supply chains. In stages, the factory of the world is shutting down.

China's turn toward totalitarianism comes not from a position of strength but rather from a position of weakness. Duesterberg's research states, "The World Economic Forum's annual assessment of countries' economic competitiveness is relevant: China has languished for the last decade in the middle of the pack of advanced economies, lagging behind countries such as Spain, the United Arab Emirates, and Malaysia as well as most of the OECD countries. Its overall global ranking is 28th out of 130 countries, and it ranks 39th in macroeconomic stability, 64th in skills, 72nd in labor markets, 27th in innovation, 36th in business dynamics and 29th in financial markets."[24] Analysts estimate that 22 percent of all loans in the Chinese banking system are nonperforming. Far from being a juggernaut, China is an also-ran in the global economic sweepstakes.

China is a classic victim of the middle-income trap in which a nation moves from poverty to sufficiency in a straightforward way yet cannot manage the final leap to high-income status. The low-hanging fruit of migration from rural to urban areas and expansion of assembly-style manufacturing with help from foreign capital has been achieved. The rise to high-income status requires high-value-added processes based on technology and innovation. China has been able to make a start in this direction with stolen technology. Now the ability to steal more has been curtailed by Western awareness and tighter security. China's economy has hit what aviators call stall speed. The plane is still in the air but it's not climbing and is perilously close to falling out of the sky.

In the face of the coming Chinese failure, reconfiguration of global commerce from Supply Chain 1.0 to Supply Chain 2.0 is well under way. Direct foreign investment is a major driver of economic growth and manufacturing capacity. This investment is increasingly aimed at Vietnam, Indonesia, Malaysia, and India. On April 11, 2022, Apple announced it had started making its iPhone 13 in Sriperumbudur, Nadu State, India, as part of an effort to reduce its reliance on China. Investment in China by Taiwan dropped 70 percent over the past ten years. Onshoring of technology investment by developed economies is also hurting China's chances to move into high-growth activities. Taiwan Semiconductor and Intel have separately announced plans to build state-of-the-art semiconductor fabs in the United States with almost $20 billion of combined investment. This is the kind of investment that might have gone to China if it had not chosen the totalitarian road. In January 2022, the National Critical Capabilities Defense Act was introduced in the U.S. Congress.[25] This act would apply national security scrutiny to direct foreign investment by U.S. investors in China and other countries of concern. Such scrutiny is the mirror image of the existing Committee on Foreign Investment in the United States, CFIUS, which examines investments by China and other nations in U.S. target companies. This type of national security review of two-way foreign investment is another impediment to hyperglobalization and efficient supply chains.

The disruption of the global supply chain would be severe if China's problems were limited to demographics, debt, and the political pivot described above. The reality may be much worse. We may be witnessing Peak China. Hal Brands and Michael Beckley raised this possibility in a series of articles in late 2021.[26] China's leaders understand that they are not economically or militarily superior to the United States. If you believed that strategic superiority was just a matter of time, you would wait until that status was achieved. In the meantime, you would avoid geopolitical confrontation and focus on growth. Brands and Beckley suggest a darker possibility. If China's growth is slowing, and the United States is entering a period of renewal due to onshoring and decoupling, then China's relative position may never be better, despite deficiencies. China's leadership may have realized the current situation is as good as it gets. If China aims to take Taiwan by force, it must proceed quickly, because the chances of success decline from here. This was the same dynamic that drove Germany to fight World War I in 1914 and Japan to attack Pearl Harbor in 1941. In neither case was the aggressor stronger than the target. It was the case that the odds of success had peaked, and the time had come to either attack or accept a subordinate position. For an ambitious, expanding power such as Germany and Japan, and now China, the logical choice is to attack.

A historical review is a good way to begin the Peak China analysis. Following the defeat of Japan in World War II, the Chinese Communist Party led by Mao Zedong and the Nationalist Party led by Chiang Kai-shek resumed a civil war for control of China that had begun in late 1928. By 1949, the Communist Party had taken control of mainland China, while Nationalist forces retreated to the island of Taiwan and some smaller nearby islands. Both forces declared themselves to be the legitimate government of China, with the Communists proclaiming the People's Republic of China (PRC), and the Nationalists proclaiming the Republic of China (ROC). The PRC dominates the comparison by size and population. Taiwan has a significantly higher per capita GDP and has emerged as a technology giant on the global stage.

The United States recognized the ROC as China's legitimate government from 1949 to 1979, at which time the United States began full diplomatic relations with the PRC. This change in policy was initiated by Richard Nixon and Henry Kissinger with Nixon's historic visit to Beijing and Shanghai in 1972. The United States has nevertheless maintained informal relations with the ROC, using various institutes and NGOs as channels. The United States is a major arms supplier to the ROC although no formal defense treaty exists.

Importantly, China has never considered Taiwan to be a separate country. It is referred to as a "breakaway province." Any country that has offered diplomatic recognition to Taiwan in any form is punished by China with severe trade and financial sanctions. Lithuania discovered this recently when it allowed Taiwan to open a representative trade office in Vilnius. Lithuanian exports to China immediately collapsed as China imposed a near-total trade embargo.

One important breakthrough in recent decades has been the rise of ROC investment in PRC and the integration of the two economies especially in the areas of high-tech and manufacturing. Those who travel from Shanghai to Taipei are familiar with the fact that flights depart from the domestic terminal, not the international terminal, since China regards Taiwan as part of one country.

A Chinese invasion of Taiwan would be the most disruptive geo-economic event possible, equivalent to an invasion of Japan or Western Europe, and just short of nuclear war. The outcome would be highly uncertain. The biggest variable is whether the United States would come to the military defense of Taiwan. The U.S. Seventh Fleet could interdict Chinese amphibious forces in the Strait of Taiwan, suppress Chinese air power, and otherwise assist Taiwan in repelling an invasion with antimissile defenses, drones, electronic warfare, and intelligence. At the same time, China could attack U.S. vessels with cruise missiles, launch its own electronic warfare, including attacks on critical infrastructure in the U.S. such as power grids and wireless communications networks, and push forward with its amphibious invasion.

Escalation would involve financial warfare, an embargo on energy imports to China, and a shutdown of a large percentage of the world's semiconductor industry. China no doubt covets control of Taiwan's semiconductor capacity, including its high-end technology and 5-nanometer production facilities. This Communist goal opens the possibility that Taiwan would destroy its own semiconductor fabs and labs before the Chinese could occupy them in a twenty-first-century version of a scorched-earth retreat.

One evolving U.S. military doctrine is called the Broken Nest. The name comes from a Chinese proverb that asks, "Beneath a broken nest, how can there be any whole eggs?" In military terms, this means if the nest (Taiwan) is broken, the eggs (global semiconductor production) will be broken too. This doctrine says the United States should not plan actively to fight China to save Taiwan. Instead, the United States and Taiwan should destroy the facilities of Taiwan Semiconductor and other semiconductor fabs in Taiwan in the event of a Chinese invasion. This would be so detrimental to China that the mere threat of destruction might be enough to deter the invasion.[27] The merits of the Broken Nest doctrine are debatable; the supply chain impact is not. The impact could not be limited to China; global commerce would grind to a near halt.

China might also deem it in its interests to invade Japan to consolidate its East Asian hegemony. Such an invasion would certainly involve the United States and likely Australia, the Philippines, and India. It could be tantamount to World War III. The outcome of such a war would be highly uncertain. The one certainty is that it would be a political and economic disaster for the world, especially for the belligerents.

Will an invasion of Taiwan happen? This is where Luttwak's definition of geoeconomics casts a light. In a preglobalized world, China might well attack. In the postglobalized world, China might refrain militarily while continuing its progress in technology, natural resources, and value-added manufacturing. This path requires cooperation, not confrontation, with the United States and Western Europe. We cannot rule out invasions of some of the smaller islands controlled by Taiwan that are quite close to the Chinese mainland, including Quemoy and Matsu. A Chinese takeover of these islands would cause further rupture with the United States and Europe yet would not be a casus belli with the West and therefore not in contradiction of the geoeconomics thesis. A sideshow invasion might be enough to enhance Xi's standing inside China without major negative side effects.

The case against such a war is contained in the scenarios above. Events would likely escalate and spin out of control. Territorial gains are possible for China only if the United States does not come to Taiwan's aid. Economic losses are inevitable and supply chain disruption will be catastrophic. Still, the risks are too high, and the costs are too great. Instead of an invasion, China will more likely continue its rhetoric and its military readiness, but otherwise bide its time.

At the same time, Xi Jinping will continue threats and economic confrontation with the West. This is the least beneficial path for China. It fails to gain the prize of Taiwan, while it also fails to gain maximum economic benefit from the West. Still, it may be optimal for the Chinese Communist Party because it feeds their greed and corruption while buying time for ideological indoctrination of the world's largest population. The state and the party are different entities. Analysis falls short when viewed through the lens of the state. One must first consider what's best for the party.

One well-regarded economic analyst with deep experience in China, Louis-Vincent Gave, suggested in an interview on May 18, 2022, that China's actions in shutting down Shanghai under its Zero COVID policy are a pretense for what is actually an economic attack on the United States. Gave says that China has weaponized its exports to the United States by intentionally disrupting supply chains in order to cause inflation, which will further undermine confidence in the U.S. government. Such a policy could be counted as aggressive decoupling. Examples of aggressive decoupling include an order by the Chinese government reported by *Bloomberg* on May 5, 2022, to all government agencies and state-owned enterprises requiring them to discontinue the use of foreign personal computers and software by 2024. While there is no direct evidence to confirm Gave's thesis, it is consistent with the facts.

Global trading powers are not waiting for either Chinese economic failure or military misadventure. Decoupling from China and the creation of alternate supply channels have already begun. The Five Eyes report outlines three paths for decoupling global supply chains from China. The first is called negative decoupling, which moves to restrict Chinese investment in the West, curtail theft of intellectual property, and reduce dependency on Chinese exports of critical goods. The second is called positive decoupling. This involves affirmative industrial policies to create leads in the critical technologies of the future, including electronics, communications, and the Future 9. The third path is called cooperative decoupling. This involves increased coordination among the Five Eyes and democratic allies to create new supply chains that are efficient without relying on China. In the words of the report, the goal is to "diversify supply chains and decentralize China as a global industrial hub."[28] These efforts are in their early stages. The Five Eyes report provides a detailed playbook for policymakers and shows the shape of things to come.

Russia Redux

The second great geoeconomic threat to global supply chains, especially those involving energy, comes from the ongoing economic war between the United States and Russia, itself the result of Russia's invasion of Ukraine on February 24, 2022. This economic confrontation, which affects goods, services, and finance broadly, cannot be understood without context that goes back to the end of the Cold War in 1989, and the collapse of the Soviet Union in 1991. The United States emerged from the Cold War as the sole global hegemon; Russia was in chaos, and China was reeling from the post-Tiananmen backlash. East and West Germany were reunified under the West German model in 1990. Central Europe was up for grabs. In 1995, NATO issued a document called the Study on NATO Enlargement, which described the process and prerequisites for adding new members. The United States and its allies moved quickly to integrate former Soviet satellites into NATO. These new members included Albania, Bulgaria, Croatia, the Czech Republic, Estonia, Latvia, Lithuania, Poland, Romania, Slovakia, Slovenia, Montenegro, and North Macedonia. Effectively the western border with Russia moved six hundred miles closer to Moscow without a shot being fired.

Russia had a pro-Western orientation in the 1990s and was trying to create as many Western-style institutions as it could, including an independent central bank, stock exchanges, free markets, and more.

This experiment ended disastrously by 2000 as oligarchs took over valuable state assets and replaced free markets with bribery and murder. Putin became president of Russia in 1999 and has remained in office as either president or prime minister ever since. Putin's main goal was to end the chaos and restore order.

While Putin had been amenable to NATO expansion, he drew the line at Lithuania, Ukraine, and Georgia. In 2004, NATO crossed Russia's red line by admitting Lithuania to membership; there was little Putin could do to stop it. In April 2008, George W. Bush nominated Georgia and Ukraine for NATO membership. In response, Putin invaded Georgia in August 2008, putting an end to the possibility of NATO membership there. Ukraine remained officially neutral, yet the possibility of Ukraine joining NATO remained open.

Events in Ukraine ran off the rails during the Obama administration. In November 2013, the CIA and MI6 sponsored a color revolution in Kyiv, which resulted in violent demonstrations in Maidan Square that came to a head in February 2014. This revolt led to the overthrow of the democratically elected pro-Russian president Viktor Yanukovych, who soon fled to Moscow. The pro-Western Petro Poroshenko became president in June 2014.

With Ukraine back on track to join NATO under Poroshenko, Putin annexed Crimea, which was home port for the Russian Navy and a key choke point between Russia's Sea of Azov and warm-water access to the Mediterranean and the Atlantic Ocean. Russia supported autonomous pro-Russian forces in eastern Ukraine, including infiltration of Russian advisers and weapons. This unstable status quo persisted until mid-2021, when Putin began surging Russian forces to its border with eastern Ukraine and positioning for a possible invasion and further annexation. The feared invasion commenced on February 24, 2022.

This historical context is critical to understanding Putin's perspective. The Western narrative that Putin is the villain bent on conquering Ukraine is false. Putin had warned the West about not pushing its advantage in Ukraine for twenty years. Bush's 2008 nomination of Ukraine to NATO was an unforced error. The 2014 Maidan revolt was not an indigenous uprising, but a coup engineered by Western intelligence agencies under the direction of Obama and UK prime minister David Cameron. Putin had been content to leave Ukraine as a neutral buffer state. The West was not and pushed Putin too hard. Putin pushed back with the mobilization of over one hundred thousand troops on Ukraine's border and an invasion.

Ukraine in NATO or even a pro-Western Ukraine is an existential threat to Moscow. The Russian border from Estonia in the north to Ukraine in the south forms the letter C, which encircles Moscow from the north, west, and south. Parts of Ukraine lie east of Moscow, opening that region to attack from the east, something that has not happened since the Mongol Empire of Genghis Khan in the thirteenth century. If Ukraine will not become neutral, then Putin must control it, at least the eastern half, by force if necessary.

Biden was bumbling in his initial response to this threat. At a press conference on January 19, 2022, Biden said the following in answer to a question about Ukraine as reported by *The Hill*:

> "It depends on what he does as to what extent we're going to be able to get total unity on the NATO front," the president said Wednesday, referring to the allies of the North Atlantic Treaty Organization.
>
> "I think what you're going to see is that Russia will be held accountable if it invades, and it depends on what it does. It's one thing if it's a minor incursion and we end up having to fight about what to do and not to do," Biden said.

Biden's green light to an invasion by Putin if it's only a "minor incursion" sent shock waves around the world. Biden offered no clarity on his definitions of "incursion" and " minor." His remarks were dangerous. Biden's clumsy effort to correct the record in the days following his remarks made matters worse because it highlighted the fact that the original comments were closer to the truth and had likely been discussed previously in a secure facility.

This incident evokes two similar blunders that both led to major global wars. At the Munich Conference in 1938, UK prime minister Neville Chamberlain allowed Adolf Hitler to peel off a slice of Czechoslovakia to appease the German chancellor. Chamberlain declared success and said, "I believe it is peace for our time." Less than one year later, World War II, the greatest bloodbath in history, had begun. On January 12, 1950, Dean Acheson, secretary of state for President Harry Truman, gave a speech at the National Press Club in Washington, D.C., in which he described a critical "defense perimeter" of the United States in the Western Pacific. Acheson did not include South Korea inside that defense perimeter. Five months later, North Korea invaded South Korea partly on the view that the United States would not act to defend the south. This was the beginning of the Korean War, which lasted until July 1953. History's lessons are clear. Weakness in action or ambiguity in words can be an invitation to aggression. The way to prevent war is not with appeasement or a green light to the enemy. The way to prevent war is through strength. Biden's weak demeanor and bumbling language amounted to an invitation for a Russian invasion.

Seeing the course of Russia's invasion of Ukraine requires a detached assessment of Russia's national interests. Putin has secured regions around Luhansk and Donetsk, which have Russian-speaking populations religiously and ethnically aligned with Russia. This has created a corridor from Donbass through Mariupol to Crimea, so that Crimea and Russia are now joined by land. The Black Sea port of Odessa just west of Crimea has become another target. Russia has no interest in Poland or Romania, although it is highly attentive to buildups of NATO forces in both places. Russia has now created buffer zones in Ukraine, Georgia, and Belarus that give Moscow some security, even if that zone is not nearly as large as the area comprised of the original Warsaw Pact nations. This outcome is a perfect illustration of Luttwak's geoeconomics definition. The goals are commercial (dependence of Western Europe on Russian natural gas), and the tools are commercial (pipelines), even though the players are sovereign states (Russia and the United States).

The United States has made it clear that it will not fight Russia in Ukraine militarily. Instead, the United States unleashed the most extensive set of economic sanctions in modern history. These sanctions include banning the Central Bank of Russia and the ten largest Russian commercial banks from the dollar payments system and the SWIFT financial telecommunications network. The United States also moved to freeze all Russian assets in U.S. banks, including U.S. offices of foreign banks, and published a list of Russian oligarchs whose assets—yachts, jets, and mansions—were subject to confiscation by local authorities wherever located. EU, UK, and allied nations both mimicked the U.S. sanctions and imposed their own sanctions tailored to bilateral ties to Russia.

As extensive and unprecedented as these sanctions were, they were just a beginning. On February 27, 2022, Western banks were prohibited from transacting in Russian rubles. This effectively prevented the Central Bank of Russia from supporting the ruble in foreign-exchange markets or making other use of its assets to support Russian institutions or its economy. On February 28, the United States targeted Russia's sovereign wealth fund, its Ministry of Finance, and the Russia Direct Investment Fund for asset freezes and prohibitions on transactions. On March 8, the United States banned all imports of Russian oil, liquefied natural gas, and coal. At the same time, the United States prohibited U.S. investment in the Russian energy sector and exports of high-tech equipment and semiconductors to Russia.

On March 11, 2022, the White House announced it would work with Congress to revoke Russia's most-favored-nation status, which offers Russia the best trade terms available to any trading partner. Removing this status allows the United States to impose harsh tariffs on Russian goods without violating WTO rules. The same announcement declared that Russia would be denied borrowing privileges at multilateral lending institutions such as the IMF and the World Bank. The United States also banned luxury goods exports to Russia such as high-end watches, expensive cars, jewelry, and designer apparel. A parallel ban was placed on U.S. imports of Russian luxury goods such as caviar and diamonds. These and other sanctions were wrapped in language that made it a criminal offense to engage in direct or indirect actions or conspiracies intended to evade or avoid the sanctions themselves.

On March 24, 2022, the White House expanded the list of sanctioned individuals to include all 328 members of the Russia Duma and 48 large Russian enterprises that comprise a large part of the defense-industrial base, including those making helicopters, precision missiles, and communications technology. The United States also prohibited all transactions involving gold held by the Central Bank of Russia, with a value of approximately $150 billion. The United States could not physically seize gold held in Russia, yet it made it impossible to sell the gold for hard currency or pledge it to support loans.

New sanctions were announced at an almost daily tempo. On March 31, 2022, President Biden announced he was releasing one million barrels of oil per day from the U.S. strategic petroleum reserve for a period of six months. This was intended to offset previous prohibitions on the importation of Russian oil. On April 6, the United States imposed a ban on all new investment by U.S. persons in Russia.

The economic impact of these sanctions went far beyond direct government action. Numerous U.S. and EU companies shut down operations in Russia or abandoned assets entirely even if sanctions did not strictly require them to do so. Among the largest shutdowns were oil exploration and production operations involving Shell, ExxonMobil, and BP. Other companies that shut down Russian operations were McDonald's, Nike, Apple, and Levi's. Over 250 companies in all had curtailed their Russian business by March 8 and more were considering similar action.

American sanctions were not limited to bilateral sales and services. The United States extended its sanctions to any country exporting goods to Russia that were manufactured using U.S. tools or U.S. technology acquired under license from the United States. In practice, this secondary boycott was aimed at China, which produces some semiconductors and other electronics under such licenses. This is the same tactic used to strangle Chinese telecommunications giant Huawei, and it proved effective in that case. While China was cool to U.S. sanctions and showed some support for Russia, the Chinese appeared to have no appetite to defy the United States in this regard. The Ukrainian government went even further than the United States in terms of the scope of sanctions. On April 11, Ukraine called on all governments in the world to seize all Russian assets, including oil tankers, and to give the proceeds to Kyiv as reparations for damages caused by the Russian invasion. These damages were estimated by a Ukrainian government economic adviser to exceed $1 trillion. There was no immediate move to act on Ukraine's request, yet the request itself was enough to add another layer of uncertainty to global commerce when it came to Russian assets.

Russia retaliated against the United States, the EU, and their allies immediately. The Central Bank of Russia announced that the ruble would be pegged to gold at a rate of RUB5,000 to 1 gram of gold. This move was best understood not as a new gold standard (because Russia limited those who could actually buy the gold for rubles), but as an effort to stabilize the exchange rate of dollars to rubles. Since gold is priced in dollars, the ruble-gold peg translated to an 80-to-1 ruble-to-dollar exchange rate using the price of $1,930 per ounce that prevailed on the date of the announcement. The gambit worked. The ruble plunged from 80 to 1 to a rate of 140 to 1 in the days following the outbreak of the war in late February, but had rallied back to 70 to 1 by early May.

Even as the United States banned exports of certain Russian goods, Russia banned exports of certain goods to its adversaries. This was more than a tit-for-tat trade war. Many of the goods affected are critical strategic metals and agricultural exports needed to avoid manufacturing shutdowns in the West and starvation in Africa and the

Middle East. Russia prohibited exports of platinum, palladium, lithium, and nickel, which are essential in automobile and battery manufacturing. Russia supplies 43 percent of the world's palladium. Ukraine itself did not prohibit exports. Still, its exports were substantially shut down by the war.

Some Russian retaliation was more sophisticated and initially beyond the ability of White House policymakers to comprehend. The United States banned semiconductor exports to Russia. Semiconductors are made as layered chips using natural resource inputs, many of which come from Russia. Critically, the circuits on the chips are etched with lasers powered with processed neon gas. Russia and Ukraine supply 90 percent of the world's neon. Over 65 percent of processed neon gas comes from a single plant in Odessa, Ukraine. The United States can cut Russia off from semiconductors, but Russia can shut down a large part of global semiconductor production by cutting off neon exports. This is a particularly pointed example of the boomerang effect of unfocused U.S. sanctions.

Russia and Ukraine together provide 26 percent of global wheat exports, 30 percent of global barley exports, and 16 percent of global corn exports. The two belligerents account for the following wheat supplies by nation: Lebanon (100 percent), Somalia (100 percent), Egypt (85 percent), Sudan (75 percent), Congo (68 percent), Tanzania (65 percent), Tunisia (56 percent), Kenya (42 percent), and South Africa (37 percent). Those and other countries among the top importers of Russian and Ukrainian wheat have a combined population of over 700 million people, almost 10 percent of the entire population of the planet. On April 12, 2022, flour mills in Kazakhstan suspended operations due to an inability to obtain Russian wheat. This outright shortage of grain exports was exacerbated by the fact that farmers all over the world were unable to plant crops in 2022, due either to fertilizer shortages or to exorbitant prices for fertilizer if it was available. In cases where alternate grain supplies could be arranged, the price was double or triple what was paid in 2021, another facet of global inflation. Ukraine tried to export grain by train across the Polish border but was thwarted by the fact that Polish and Ukrainian trains run on different track gauges. This means that goods cannot simply transit the border but must be unloaded from Ukrainian wagons and reloaded onto Polish wagons or trucks. Reuters reported that as of April 7, 2022, over 24,190 Ukrainian wagons were waiting to cross the border, a logistical nightmare. One grain vessel from Ukraine did manage to arrive in Lebanon, only to find its entire cargo spoiled by moisture. It seemed likely that deaths from starvation due to a lack of grain exports would greatly exceed deaths from the war itself.

As the prospects for mass starvation became more clear by the spring of 2022, Western media outlets such as *The Economist* and *The New York Times* launched a new narrative that any such catastrophe would be the fault of Russian president Vladimir Putin. Russia is responsible for the invasion of Ukraine, yet food shortages are the result of U.S.- and EU-led economic sanctions. Notwithstanding the war, Russia could continue to export grain, fertilizer, and energy but for the sanctions. Blame for the coming starvation will lie as much at the feet of Biden as Putin.

Suspension of Russian exports of aluminum and titanium caused delays in aircraft manufacturing by Boeing and Airbus, which both depend on Russian supplies to keep the manufacturing and assembly processes moving. Boeing gets 35 percent of its titanium from Russia; Airbus gets 50 percent. Russia and Ukraine supply over 30 percent of all the titanium in the world. Volkswagen announced in late February 2022 that it was shutting down its Zwickau plant in eastern Germany due to its inability to get automobile wiring systems from its sole supplier in Ukraine. BMW also closed plants due to the failure of Ukrainian suppliers to deliver customized wiring harnesses for its high-end automobiles. Those harnesses guide over three miles of wiring inside each car; they are highly customized to the vehicle and not easily replaced by other suppliers. Over twenty-two tankers jammed the Kerch Strait, a Russian-controlled passage near Ukraine, because of port closures. Russia and Ukraine combined provide 32 percent of global steel exports, 28 percent of global uranium exports, 22 percent of global fertilizer exports, 16 percent of global nickel exports, and comparable large percentages of global exports of coal, silver, iron, vegetable fats, and wood. The impact on global supply chains from the war in Ukraine was not a disruption; it was closer to a catastrophe.

Russia's military success in the Donbass region of Ukraine gave it control over 57.5 billion tons of coal reserves located there. This tightens Russia's control of global coal supplies and facilitates Russia's promised delivery of 100 million tons of coal to China in the years ahead. This prize also increases Russian leverage over Western Europe in the oil and natural gas sectors since coal is the easiest substitute and it will no longer be available from Ukraine.

The initial effects of the war on supply chains were somewhat muted partly because intermediate manufacturers and distributors had safety stock and goods in transit they could draw on to meet demand, and because price increases at the input level take time to work through to higher prices at the pump or on supermarket shelves. Investors and Wall Street gurus seemed not to notice that many of the sanction announcements had 30-, 60-, or 90-day delayed effective dates, so the impact of March 2022 orders did not commence until June 2022 in some cases, and the economic consequences took even longer to come into view. Those cushioning effects did not last long. In an age of just-in-time inventory and automated information sharing, the shortages and price spikes soon hit supply chain participants from industrial-scale manufacturers to retail boutiques. This fed the inflationary wave that had formed before the war and amplified it to levels not seen since the 1970s.

Curiously, the commodities least affected by the war were those for which disruptive effects were most feared—oil and natural gas. The reason was clear: the implications of shutting down oil and natural gas deliveries from Russia (many of which pass through pipelines in Ukraine) were so cataclysmic they could scarcely be contemplated. Germany, the world's fourth-largest economy and an export powerhouse, relies on Russia for 49 percent of its natural gas. Italy, the world's eighth-largest economy, receives 46 percent of its natural gas from

Russia. France, which has a more robust nuclear-generating capacity, still gets 24 percent of its natural gas from Russia. The figure for Austria is 80 percent and that for Poland is 40 percent. Several smaller European economies, including Latvia, Finland, Moldova, Bosnia and Herzegovina, and North Macedonia, receive between 90 and 100 percent of their natural gas from Russia. Simply put, these economies would shut down if Russian natural gas were not available. The lucky ones might be able to ration enough gas to keep the lights turned on in most homes. The unlucky ones would freeze in the dark.

The White House acknowledged that European natural gas reserves "are, obviously, at significantly low levels."[29] The administration's plan was to draw down reserves close to zero to buy time while natural gas exporters reroute supplies. The goal was to identify companies "that have the capacity to surge their actual production of gas that they would not normally do," and "look at the ability to increase by a few cargoes—different suppliers increasing by a few cargoes each." The plan was half baked. The idea of surging supply and diverting cargoes ignores the problem of whether vessels are even available to transport the surge and whether ports are able to receive the cargoes on arrival. If any link in the supply chain failed, Europe could literally run out of energy in some sectors if it had drawn reserves to zero waiting for the surge. The plan also ignores the fact that many producers are already running flat-out to supply demand from China; the ability to surge anything is doubtful. At best, this might be a zero-sum game, where rerouting supplies to Europe would cause shortages elsewhere. Whether the plan can succeed or not, the impact on global supply chains will be highly deleterious as output and shipping capacity are stretched to their limits and jammed ports become more jammed. In any case the plan remained just a plan through the summer of 2022. Notwithstanding Western indecision, Russia began to reduce flows of natural gas to Germany and other nations, citing pipeline maintenance and repair issues as a reason. This was clearly a warning to expect worse as winter neared for those who continued to aid Ukraine.

The same analysis applies to exports of Russian oil. Russia provides about 10 percent of all the oil produced in the world. Russia, Saudi Arabia, and the United States combined produce over 33 percent of all the oil in the world. It's simply impossible to sanction Russian oil sales. Any interference in Russian oil sales would cause global hyperinflation and global economic collapse at the same time. The irony was that Russia continued to earn billions of dollars of hard currency on its sales of oil and natural gas despite the war and despite the sanctions. These dollar payments were routed to accounts at Russia's Gazprombank, which were exempted from the initial round of sanctions. An even greater irony was that Ukraine continued to earn about $2 billion per year in transit fees for allowing the Russian natural gas through its pipelines. European demand for Russian energy was financing both sides in a bitter war.

Even if the United States and the EU ban imports of Russian energy, an unlikely prospect, the impact on Russia will be marginal; it has a waiting list of customers for the oil and natural gas in China. India also emerged as a major buyer of Russian oil despite U.S. warnings to avoid deals with Russia. The impact on Western Europe, especially Germany, will be devastating. Germany has spent the past decade shutting down its nuclear and coal-fired electric-generating capacity and is dependent on Russian natural gas for its manufacturing, light, and heat. U.S. promises of substitute energy sources are mostly empty either because Middle Eastern sources are already committed to China or because U.S. sources will take too long to organize. Posturing didn't help. The EU announced a ban on imported Russian coal in April 2022, but the ban did not take effect until August. It seemed almost as if the EU were hoping the war would be over by then with no real sacrifice required. A presumed "energy airlift" for Germany would come in the midst of a global energy shortage, making failure all the more likely. Russian countermeasures would involve cyber warfare, including shutdowns of U.S. and European critical infrastructure such as banks and stock exchanges. The impact of cyberattacks on global supply chains will be as devastating as the sanctions that gave rise to the attacks.

The seizure of Russian oligarch assets such as yachts and town-houses is best understood as a favor to Russia. Putin's power base is the military, intelligence services, the Orthodox Church, and every-day Russians. He has always regarded the oligarchs as a rival power center and was hesitant to seize their assets. Now the United States and UK are doing Putin's dirty work by rolling up oligarch assets outside of Russia. One irony is that oligarchs are repatriating capital to Russia when they can as a new safe haven relative to the rest of the world. Sanctions have a feel-good quality from the perspective of Western pol-iticians but they accomplish little and even help Putin in some ways.

The effect of U.S. and EU economic sanctions has been a total fail-ure measured against their strategic goals. Russia continued to make steady progress in its war aims of controlling the Ukrainian coasts on the Sea of Azov and the Black Sea and in building a land bridge from Russian territory to the recently annexed Crimea and beyond. Russia has consolidated its gains in the south and east of Ukraine and has ensured that Ukraine will not join NATO. Sanctions had no impact on the realization of these objectives.

Of course, the sanctions did have a catastrophic impact on global supply chains and inflation. Russian citizens are suffering higher costs and shortages. Still, U.S. citizens are suffering even more in economic terms. Over the course of 2022, gas prices more than doubled, and food prices nearly doubled. Bare shelves in stores were even more ob-vious than they were in late 2021 when the supply chain crisis first came to national attention. The prospective damage to U.S. citizens is even worse. Saudi Arabia and China are in discussions to price oil in yuan—a potentially fatal blow to the historic petrodollar standard worked out by Richard Nixon and Henry Kissinger in 1974. Ameri-can trading partners all over the world began to consider ways to re-duce their U.S. dollar reserve positions in view of the ease with which the United States seized or froze the dollar assets of Russia, its central bank, and its citizens. The United States justified this as an act of war, yet the rest of the world rightly saw it as a default on U.S. Treasury notes. Taken together, the asset freezes, currency shifts, and movement away from dollar-denominated assets could mark the beginning of the end of the U.S. dollar's privileged position as the world's leading reserve and payment currency. Alternatives to dollar reserves were not readily apparent. Still, gold was an obvious candidate. The price of gold rose steadily throughout early 2022. Russia did not inflict this damage on the United States. The damage was self-inflicted due to the ignorance of U.S. officials of the dense interconnectedness of global finance and the boomerang effects of all-out economic warfare. Financial sanctions will reduce global liquidity, increase market uncertainty, and possibly trigger a global financial panic of the kind seen in 2008. Inflation is the first and most obvious symptom; it will be far from the last.

The point of this expansive list of supply chain impediments is that none are going away soon. Climate change alarm is an effective channel for globalist ambitions in the financial sector. It will not fade quickly, even as its unfounded claims are increasingly disproved. Energy shortages and higher energy prices go hand in hand with the elites' green agenda promulgated from the bastions of academia, government, and banks. This damage will last for years. The turning point may not occur until elites themselves are freezing in the dark. China's conscious decoupling from existing supply chains is part of a broader strategy of self-reliance driven by Xi Jinping's insecure standing and a candid acknowledgment that the West is decoupling from China in any case. Chinese decoupling will take decades unless interrupted by regime change, which will be even more disruptive. In the West, onshoring and reshoring to democratic locales as advocated by the Five Eyes is under way yet will also take decades. The result will be higher costs for consumers, offset by better-paying jobs with benefits and higher-quality products. Russia's ambitions in Eastern Europe and Central Asia will play out over decades as well. That's in the nature of empire building, or in this case, rebuilding. Aftereffects of the pandemic will last until the 2050s in the same manner that the frugality of the Great Depression did not fade until the 1960s. Mental-health effects and adaptive behavior last longer than viruses. Dominating all these trends is a demographic disaster the likes of which has not been seen since the Black Death, maybe ever. The demographic ship cannot be turned to a healthier path until 2070 or later.

Supply chains were nearly perfected over the thirty years from 1989 to 2019. They were disrupted in a mere three years by trade wars, pandemic, climate alarm, decoupling, energy shortages, geopolitics, and demographics. They will be rebuilt in time, but not quickly. In the meantime, money is the medium through which supply chain stress is relayed. In part 2, we turn to the impact of supply chain disruption on money as seen through the lens of current inflation and coming deflation.

PART TWO

The Role of Money

———

Will Inflation Linger?

The idea of investing in bricks and mortar, if such could be afforded, was tempting all the same. For those who, unlike the pensioners and the impoverished middle class, and the hand-to-mouth working class, had spare money over and above what was needed for subsistence, acquiring "things," material assets, was the key to surviving and even prospering in these uncertain times. More important than anything was to get rid of your cash, which might tomorrow be worthless.

— FREDERICK TAYLOR
The Downfall of Money (2013)[1]

The fundamental paradox about banks is that they are illusory but stable so long as everyone buys into the promise that the money is there.

— ADAM TOOZE
Ones and Tooze podcast (2022)[2]

It's Back

Inflation is back in the United States and around the world. On July 13, 2022, the U.S. Labor Department reported that the consumer price index for June surged 9.1 percent, the highest increase since November 1981, over forty years earlier.[3] The components were worse: food rose 10.4 percent. Fuel oil to heat homes rose 98.5 percent. The most visible price hike, gasoline, rose 59.9 percent. That June surge followed inflation of 8.6 percent for May and 8.3 percent for April. This was part of a trend, not an anomaly.

From December 2020 to December 2021, consumer prices rose 7 percent, the highest year-over-year change since 1981.[4] Food prices considered separately rose 6.3 percent year over year compared to a still-high 3.9 percent increase in 2020. The Bureau of Labor Statistics, which compiles inflation data, measures twenty-nine broad categories of prices with thousands of individual items in each basket. Those categories with the highest price increases from December 2020 to December 2021 were gasoline, cars, energy, meats, poultry, fish, and eggs. In other words, the items that went up the most in price were those items that Americans buy on a daily basis. Inflation was not buried in more discretionary categories like apparel and recreation. It was staring you in the face at the gas pump and checkout counter.

Individual price increases were striking. On a year-over-year basis from 2020 to 2021, gasoline prices rose 49.6 percent, natural gas prices rose 24.1 percent, energy prices rose 29.3 percent. Electricity prices increased 6.3 percent. Prices for meats, poultry, fish, and eggs rose 12.5 percent. The price of new vehicles rose 11.8 percent. Yet new vehicles were often not available due to supply chain difficulties. If you turned to the used-car market, the sticker shock was far worse—used-car and truck prices rose 37.3 percent in 2021. That was the largest year-over-year price increase in the history of that index. Household furnishings rose 7.4 percent. If the shock of price increases caused you to take up smoking, there was no relief—tobacco prices rose 9 percent.

Even the more modest price increases were troubling. If 3 percent inflation sounds benign, it's not. An inflation rate of only 3 percent cuts the value of a dollar in half in twenty-three years, about the time it takes from birth to college graduation. In another twenty-three years, from college graduation to midcareer, 3 percent inflation cuts the value of the dollar in half again, or only one quarter of what the dollar was worth at birth. That's the right context in which to consider 2021 inflation of 4.1 percent for shelter, 3.3 percent for rent of a primary residence, and 3.3 percent for hospital services. There is no such thing as good inflation. All inflation is a form of theft from those on fixed incomes or salaries. The stolen loot is handed over to banks and borrowers. Since the U.S. government is the biggest borrower in the world, it is also the biggest winner from inflation.

This inflationary surge was hardly limited to the United States. Inflation was emerging all over the world as measured in various currencies. The International Monetary Fund's World Economic Outlook showed that for the year ending December 2021, fifteen out of thirty-four advanced economies experienced inflation in excess of 5 percent, the highest number in more than twenty years. Eurozone inflation in December 2021 was 5 percent (annualized). Inflation in the UK for the same period was 5.4 percent. Looking at individual nations in the Eurozone, December 2021 inflation was 6.4 percent in the Netherlands and 6.7 percent in Spain. Germany's inflation in November 2021 was 6 percent, a shockingly high rate in a country known for its aversion to inflation at any level. In December 2021, German inflation fell back slightly to 5.5 percent, still quite high by German standards. In the Baltic states, inflation had already hit double digits by late 2021. The Bank of England followed the U.S. Federal Reserve in monetary tightening in response to inflation. Even the European Central Bank, famous for its negative interest rates, announced a 0.50% rate increase on July 21, 2022. The ECB is betting inflation will abate on its own, its version of chairman of the Federal Reserve Jerome Powell's transitory perspective. Powell abandoned his position on transitory inflation in the United States. If the ECB sticks to this view and gets the forecast wrong, inflation will surge even higher in Europe over the course of 2022 and beyond.

The 7 percent year-over-year inflation in the United States in 2021 was the highest annual rate since 1981, as noted. That's a striking statistic, yet it's even more troubling when put in context. Inflation rates in the twenty-first century are among the lowest on record. Here's the annual inflation track record for the consumer price index for 2000 to 2020, as compiled by the Federal Reserve Bank of Minneapolis:[5]

2000	3.4%
2001	2.8%
2002	1.6%
2003	2.3%
2004	2.7%
2005	3.4%
2006	3.2%
2007	2.9%
2008	3.8%
2009	-0.4%
2010	1.6%
2011	3.2%
2012	2.1%
2013	1.5%
2014	1.6%
2015	0.1%
2016	1.3%
2017	2.1%
2018	2.4%
2019	1.8%
2020	1.2%

In this twenty-one-year time frame, the average annual inflation was 2.1 percent. Nine of the twenty-one years show inflation below 2 percent. Only five of the twenty-one years show inflation above 3 percent. None of the annual inflation measures was above 4 percent. One year, 2009, showed a negative inflation rate, or deflation. The 7 percent rate for 2021 was not just high, it was almost double the highest rate since the turn of the millennium. If you're under the age of forty, you've never seen the like in your adult lifetime. If you're under the age of sixty, you have to go back to your teenage years to recall inflation of this kind. Inflation of 7 percent in 2021 was not just high, it was close to a once-in-a-lifetime event. By mid-2022 it was worse.

Headlines about "the highest inflation in forty years!" were accurate, yet they don't tell the whole story of inflation in the late 1970s and early '80s. Inflation in 1981 was 10.3 percent, significantly higher than the 7 percent of 2021. Yet 1981 was not an outlier. It was part of a ten-year stretch that encompassed the worst inflation since the end of World War II, and before that the aftermath of World War I. That stretch of inflation unfolded as follows:

1973	6.2%
1974	11.1%
1975	9.1%
1976	5.7%
1977	6.5%
1978	7.6%
1979	11.3%
1980	13.5%
1981	10.3%
1982	6.1%

Average annual inflation over this ten-year stretch was 8.7 percent. Four of the ten years featured double-digit inflation. Only one year, 1976, came in below 6 percent. The U.S. dollar lost 57 percent of its purchasing power from 1973 to 1982, measured by the Consumer Price Index. Measured by weight of gold, the dollar lost 75 percent of its purchasing power. For those who guess that inflation is associated with boom times in the stock market, the opposite is true. The Dow Jones Industrial Average was 1,031.68 on January 2, 1973, and closed at 1,046.54 on December 31, 1982, essentially unchanged for ten years. Over the same ten-year inflationary episode, the Dow traded as low as 632.04 at the start of 1975, a 38 percent drop from the level two years earlier. Of course, that's a drop in nominal levels. When the index is adjusted for inflation, the drop was even steeper. The period was also marked by three recessions—1973 to 1975, 1980, and 1981 to 1982. That's the legacy of inflation from 1973 to 1982—a flat stock market, three recessions, and the purchasing power of a dollar cut by more than half.

The most important question in economics today is whether the 7 percent inflation in 2021 and 9 percent inflation in mid-2022 is an anomaly—what Jay Powell called "transitory"—or whether it's the start of a new inflationary episode of the kind seen in the late 1970s and early '80s, with stagnant stocks, high unemployment, and lost wealth from a crashing dollar. If inflation were to persist, an investor's response would be straightforward. One would sell bonds, increase leverage, buy hard assets such as real estate, gold, and fine art, and allocate funds to private and public equities with underlying hard assets such as oil companies, mines, and agribusinesses. If inflation is transitory, because either the Fed chokes it off with interest rate hikes or exogenous factors including pandemic effects, supply chain failures, and demographics impede growth, one would buy Treasury securities, reduce leverage, and increase allocations to equities on the view that stocks have higher valuations when competing rates on fixed-income products are low. If one were genuinely uncertain and had no strong views on how inflation would evolve, the investor would increase his allocation to cash and wait on the sidelines until economic visibility improved. Currencies act as conveyor belts to move inflation and deflation from one country to another through import-export prices and the terms of trade. Global asset allocators would be weighing the same factors described above, adjusted for exchange-rate fluctuations relative to a chosen base currency or gold. The response functions are easy. The forecast is hard. Inflation asks the same question lyricist Mick Jones posed in 1981: Should I stay or should I go?

The best predictive analytic method does not rely on linear extrapolation. That always produces deficient results except on rare occasions when it's right by chance. This does not mean the past has no lessons for the future. The history of inflation has valuable lessons for forecasting inflationary trends, yet they don't derive from simple projections of trends. They derive from the ability to identify causal factors, mapping those factors (and new factors) into a network of nodes, populating each node with data and natural language inputs, estimating the direction and strength of nodal outputs, and aggregating those outputs into a single inflation forecast. In plain English, history matters because you can derive causes, not because it's ever the same twice. People, even policymakers, learn. Behavior is adaptive. When society passes through an adverse phase such as the late 1970s inflation, officials resolve not to let it happen again. That doesn't mean inflation won't happen again. It doesn't mean officials won't make new mistakes; they usually do. It does mean that certain response functions are highly predictable as to both policy and timing. It's the PhD equivalent of closing the barn door. This makes it easy to predict that the barn door will be closed. That gives you a head start on what comes next.

The inflation that exploded in the mid-1970s had its roots in five factors from the mid-1960s onward: Great Society plus Vietnam War spending (1964), the Baby Boom coming of age (1966), the end of the gold standard (1971), Nixon's reelection (1972), and the Arab oil embargo (1973). This sequence of events was like a countdown on a ticking time bomb that detonated in 1973–74. The same factors will not repeat in the same sequence. Still, these factors can be generalized and applied in any period. The generalized version of the 1964 to 1973 sequence is: deficit spending, demographics, monetary policy, politics, and supply shocks. That's the beginning of an analytic model. One can build from there.

While inflation took flight in 1973, it did not come out of nowhere. Inflation hit 5.5 percent in 1969 and 5.8 percent in 1970 before cooling down to 3.3 percent in 1972. Those 1969–70 inflation figures contrasted sharply with levels that had never exceeded 1.6 percent from 1959 to 1965. In other words, there were clear warning signs as early as 1969 that inflation was becoming problematic, yet those signs were mostly ignored. This was due to a belief at the time that the Fed and fiscal policy experts could "fine-tune" the economy. A mild recession in 1969–1970 also helped to break the budding inflationary fever. The lesson for predictive analytics is that major developments are almost always presaged by clear warnings. The best method is to put weight on the warnings and not treat them as anomalies.

Predicting inflation is not the only challenge. It's also critical to predict the policy response function and the aftermath. Again, history is helpful. The response to the 1973–82 inflation was a brutal monetary tightening led by Paul Volcker, who became Federal Reserve chairman in August 1979. The Federal Open Market Committee (FOMC) led by the Fed chairman uses monetary policy to target what is called the Fed Funds rate, the rate at which banks lend reserves to each other on an overnight basis. When Volcker became chairman, the effective Fed Funds rate was 10.94 percent. Volcker raised the target rate to 11 percent (technically a range of 10.75 percent to 11.25 percent) on August 14, 1979, and continued raising the target in stages until the effective rate hit 19.08 percent in January 1981. In October 1981, the ten-year U.S. Treasury note hit a yield to maturity of 15 percent. As late as June 1982, the Fed Funds effective rate was still 14.15 percent. This rate did not fall below 10 percent until September 1982. Volcker's shock therapy worked. Inflation fell to 3.2 percent in 1983 and was a mild 1.9 percent in 1986. That's generally regarded as the start of the Great Moderation, during which annual inflation never again reached 6 percent until 2021 and was predominately below 4 percent for thirty-five years.

Still, Volcker's victory over inflation came at a steep cost. The U.S. economy entered a recession in January 1980, just five months after Volcker's rate hikes began. This recession was over in six months; still, GDP declined 2.2 percent from peak to trough and unemployment reached 7.8 percent. This was followed by a more severe recession that lasted from July 1981 to November 1982, during which GDP declined 2.7 percent from peak to trough and unemployment reached 10.8 percent. The 1980 and 1981–82 recessions are often combined by economists into one long recession or referred to as the double-dip recession. It was the worst economic collapse in the U.S. economy since the Great Depression. The payoff began in 1983 with a recovery that produced some of the strongest growth in U.S. history through 1986, and continued growth until a mild recession in July 1990. Growth resumed in 1991 and continued for ten years until another mild recession in 2001, followed by another six years of growth until the 2008 global financial crisis. The Volcker experiment was brutal, but it was followed by twenty-five years of near continuous growth and low inflation. The market's lesson from Volcker's reign, recited to this day, is that high inflation must be crushed at any cost, and the long-term gains are worth the candle.

This history gives us a nearly sixty-year chronological model of high inflation. It begins with low inflation and increased deficit spending (1965), offers some early warning signs of inflation (1968–69), hits a takeoff stage (1973), reaches a peak (1980), gradually comes under control (1983), and then offers decades of low inflation and well-managed inflationary expectations (1984–2020). The 2008 financial panic and the 2020 pandemic panic broke with the pattern of steady growth that began in 1983, but did not break with the pattern of low inflation. Inflation in 2009, when the stock market hit bottom, was negative 0.4 percent, and inflation in 2020 was only 1.2 percent. The first warning sign of higher inflation, perhaps comparable to 1968, was the 7 percent inflation of 2021.

Inflation Dynamics

We have already identified five factors that may cause higher inflation: deficits, demographics, monetary policy, politics, and supply shocks. Before turning to those factors in the present context, we should consider the dynamics through which the factors operate. Put differently, if the five factors are rocket fuel, how does the rocket itself work? What are the valves, hoses, gaskets, and insulators that keep the rocket from blowing up on the launchpad? What systems can cause disaster if they fail? We'll look at two of these in detail and return to the five factors to see where inflation goes from here.

The first and most important system element is velocity. That's the technical term for a measure of the turnover of money. It tells you how quickly people are spending their money. The definition is simple. You take GDP (the total value of goods and services in the economy) and divide by the money supply, and the result is the velocity of the money supply. For example, if GDP is $24 trillion and the money supply is $8 trillion, then velocity is 3 (24 ÷ 8 = 3). Of course, monetary economics are never quite that simple. Before making the calculation, you have to settle on a definition of money supply. The Fed publishes what it calls the Monetary Base (M0). It also publishes M1 (currency, demand deposits, and other liquid deposits such as checking accounts), and M2 (M1 plus small time deposits and money market funds). These definitions of money supply are quite different, so the math produces different measures of velocity. For our purposes, we'll use M1 because it's close to M2 and most closely matches what everyday Americans consider their spending money. For GDP, we'll use $24 trillion, which almost exactly matches what the Commerce Department reported as of December 31, 2021. If we divide $24 trillion of GDP by M1 of $20.67 trillion as of December 2021, then velocity of M1 = 1.16. That means every $1 of M1 supports $1.16 of GDP.

Here's the shocking part: velocity has been in a state of collapse since 2008. At the end of the fourth quarter of 2007, before the worst of the global financial crisis, velocity was 10.70. In December 2007, every dollar of M1 supported $10.70 of goods and services, compared with $1.16 today. Velocity went into free fall as the global financial crisis hit. It fell to 8.70 by September 30, 2009, following the stock market crash and 2007–9 recession. That was just the beginning of a long, slow decline. Velocity slid downward to 5.23 immediately prior to the pandemic in January 2020. That's less than half the level of late 2007. The ability of money to produce economic growth was melting like an ice cube on a hot day. What came next more closely resembles a Red Bull cliff dive. Velocity drops vertically from January 2020 to September 2020. By the end of the third quarter of 2020, after six months of lockdowns and quarantines, velocity was 1.25. It shows no signs of turning up from that level and has fallen slightly since. From December 31, 2007, to December 31, 2020, the velocity of money fell 89 percent. Simply put, your money doesn't work anymore.

The reasons for this are straightforward even as the policy implications are almost unthinkable. The global financial crisis of 2008–9 saw the sequential collapse of major financial institutions including Bear Stearns, Fannie Mae, Freddie Mac, Lehman Brothers, and AIG. Major investment banks including Morgan Stanley and Goldman Sachs were only days away from failure and were rescued by rapid conversion to bank holding companies, which put them under the Fed's protective umbrella. While major banks were bailed out, individual citizens and small businesses were not. Unemployment soared, business failures multiplied, the stock market crashed, and the economy suffered through the worst recession since the end of World War II. In response, Americans slashed spending and adopted what economists call precautionary savings. This means increasing savings beyond normal levels in case hard times should persist or return unexpectedly. When incomes are falling and savings are rising, the result is less money available for consumption. This was a main driver of the decline in velocity.

In turn, crashing velocity is the clue to low inflation from 2009 to 2019. That was the longest yet also weakest recovery in U.S. history. The entire eleven-year span was peppered with warnings of imminent inflation emanating from both monetarists and classical Austrian School economists. The warning was captured in monetarist Milton Friedman's famous 1963 epigram, "Inflation is always and everywhere a monetary phenomena." Austrians looking to Friedrich Hayek and Ludwig von Mises adhered to the same view, although Austrian economics is considerably more sophisticated than Friedman's relatively simple views.

There was no question about the monetary side of the equation in the post-2009 recovery. The Federal Reserve's monetary base (M0) was $840 billion in June 2008, shortly before the September 15, 2008, bankruptcy of Lehman Brothers. This figure rose to $1.7 trillion in January 2009 then to $4.0 trillion in August 2014, as the Fed pursued quantitative easing (QE) in stages known as QE1, QE2, and QE3. Yet inflation did not appear despite the doctrines and warnings. From 2009 to 2019, inflation never exceeded 3.2 percent (in 2011), and ran below 2 percent in seven of those eleven years. Why did no significant inflation emerge despite the Fed increasing the base money supply by 375 percent in six years? The answer is that while base money rose 375 percent, velocity fell over 40 percent. Velocity crashed even further in the years from 2014 to 2021.

It turns out that the only economist who got the money-inflation analysis right was the legendary Irving Fisher, who was regarded by Joseph Schumpeter as "the greatest economist the United States ever produced." Long before Milton Friedman, Fisher pioneered the quantity theory of money and inaugurated what later became known as monetarism. Fisher recognized that money supply alone did not drive inflation. It was the combination of money and velocity that caused inflation. And velocity is a behavioral phenomenon outside the control of central banks.

In its simplest form, the quantity theory of money states:

$$M \times V = P \times Y$$

Where
M = money supply
V = velocity of money
P = price index, and
Y = real output

Real output (Y) times the price index (P, which can represent inflation or deflation) is equal to nominal GDP. Nominal output ($P \times Y$) equals money supply times velocity ($M \times V$). When inflation exists, nominal output will be greater than real output.

Friedman's view was that real output in a developed economy is limited to about 3 percent per year, a reasonable assumption. He further suggested that P should equal 1, which means real output and nominal output are the same; there's no inflation or deflation, another reasonable aim despite the Fed's preference for 2 percent inflation (which is like stealing small amounts from people in the hope that no one will notice). Where Friedman failed is in his assumption that velocity was constant. If V is constant and P is targeted at 1, then it is true that real output (Y) can be targeted by controlling the money supply (M). Friedman thought of the money supply like a thermostat that could be dialed up or down to produce a desired result. In that world, it is reasonable to say that inflation is always a monetary phenomenon.

Fisher knew better. Fisher understood that velocity is not constant. He also understood that velocity is the result of consumer and investor psychology. Velocity is based on a consumer's experience with recent inflation. That experience drives consumer decisions in real time. This creates a recursive function in which experience with recent inflation results in further inflation as consumers race to beat price increases, an example of what the great sociologist Robert K. Merton named the self-fulfilling prophecy. I lived through the late 1970s and early '80s at the start of my career. If you needed a new car or some furniture, there was an urgency about the purchase. You were driven to buy the item right away "before the price went up." That behavior is called demand-pull inflation by economists. Fear of inflation pulls demand forward. Of course, this behavior creates shortages, bids up prices (as consumers compete for scarce items in a kind of auction dynamic), and drives velocity higher. No sooner did you buy one item than you were out to buy another before its price went up too. Borrowed money was a way to make money as long as inflation rates were rising faster than interest rates. Volcker changed the psychology by raising interest rates to 20 percent, putting 10 percent of the labor force out of work and sinking GDP by 5 percent over the course of two recessions.

It worked, but the cost was extraordinary. Inflation has remained well behaved in the anodyne jargon of the Fed ever since.

Fisher had a third insight possibly even more important than his views on velocity and behavior. He understood that an application of the quantity theory of money would turn crucially on the definition of money itself. Fisher fashioned the phrase "money illusion." This was meant to highlight the difference between the nominal value and real value of money. The difference is inflation. Since inflation can proceed slowly at first and appear in some goods and services before others, consumers often don't see it coming and cling to nominal values that are actually shrinking. Fisher went further to say that base money (M0), the kind controlled by the Fed, was not the right yardstick for calculating velocity or inflation. Fisher insisted on using metrics closer to today's M1 money supply. The difference is not just one of size. M0 is created by central banks. M1 is created by commercial banks. If M0 doesn't matter, then central banks don't matter. They are impotent. What matters are commercial banks in their role as lenders and the appetite of borrowers for new loans. The only important role of central banks is to prop up commercial banks in a panic. Commercial banks and their borrowers are the drivers of money supply and inflation. Again, this points to the behavioral root of inflation rather than so-called central bank money printing.

The fact is, Fed money printing has little to do with inflation. Commercial bank money creation is more relevant. Consumer inflationary psychology is most relevant of all. This is why inflation did not emerge when the Fed bloated its balance sheet from 2009 to 2019. It's also why inflation may emerge today despite Fed tightening. The Fed is not in charge. To paraphrase James Carville: It's the psychology, stupid.

Another system element that can drive inflation in addition to velocity is the role of base effects. When the U.S. Bureau of Labor Statistics calculates inflation, it looks at the reporting period (usually monthly) and compares it to the same period in the prior year. For example, inflation for December 2021 would be measured in comparison to December 2020 and then stated as an annualized amount. That is the figure you see in the headlines and hear about on financial TV. Inflation in the United States gained attention in April 2021 when the year-over-year inflation rate that month was reported at 4.2 percent, the highest since September 2008. This inflation persisted through the year, hitting 5 percent in May and 5.4 percent in June, before finally reaching 7 percent by December 2021. Still, these rates were computed year over year. This means that the monthly rates in 2020 were the baseline on which the 2021 calculations were made. Of course, 2020 was the first year of the pandemic and the first year of widespread lockdowns. The second quarter of 2020 produced the worst quarterly economic collapse since 1946. A look at 2020 inflation figures from the April to June period bears out this weakness:

MONTH/YEAR	INFLATION YEAR OVER YEAR
APRIL 2020	0.3%
MAY 2020	0.1%
JUNE 2020	0.6%

This three-month segment corresponds with the worst part of the 2020 recession and the most severe stage of the lockdown. Those inflation figures were the lowest since 2015. When you had such a low base for comparison, it came as no surprise that inflation showed significant year-over-year increases in 2021. An increase in inflation the year following quite low inflation is a statistical quirk called a base effect. Base effects are typically muted because inflation or disinflation does not vary that much year to year, although there are exceptions. Statistically it's difficult to untangle base effects from new inflationary trends. Still, the best analysis suggests that reported inflation in April, May, and June 2021 was roughly half due to base effects and half due to a new rise in inflation. This means that the 4.2 percent inflation in April 2021 might be regarded as 2.1 percent new inflation plus 2.1 percent base effect. Likewise, May 2021 could be regarded as only 2.5 percent new inflation and June as 2.7 percent new inflation once base effects were stripped out. These numbers were still high but were less troubling than the headline numbers. This was the basis on which the Fed showed no particular concern from a rate policy perspective and Jay Powell embraced the idea that inflation was "transitory." It would soon fade.

But it didn't. Just as the 2020 second quarter fall in GDP was one of the worst in U.S. history (−31.4 percent annualized), the third-quarter recovery was one of the strongest in U.S. history (+33.4 percent annualized). The recession was over, and the base effects faded. By August 2020 inflation was 1.3 percent. It was 1.4 percent in September, and 1.2 percent in October. This implied that 2021 year-over-year inflation figures would moderate. That didn't happen. The August 2021 rate was 5.4 percent, September was 5.4 percent, and October was 6.2 percent. Those who expected inflation to moderate didn't have base effects to lean on anymore. The year-over-year inflation was high and growing. New forces, not just base effects, drove the inflation figures higher. When asked about transitory inflation by Congress on November 30, 2021, Jay Powell said it's "probably a good time to retire that word." By then, the Fed had already begun the taper and raised the prospect of interest rate hikes. By March 2022, the taper was complete and a new wave of rate hikes had started. The battle to nuke inflation had begun.

Now we'll look at our five factors—deficits, demographics, monetary policy, politics, and supply shocks—along with our systemic elements—velocity and base effects—to infer where inflation goes from here.

Deficits are the obvious place to begin because both the condition is well understood by the public and the impact on economic growth is clear. The United States distinguished itself on February 1, 2022, when it was reported that the U.S. national debt surpassed $30 trillion for the first time. That number itself is impressive yet it does not mean much unless considered in the context of economic output. A trivial amount of debt can lead to bankruptcy if you have no means to service it. A mountain of debt is manageable if you have enormous output and liquidity with which to pay interest and the creditworthiness with which to roll over maturing instruments. With that in mind, the best way to consider debt is the debt-to-GDP ratio; you put the debt in the context of the gross income needed to service the debt. That metric is useful analytically but does not provide much comfort. The best estimate for annual U.S. GDP as of December 31, 2021, is $24 trillion. The result is a U.S. debt-to-GDP ratio of 125 percent ($30T ÷ $24T = 1.25). Another estimate put the ratio at 129 percent as of December 31, 2021. Those ratios (and projected ratios for future years) are the highest in U.S. history, higher even than at the end of World War II, when it was 119 percent.

The United States was able to work off its World War II debt on a bipartisan basis through slow, steady inflation and high growth until the ratio bottomed at a comfortable 31 percent when Ronald Reagan took office in 1981. The debt-to-GDP ratio rose to 61 percent during the Reagan–Bush 41 years and remained at about that level through the Clinton–Bush 43 years, ending at 68 percent in 2008. The explosion in the ratio occurred during the Obama-Trump years. Obama took the ratio to 105 percent by 2016 largely due to the bailout spending in 2009. Trump took the ratio to 129 percent largely due to pandemic relief spending in 2020. Biden is on track to push the ratio even higher with his infrastructure spending, most of which does not involve infrastructure, and his plans for a Green New Deal. The difference between 1946 and 2022 is that after World War II the United States was an industrial and financial juggernaut while Germany and Japan were in ruins, the UK was broke, and Russia and China were under the Communist thumb. The United States had the global economic playing field to itself, and policymakers knew exactly what to do. It just took time. Today the United States faces economic competition in every corner, and there is no plan. For added context, other important nations with a debt-to-GDP ratio comparable to or higher than that of the United States are: Canada (118 percent), France (116 percent), Greece

(206 percent), Portugal (134 percent), Italy (156 percent), Singapore (131 percent), and Spain (120 percent). Two economies in the intensive-care ward are Lebanon (172 percent) and Venezuela (350 percent). Among developed economies, Japan is in a league of its own at 266 percent. By comparison, Australia's ratio is a comfortable 25 percent, and Germany is at a still manageable 70 percent. These ratios are based on national government debt. In China, the lines between the national government, provincial governments, SOEs, and state-controlled banks are blurred. A proper analysis would put the Chinese ratio at 300 percent, although the official figure is 67 percent. As for the United States, when Greece, Portugal, and Italy are in your peer group, it may be time to look in the mirror.

Does the debt-to-GDP ratio matter as far as inflation is concerned? Yes and no. In the short run, probably not. There's extensive economic literature that shows high debt-to-GDP ratios slow economic growth and put the economy on a disinflationary path. Advocates of modern monetary theory, prominently Stephanie Kelton of the State University of New York, claim that national debt is not like household debt, and a country can spend as much as it wants unless inflation emerges, at which point higher taxes can be used to mute inflation.[6] The impact of high debt-to-GDP ratios is considered in chapter 5. For now, it's enough to say that economies with high debt-to-GDP ratios often flip from disinflation (or deflation) to hyperinflation almost overnight as citizens and creditors suddenly realize that inflation is the only way to escape the room. (Default is the preferred technique for debt denominated in a currency you don't print. If your debt is in your national currency, default is unnecessary; you just print what you need to pay the debt.) Modern monetary theory analysis is deficient since practitioners treat the U.S. economy as a closed system. It's not. Inflation can appear almost overnight through the foreign exchange channel, a phenomenon on which Kelton and her ilk display no learning. In the short run, high debt levels are not inflationary. In the long run, they are almost certainly inflationary. The phase transition from one state to the other will be both unexpected and sudden, recalling Hemingway's description of bankruptcy. As with all phase transitions, the timing is unclear, but the outcome is certain. It's like watching a pot boil. Give it time.

Like debt, demographics are a powerful yet slow-moving force. Unlike debt, we can forecast demographics with high precision. Everyone in the world who will be forty years old in 2042 is alive today, twenty years old to be exact, minus an actuarially reliable fatality rate. One can debate the impact, but we know the numbers. If you favor economic growth (many elites do not), it's not a pretty picture. The two best works on the topic are *Empty Planet* by Darrell Bricker and John Ibbitson and *The Great Demographic Reversal* by Charles Goodhart and Manoj Pradhan.[7] These works put paid to Paul Ehrlich's *The Population Bomb*, an ideological screed published in 1968 that predicted global famine in the 1980s due to overpopulation and called for population control, including mass sterilization. In fact, population growth declined precipitously soon after that book's publication. Ehrlich, a Stanford professor, was wrong about almost everything, yet his book had enormous impact on public policy, including China's murderous one-child policy. Working with the latest highly accurate data, Bricker and Ibbitson focus on sociological and political implications of demography, while Goodhart and Pradhan take aim at the economic implications. They agree on one high-level implication—the human race is dying out. Put more precisely, we are living longer but our replacement rate is collapsing. Populations are aging and shrinking at the same time. There is a missing link in the human supply chain—children.

The number of children each woman must bear on average to maintain a population at a constant level is 2.1. A higher rate will expand population, a lower rate will decrease it. We explored the demographic situation in China in chapter 3. Following is a broader view of the global demographic situation. The declining birthrate in developed economies is at an acute stage. Below are birthrates for major developed economies as provided by the World Bank:

U.S.	1.7
UK	1.6
GERMANY	1.5
FRANCE	1.9
SPAIN	1.2
ITALY	1.3
NETHERLANDS	1.6
SWEDEN	1.7
JAPAN	1.4
AUSTRALIA	1.7
AUSTRIA	1.5
DENMARK	1.7
CANADA	1.5

The figures for important economic aggregations are no better:

EUROPEAN UNION	1.5
EURO AREA (€)	1.5
CENTRAL EUROPE	1.6
OECD MEMBERS	1.7
NORTH AMERICA	1.7

These figures are not merely low, they are a demographic disaster. Once birthrates fall below replacement rates for a sustained period of time, it becomes impossible to regain the replacement rate for decades. With each age cohort smaller than the one before, and with the persistence of the demographic drivers of education, urbanization, and women's emancipation, no amount of government policy or official cheerleading about "big families" can bend the curve in less than forty or fifty years.

Here are some of the grim realities that emerge from these birthrates: In certain parts of Spain, there are two deaths for every birth. Madrid estimates that Spain's population will decline by one million people by 2030 and will decline by 5.6 million by 2080. Spain's population today is 46.7 million, so the 2080 projection represents a 12 percent population decline. Japan's population will decline 25 percent between now and 2055, taking the population from 127 million to 95 million. Bulgaria's population has fallen from 9 million in 1989 to 7 million today and is expected to drop another 30 percent to 4.9 million by 2050. These examples are not outliers. They're entirely typical of many other countries, from Switzerland (1.5) to Singapore (1.1). Rapidly declining populations are a fact of life for the remainder of the twenty-first century.

Reliance on developing economies to sustain high birthrates to make up for declining birthrates in developed economies is misplaced. The developing economy birthrates are collapsing also. Here are birthrates for some of the highest-population countries among the developing economies:

NIGERIA	5.3
CHINA	1.7
INDIA	2.2
INDONESIA	2.3
BRAZIL	1.5
PAKISTAN	3.5
BANGLADESH	2.0
RUSSIA	1.5
MEXICO	2.1
PHILIPPINES	2.5
EGYPT	3.3
VIETNAM	2.0

These twelve developing-economy population giants have a combined population of 4.58 billion, equal to 60 percent of the global population. The striking aspect of these numbers is how many developing-economy populations are already at or below the 2.1 replacement rate, including China (1.7), Brazil (1.5), Bangladesh (2), Russia (1.5), Mexico (2.1), and Vietnam (2). India (2.2) and Indonesia

(2.3) will fall below replacement level soon. Depopulation in developing economies is not the trend of the future—it's already here. There are developing economies with materially higher birthrates, including Nigeria (5.3), Pakistan (3.5), and Egypt (3.3). Those focused on global population trends should not expect that these high-birthrate countries will offset the impact of low birthrates in the developed world. The reason is that these high birthrates are collapsing fast based on the drivers described above. Major urban complexes are expanding in Lagos, Nairobi, Mombasa, Cairo, Dhaka, and elsewhere in sub-Saharan Africa and Southeast Asia. New arrivals from the countryside succumb quickly to the influence of cities, where large families are a burden and peer pressure can change attitudes. In many cases, especially Brazil, women have one or perhaps two children and use the customary maternity process to have additional procedures for sterilization. This caps their reproduction at 1 or 2 each, for an average of 1.5, well below the 2.1 replacement rate.

On trend, the human race will die out, although one might expect the trend to reverse or at least stabilize by the twenty-second century. While the demographic projections are clear, the implications for inflation are less so. Bricker and Ibbitson look at the simplest definition of gross domestic product, which weighs working-age population and productivity. China and India are not only dying out, they are aging rapidly. This is correlated with dementia and other disabilities. It follows that overall output will decline in line with the decline in working-age populations. At the same time, more prime-age workers will be involved with eldercare, which is an admirable occupation yet not one that lends itself to productivity gains. This amplifies the output losses beyond the mere number of workers. It follows that lower output will have a deflationary tilt as happened during the Great Depression. Bricker and Ibbitson point to other dysfunctions, such as a crisis of legitimacy for the Communist Party of China as the party fails to deliver on its promise of high growth or even a slightly improved standard of living.

Goodhart and Pradhan reach the opposite conclusion on inflation. The same demographics that point to an aging society, sharp declines in prime-age workers, and diversion of more workers to low-productivity eldercare mean that remaining workers will be able to demand real wage increases. This will add to costs of production and a gradual increase in the final price of goods for consumers. China will move from being a kind of low-cost deflation pump for the world to the opposite—a manufacturing base that will gradually increase costs. Rather than point to the Great Depression as a model, economists can look to the labor shortages and real wage gains in the late fourteenth and early fifteenth centuries following the Black Death.[8] As analyzed by Walter Scheidel in his work *The Great Leveler*, the extreme depopulation of Europe, North Africa, and the Middle East resulting from the bubonic plague, which peaked between 1347 and 1351, resulted in higher wages and reduced income inequality for about seventy-five years following the plague. Returns to labor rose. The causes are different (reduced childbearing versus bubonic plague), but the result will be the same—increased returns to labor and higher input costs. Relocating factories to Vietnam and Indonesia will be unavailing since those countries will experience their own demographic implosions. The dynamic is global.

As with increasing debt-to-GDP ratios, demographics seem likely to produce inflation, yet the process will be a slow one, playing out over twenty years or more. We do not need peak debt repudiation or peak demographic collapse to produce inflation. Consumers, investors, and economists will see it coming. Inflation will accelerate before the causes reach critical mass, in the same way the core of a nuclear reactor will heat up before it melts down. Still, these phenomena will play out over decades rather than months or years.

Monetary policy, our third factor, is at the top of most lists as a likely cause of inflation in the short term. In fact, it will have no inflationary impact at all and is more likely to be disinflationary. The popular view is that excessive Fed money printing must inevitably cause inflation. As discussed above, the Fed creates so-called base money by buying Treasury securities from banks. Those banks simply return the money to the Fed in the form of excess reserves. So that money does not enter the real economy and plays no role whatsoever in consumption or other activities that could lead to consumer price inflation. The only form of money that might lead to higher inflation is M1, the money created by commercial banks when they make loans or extend other forms of credit such as guarantees or standby lines of credit. Increased lending of that sort may or may not happen, but it will have little to do with the Fed. Commercial banks do need some level of reserves to support increased lending on their balance sheets, but the level of excess reserves today is so high that banks are far from constrained in their lending and will remain essentially unconstrained for the foreseeable future. An increase in commercial bank lending requires individuals or businesses who are willing to borrow. It takes two to tango.

One area where Fed policy does touch the real economy is the creation of asset bubbles. The Fed's zero- and low-interest-rate policies do support leverage on bank and hedge fund balance sheets that is diverted into stocks, bonds, and real estate, among other asset classes. Asset bubbles are not inflationary by themselves, but they are real and can have important economic consequences. The Fed imagines there is a so-called wealth effect through which higher asset values in portfolios leave consumers feeling richer and therefore more willing to spend. The empirical evidence for the wealth effect suggests that it is a mirage—just another flawed model that Fed economists cling to for no good reason. Instead, higher portfolio values cause investors to increase their investments in their portfolios, causing the asset bubbles to expand even more. This behavior enriches the wealthy, who have the largest allocations to bubble assets. It does not help lower-income individuals who have little or nothing invested in stocks, bonds, or real estate with which to enjoy the ride. This pattern persists until the bubble bursts. The tempo of bubbles inflating and bursting is asymmetric. The expanding phase lasts for years or even decades. The collapse comes in weeks or months (although the 1929 stock market crash took almost three years from peak to trough, dropping 82 percent from October 1929 to June 1932). Expanding bubbles are not particularly inflationary because the animal spirits are directed at stocks and bonds rather than consumption. Bursting bubbles can be disinflationary because they tend to change psychology in the direction of reduced consumption and higher unemployment. In short, there's little reason to believe that current asset bubbles will contribute to inflation. There is some reason to expect that current Fed tightening through asset sales and rate hikes will cause asset bubbles to deflate, which could feed through to reduced consumption.

Today, banks are not willing lenders because of weak business conditions. Customers are not willing borrowers because of increased precautionary savings and a generally weak economy with poor prospects for the kind of growth needed to support the borrowings. This will only change when bank customers change their inflationary behavior. It is possible that current inflation will lead to actions that cause more inflation in the future. In turn, that could lead to increased borrowing and spending as consumers attempt to beat price increases and as businesses expand staff and inventories to take advantage of increased demand. Yet those behavioral changes are psychological and conditional and have little to do with Fed policy. They depend on exogenous factors discussed below. The Fed and monetary policy are impotent to effect changes in inflationary behavior. The Fed is essentially a bystander with no material role to play. Policy is all for show.

Politics, the fourth factor, has had a clear inflationary impact, although the effect may be short-lived. Politics was the driver of massive pandemic relief packages that directed trillions of dollars to individuals, small businesses, and global corporations from March 2020 to November 2021. New relief packages are still being considered, although the momentum for additional spending waned as infections from the omicron variant of the SARS-CoV-2 virus faded in February 2022, and as inflation from past spending packages accelerated. The inflationary impact of this spending came not from higher deficits or Fed monetization of the debt; those are long-term problems. The inflation came from the fact that money was pumped straight into the hands of consumers and CEOs at a time when output was constrained by lockdowns and supply chain breakdowns. The result was a spending spree in the goods sector when the goods were often hard to find. That's a classic recipe for both cost-push and demand-pull inflation.

The first dose of fiscal stimulus in response to the pandemic came on March 25, 2020, with the signing of the Coronavirus Aid, Relief, and Economic Security Act, called the CARES Act, by President Trump. The CARES Act provided $2.7 trillion of new spending equal to 10 percent of U.S. GDP at the time. CARES provided $1,200 checks sent directly to most Americans. These direct payments were the closest thing to helicopter money, which had been theorized by both Milton Friedman and Ben Bernanke in the decades before the pandemic. The total given in direct aid as either handouts or extended unemployment benefits was $610 billion. Health-care service providers received $185 billion in assistance. Another $525 billion was directed to large corporations, with $600 billion allocated for small-business support. A separate allocation of $160 billion was for the airline industry, much of that handed out in $10 billion scoops each to major airlines such as Delta, United, and American Airlines. The largest single line item was $669 billion to fund the Paycheck Protection Program, which was used for loans to qualifying businesses that agreed to avoid layoffs among their employees. Upon certification one year after the loan that employees had been retained (or that the funds were used for other approved purposes such as office rent), the loans were forgiven without the tax consequences that normally come from loan forgiveness.

CARES was the largest direct deficit spending effort to support the U.S. economy ever. Interestingly, the direct impact of this massive deficit spending program on inflation was slight. Average inflation for all of 2020 was 1.2 percent, and there was no significant increase in inflation from August through December 2020, when most of the rescue money was being spent. Of course, it could be argued that without the aid the United States would have slipped into deflation, so even modest inflation in late 2020 was evidence of inflationary impact relative to the alternative. One group that definitely did not spend most of their CARES money were individuals who received the $1,400 checks. Most of this money was saved, not spent. In April 2020, after the checks had been distributed, the U.S. savings rate spiked to 32.2 percent, the highest ever. Americans were living through a rainy day and were saving more in case the rain didn't end soon. That said, some of the money was spent on imported high-priced items such as washing machines, refrigerators, and big-screen TVs. This amplified the supply chain breakdown as new orders for consumer goods surged even as factories abroad struggled to stay open.

The next fiscal shot in the arm came in December 2020, near the end of Trump's term as president. On December 27, 2020, Trump signed a second coronavirus relief bill that pumped an additional $900 billion into the economy through deficit spending effectively monetized by the Fed. This spending continued some unemployment and other benefit programs set to expire on December 31, 2020. It also provided an additional $600 check to almost every American, bringing the total amount of helicopter money per person to $2,000. The political pressure to pass this bill was overwhelming, but the economic case was decidedly weak. The U.S. economy had turned in one of its strongest performances ever in the third quarter of 2020. Unemployment was dropping steadily. Former Treasury secretary Larry Summers warned this second stimulus package risked causing inflation.[9] He was right. The final package was less than Trump had demanded just a few days earlier, yet Summers's analysis still applied. He said that when handouts in the form of discretionary income exceeded the economy's productive capacity, inflation would be the result. Unlike the March 2020 rescue spending that barely moved the inflation needle, the results of the December 2020 spending were immediate. The money was distributed in January 2021 and later. By March 2021, inflation had ticked up to 2.6 percent, the highest since August 2018. The following month, inflation hit 4.2 percent, the highest since September 2008. By the end of 2021, inflation was running at a 7 percent rate, the highest since 1982.

These inflationary trends were made worse by a third round of government deficit spending for pandemic relief early in the new Biden administration. On March 11, 2021, Biden signed the American Rescue Plan Act of 2021, or ARPA, which provided $1.9 trillion of deficit-financed stimulus and pandemic relief. This bill offered extended unemployment benefits with a $300 weekly supplement through September 2021. It also provided a third round of helicopter money, this time a $1,400 check for almost all individual Americans. It was becoming apparent by March 2021 that Larry Summers was right about the $600 checks from the December 2020 law causing inflation. Now the situation grew worse for the same reason—helicopter money was exceeding the productive ability of the U.S. economy and, through import channels, the global economy. Inflation took off after March 2021 as the Biden bailout bill amplified the impact of Trump's December 2020 handouts. Retail sales rose sharply. Prices followed in lockstep.

Congress had one more ace up its sleeve. On November 15, 2021, Biden signed the $1 trillion Infrastructure Investment and Jobs Act funded with deficit spending and Fed monetization. The infrastructure bill did not include helicopter money, and it called for spending on long-term projects over a five-year horizon. Therefore, it was unlikely to have the immediate inflationary impact of CARES, the December coronavirus relief, or ARPA. Still, the damage was done. Over $5.5 trillion in deficit spending (excluding the infrastructure bill), including $3,200 per individual in helicopter money monetized by the Fed, did the trick. Inflation was off and running at levels not seen in forty years.

Supply shocks are the fifth factor that drives inflation. This kind of inflation is caused by the supply side rather than the demand side of an economy. It can take two forms. The first is an outright shortage in supply, which causes customers to bid up the price of what remains. The second is an oligopolistic price hike against which there is no recourse because there are no alternate sources or feasible substitutes.

Both scenarios rely on inelastic demand for essential goods to make the price hikes stick.

The most famous example of a supply shock driven both by artificially induced shortages and by oligopolistic price hikes was the Arab oil embargo that began on October 17, 1973. This was led by Saudi Arabia and targeted countries that supported Israel in the October 6, 1973, Yom Kippur War, including the United States. Between October 1973 and the end of the embargo in March 1974, the price of oil increased almost 300 percent from three dollars per barrel to twelve dollars per barrel. Americans alive at the time, myself included, recall waiting in lines an hour or more for a turn at the pump to put gas in our cars. We were often limited to just a few gallons each. Some locales instituted even- or odd-day access to the gas pump based on the last digit on your license plate. In many cases the gas stations themselves ran dry and closed until new deliveries could be arranged. The United States had left itself vulnerable to the Arab oil weapon by allowing domestic oil production to decline precipitously in the early 1970s, a policy similar to that being pursued by Biden today. The impact on U.S. inflation was immediate. From a baseline of 3.3 percent inflation in 1972 before the embargo, it rose to 6.2 percent in 1973 and spiked to 11.1 percent in 1974 despite a sharp recession.

The same supply shock cost-push inflation occurred during the second oil crisis in 1979. That price shock came as a result of a sharp decline in oil output due to the Iranian Revolution that year. While there was no formal oil embargo in 1979, the output shortage did the same damage. The price of oil rose from twenty dollars per barrel to forty dollars per barrel over the course of 1979, beginning with the fall of the shah of Iran on January 16, 1979, followed by the arrival of Ayatollah Khomeini as the new leader. Gas lines returned at U.S. gas stations. The United States printed gas-rationing coupons, although they were never actually issued to citizens. Inflation also returned. From a 1978 baseline of 7.6 percent inflation, the inflation level rose to 11.3 percent in 1979 and 13.5 percent in 1980. Of course, by 1979 there were other inflationary factors in play, including higher inflationary expectations and steeply rising velocity. Still, the supply shock of the 1979 oil crisis was a significant element in soaring rates of inflation.

Now evidence is emerging that the U.S. and global economies are experiencing a new round of supply shocks. Instead of coming from a single commodity (oil) and a single source (the Middle East), the new supply shocks are coming from all directions as the cumulative effects of trade wars, pandemic lockdowns, and supply chain breakdowns are felt.

Bare shelves in supermarkets are the most obvious symptom of supply shocks. Still, the shelves are superficial symptoms of deeper problems. Increased costs for fertilizer (partly due to higher energy costs) are causing farmers to shift acreage from corn to soybeans, which use less fertilizer. There are limits to that shift because of soybean seed shortages; still, the shift is under way. One result by late 2022 will be a glut of soybeans, an example of the Bullwhip Effect, and a shortage of corn. This has widespread implications because corn derivatives are an additive to an enormous number of consumer products. More importantly, corn is used for ethanol and feed for livestock. Higher corn prices due to reduced supplies will result in higher prices for ethanol and for beef and pork. Higher fertilizer prices will feed through to higher prices for other agricultural produce, including coffee. More severe outcomes include starvation for some in Africa as fertilizer shortages cause declines in food production available for the world's poorest populations.

Labor shortages are another driver of inflation. There is no shortage of prime-working-age individuals. There is a shortage of those individuals actually looking for work or with jobs. The difference between the unemployment rate, which considers only those with jobs or looking for work, and the large number of potential workers who are simply not looking is captured in the Labor Force Participation Rate, or LFPR. This is a rate determined by dividing the total number of workers by the entire labor force without regard to whether an individual is looking for work or not. It's a more meaningful measure than the unemployment rate because it captures the true labor supply.

The LFPR peaked at 67.2 percent in March 2001, immediately prior to the recession that began in the wake of the dot.com stock crash that year. (This rate is never near 100 percent because there are many reasons for individuals not to be in the labor force, including early retirement, disability, education, childcare, and health care of those affected by the pandemic.) The rate began a steady decline, hitting 63.4 in February 2020, just before the impact of the pandemic was felt. At the depths of the pandemic-related market crash and economic lockdown in April 2020, the rate plunged to 60.2 before bouncing back somewhat to 62.2 by June 2022. That rate is still almost five percentage points below the all-time high, and over a full percentage point below the prepandemic low. With a labor force in January 2022 of over 162 million individuals, the five-percentage-point decline from March 2001 implies that 8.1 million individuals have dropped out of the labor force compared to levels that prevailed then. Even the regular unemployment report produced by the Bureau of Labor Statistics showed 524,000 fewer employed workers than before the pandemic. By either measure, there is a shortage of willing workers even if there is no shortage of potentially available workers. The primary means for employers to tap into this pool of unattached workers is to offer higher wages and benefits. The June 2022 employment report revealed a year-over-year increase in average hourly earnings of 5.1 percent. Gradually jobs are being filled from the pool of unemployed workers, but the price is higher wages, which will be passed through in the form of higher prices for consumers.

Energy prices are a primary cause of the recent rise in inflation because of both their direct impact in terms of gas at the pump and the wider indirect impact as an input in electricity generation and diverse intermediate processes including the creation of plastics and chemicals. The price of crude oil has staged a relentless surge from $12.78 per barrel on April 28, 2020 (following an anomalous dip to negative $37.63 per barrel on April 20, 2020, for technical reasons related to futures trading) to $104.54 on April 4, 2022. That 720 percent gain in two years showed few signs of cooling off in 2022. Oil over $120 per barrel was expected by some market analysts. The price of gas at the pump was also on a tear. The average price of regular gas in the United States rose from $2.16 per gallon on January 4, 2021, to $4.41 per gallon on July 22, 2022, a 104 percent spike in 18 months. Prices rose even higher in some regional markets. Americans did not need a PhD to understand inflation; higher prices were being paid right out of their purses.

Unlike the oil supply shocks of 1973 and 1979, this price shock was not caused by an embargo nor was it driven by panic buying or spiking inflationary expectations. It was the result of poor policy choices by the Biden administration. These policies included shutting pipelines, restricting new exploration leases on federal lands, and adding new regulations on fracking operations. Biden's blunders were matched by former German chancellor Angela Merkel, who shut down German electricity production from nuclear plants and coal-fired plants and left Germany completely at the mercy of Russia for incremental energy supplies. These unforced errors were exacerbated by the Ukraine war, which could potentially result in a shutoff of natural gas supplies to Europe. Finally, energy supplies were disrupted in China because of both the logistical challenges of its Zero COVID policy and the shortsightedness of its trade war with Australia that interrupted coal shipments. The result was a mad scramble for oil and natural gas imports by China and resulting higher prices.

Food, labor, and energy are the three most important inputs for a commercial and industrial society—indeed, for civilization itself. All three, and their derivative products, were moving higher in price in 2022.

Is Inflation Here to Stay?

This analysis brings us full circle. Inflation is certainly on the rise, yet will it persist or fade due to offsetting factors? In the short run, inflation will persist at or about current levels (7 percent year over year). Once momentum is established, a trend rarely stops on a dime unless there is a new shock comparable to the pandemic that appeared in 2020. The better form of the question is whether inflation is on the rise to levels of 8 percent or higher over the course of 2022 and 2023 or will retreat to the 5 percent level and eventually levels below 3 percent that were the norm from 2009 to 2020. A summary of our five factors viewed through the lens of velocity and baseline effects provides the answer.

Excessive debt and dismal demographics may be considered together for purposes of this analysis because they produce the same result over roughly the same time horizon. Neither will contribute to inflation over the next several years. Each will guarantee inflation beginning in ten to twenty years. An increase in debt as measured by the debt-to-GDP ratio may continue for some time before the inflation needed to melt the debt becomes a matter of policy. The taming of the post–World War II mountain of debt took thirty-five years (1946–81). It also took cooperation between the Fed and the Treasury, including a Treasury-imposed cap on interest rates from 1942 to 1951 and the subsequent Treasury-Fed accord beginning in March 1951. The effort was bipartisan as it ran under Democrats (Truman, Kennedy, Johnson, and Carter) and Republicans (Eisenhower, Nixon, and Ford). It was a slow but steady success.

Most of these elements are missing today. Bipartisanship is dead. Any sense that high debts are a problem to begin with has been muted by both modern monetary theory and the perceived necessity of bailouts as seen in 2008 and 2020. The Fed failed to maintain even modest inflation above 2 percent despite targeted efforts for the twelve years prior to 2021. It's a sad day when a central bank wants inflation and can't get it. Still, debt is a problem. It actually works to cause deflation rather than inflation until the critical state arrives. The United States will not default on its debt because it can print the money needed.

The crisis will come when the money printing itself causes a loss of confidence, perhaps due to higher interest rates, compounding effects, or sheer volume, and a flight from the dollar commences. At that point, inflation will appear quickly and possibly morph into hyperinflation. So, yes, excessive debt will cause high inflation—but not yet.

The same is true for demographics. Goodhart and Pradhan have it right that the coming demographic collapse will put a premium on available labor. Yet the same labor shortage will lower output, even if supplemented with robotics and increased computational capacity. An aging society and attendant eldercare will be a drag on productivity. Robots don't give baths. The combination of higher returns to labor with lower overall productivity is practically the definition of inflation. These effects are starting now but will take a decade or more to reach a critical state. Like excessive debt, demographics will cause high inflation—but not yet.

Monetary policy conducted by the Fed is irrelevant to inflation (because of falling velocity) yet is highly relevant to asset bubbles. On balance, the Fed's current efforts at monetary tightening will collapse asset bubbles in a disorderly way, which will be deflationary in its impact, contrary to Fed expectations. For this reason, the Fed will not be a source of inflation in the near term. Commercial banks and borrowers could cause inflation if they gin up the lending and spending machine to create M1. Yet this requires improved business conditions and some combination of animal spirits and inflationary expectations. Neither are present currently. Bank finance is directed to asset inflation rather than inflation in the price of goods and services. That will continue until the bubbles burst, at which point any consumer price inflation will go in reverse.

Politics will also not contribute to inflation in the near future. There's clear evidence that the $5.5 trillion in deficit spending between March 2020 and March 2021 (excluding $2 trillion of baseline budget deficits and $1 trillion of infrastructure spending) was a cause of the inflation that emerged in 2021. In particular, the $3,200 per individual in helicopter money that was handed out with no strings attached fueled surges in retail sales in 2021 that contributed to supply chain bottlenecks and rising prices. The difficulty is that these surges faded once the money was spent. The impact was temporary, not lasting. This is consistent with the view that excess debt and deficits are more deflationary than inflationary beyond certain levels (and the United States is well beyond those levels). More to the point, no further stimulus or helicopter money is in the cards absent another pandemic or comparable disaster such as a war. There is no majority in the U.S. Senate for more spending of the kind that Trump and Biden pushed through in the year following the outbreak of the virus. Pandemic spending had its day, but that day has come and gone.

Debt and demographic inflation effects are long term. Monetary policy and politics will not produce inflation under current conditions. Is there a factor that can drive inflation higher in the short run and possibly change behavior to produce a recursive function that drives prices even higher? Yes. That factor is the supply chain and the emergence of supply shocks that play out in higher prices. This dynamic is not transient like helicopter money. It does feed on itself if not cured quickly. It is beyond the control of policymakers because of the complexity of supply chains.

We're seeing supply-shock inflation play out in front of our eyes. Inflation is at the gas pump, the grocery store, and the nail salon. Businesses that were shut down in the spring of 2020 have reopened, but with higher costs for energy and labor and therefore higher prices for consumers. The supply chain price shock is also present in myriad ways that consumers cannot see, such as shipping costs, container costs, docking fees, warehouse fees, demurrage, fines and penalties, and the costs of thousands of other logistics links in global chains. Energy costs are rising due to Western policy blunders and Eastern geopolitics. At an even higher level, the decoupling of China and the United States and the rebuilding of supply chains around new suppliers and customers will add to costs for years to come. These costs may be worth it from a national security perspective and in the name of human rights, but consumers will pick up the tab.

Across-the-board inflation from failing supply chains is happening and will persist. The issue then is whether countervailing forces of disinflation can stop the inflation train in its tracks. That's the topic of chapter 5.

CHAPTER FIVE

Is Deflation the Threat?

———

With the clear danger of an equity bubble revealed in 2000 to 2002, the even greater dangers of a housing bubble in 2006 to 2010, and the extra risk of doing two asset bubbles together in Japan in the late 1980s and in the U.S. in 2007, what has the Fed learned? Absolutely nothing.

—JEREMY GRANTHAM
"Let the Wild Rumpus Begin" (2022)[1]

The Case for Deflation

With recent U.S. inflation running at forty-year highs, and supply chain disruptions forcing prices higher due to shortages, the case for disinflation or outright deflation seems difficult to make. It's not. It's a matter of whether price increases will abate in the face of more powerful fundamental factors. It's also a matter of whether the Fed's inflation-fighting policy will prove poorly timed and overdone. There's good reason to conclude that both trends are true—the economy is fundamentally deflationary, and the Fed will fail in its policy efforts, as it did in 2018. Current conditions are not a case of returning to the 1970s. In fact, we may be fortunate to avoid a repeat of the 1930s.

Before diving into the dynamics that presage deflation, it's important to clarify the distinction between deflation and disinflation. Deflation means actual price decreases. This happened on a global basis in the 1930s. Disinflation means prices are still increasing, but at a lower rate. If inflation falls from, say, 4 percent to 1.5 percent, that's an example of disinflation; you still have 1.5 percent inflation but that's materially less than the prior rate. If disinflation is still inflation, why did I not discuss it in the previous chapter on inflation? The answer has to do with the impact of disinflation on real interest rates and behavior. In those respects, disinflation has more in common with deflation than inflation. If the two are not twins, they are at least close cousins. Some examples will clarify this point.

In deflation, even interest rates of zero can still be high real rates. If interest rates are zero, and deflation is 3 percent (inflation of negative 3 percent), the real interest rate is positive 3 percent. The math is: $[0 - (-3)] = 3$. Compare that to a case where nominal interest rates are 3 percent and inflation is 4 percent. In that case, the real interest rate is negative 1 percent. The math is: $3 - 4 = -1$. The math is simple, yet psychologically you have gone through the looking glass. Real rates go higher in deflation even as nominal rates go lower. This is where disinflation resembles deflation more than inflation. If nominal interest rates stay at 3 percent as inflation drops from 5 percent to 1.5 percent (an example of disinflation), then real rates rise from negative 2 percent ($3 - 5 = -2$) to positive 1.5 percent ($3 - 1.5 = 1.5$). That trend toward higher real rates is what joins deflation and disinflation as similar phenomena. The same is true for consumer behavior. If inflation rises from 3 percent to 7 percent, it is likely (not certain) that everyday Americans will expect that trend to continue or get worse. In that case, adaptive behavior including accelerating the timing of big-ticket purchases and hoarding goods can cause prices to rise in a self-fulfilling prophecy. Conversely, if inflation falls from 3 percent to 1 percent, Americans may expect it to fall further or at least not rise, in which case purchases may be deferred since there is little risk of much higher prices. Both 7 percent and 1 percent are species of inflation, yet what matters is not the level but the trend. Disinflation points away from more inflation toward possible deflation. Disinflation and deflation both point toward higher real rates, slower growth, and deferred or diminished consumption. That's why we treat them under the same heading even though they are on two sides of the looking glass. We will be precise in our use of the terms. Still, reference to disinflation should be taken as akin to deflation and with many of the same effects.

The case for disinflation or deflation in the United States today begins with a comparison to conditions in the 1970s, the last time inflation surged and required extreme tightening by the Federal Reserve to subdue. Curiously, the causes of inflation in the 1970s are still hotly debated by economists and not widely agreed. Economist Dan Alpert has identified three schools of thought on this: He breaks these camps into the conservatives who blame budget deficits and easy monetary policy beginning in 1969, the institutionalists who blame the Nixon Shock that ended the Bretton Woods gold standard in stages between 1971 and 1973, and liberals who take a Keynesian view and blame the twin oil price shocks of 1973 and 1979.[2]

Alpert dismisses the conservative perspective simply because there is no strong correlation between budget deficits and low interest rates on the one hand and inflation on the other. This lack of positive correlation is more prevalent today than it was in the 1970s, which is the period Alpert examined. In fact, the relationship is moving toward negative correlation, where larger deficits produce lower inflation or disinflation. The reason then and now is the same—declining velocity. If velocity declines enough, the money printing doesn't matter; it's not inflationary. Alpert gives more credit to the liberal and Keynesian perspective, which blames inflation on the twin oil embargoes. Those events neatly fit the model of cost-push inflation, where an exogenous supply shock hits the economy and causes ripple effects in intermediate and finished goods. In time, that kind of shock can feed back as raised inflationary expectations and demands for higher wages, or demand-pull inflation. Still, the source was from the supply side.

Alpert gives the most weight and credence to the institutionalist

Nixon Shock view. When President Nixon suspended the convertibility of dollars into gold by foreign trading partners, this did not lead to a return to a gold standard at a devalued exchange rate as intended. It led to the end of the gold standard and the advent of floating exchange rates, which the world has lived with ever since. One consequence was a rapid increase in the dollar price of gold. Gold now traded freely in global markets and began a steady ascent. From $35 per ounce on the day of Nixon's announcement, August 15, 1971, gold rose to $137 per ounce by the end of 1973, then to $450 per ounce at the end of 1979. Gold briefly touched $800 per ounce in mid-January 1980 but retreated from there. The average price in January 1980 was $625 per ounce. This market activity was widely perceived as a rise in the price of gold. Yet gold is an inert metal with few uses other than as money. The rise in the price of gold is better understood as a collapse in the value of the dollar. In July 1971, one dollar would purchase 1/35 of an ounce of gold. In December 1979, one dollar would purchase 1/450 of an ounce of gold. An ounce of gold had not changed. Instead, the dollar had collapsed. The time series of gold prices shows the value of a dollar crashed by 92 percent from 1971 to 1979. That's a worse collapse in percentage terms than the stock market at the start of the Great Depression.

Gold is the only neutral metric for measuring the dollar's collapse in this context. Other currencies are not a useful frame of reference because those currencies were also collapsing against gold, which muted their collapse relative to each other. In the late 1970s, all major currencies were in free fall against gold, silver, land, oil, and other hard assets.

This collapse of the dollar casts the oil price increases of the 1970s in a new light. Oil rose 300 percent from $3 per barrel to $12 per barrel between late 1973 and early 1974 in the first oil crisis. Then oil spiked 100 percent from $20 per barrel to $40 per barrel in 1979 during the second oil crisis. Taking the entire period from 1973 to 1979, oil rose 1,200 percent. Gold rose from $137 per ounce at the end of 1973 and reached $450 per ounce at the end of 1979. That's a 70 percent devaluation of the dollar from 1973 to 1979. Arabs were charging more dollars for oil, but each dollar was worth less. The 1979 dollar was only worth $0.30 compared to the 1973 dollar. This means that $40 oil was really $12 oil when adjusted for the lost purchasing power of the dollar. The price of oil did go up in the 1970s but only by 300 percent in real terms, not 1,200 percent. Compared to 1971, the real price of oil actually rose only 7 percent from $3 per barrel to $3.20 per barrel over nine years, less than 1 percent per year. In short, there was no oil price shock in the 1970s in real terms. What happened was a dollar collapse and borderline hyperinflation. The Arabs can hardly be blamed for raising the price of oil. They were just trying to break even against the decline of the dollar.

The point of this review of energy prices in the 1970s is that it can't happen again, at least not in the same direct manner. There is no gold standard to abandon and set off a chain reaction of higher inflationary expectations. The dollar has been getting stronger, not weaker, over the course of 2021 and 2022 as measured by currency indices. Oil prices have been going up in real terms since 2021. That's important because real oil price increases contain the seeds of their own decline. As energy prices rise in real terms, consumers have less discretionary income for other purchases, energy users seek substitutes, and energy producers increase output. Gradually the economy slows, and oil prices revert to lower levels. The real price mechanism is self-correcting, whereas the inflationary (nominal) price mechanism is self-reinforcing. One exception is a major war; even then the war could invite price controls, major releases from the strategic petroleum reserve, and an easing of current restrictions on fracking, new exploration, and pipelines. Oil prices and energy prices more broadly will not have the same impact in the 2020s as they did in the 1970s because initial conditions are entirely different. The abandonment of a gold standard means the dollar cannot break against gold all at once to set an inflationary train in motion. In an age of King Dollar, oil price increases are real, not just nominal, which means there are practical and political limits on how far they can go.

The second part of Alpert's disinflationary thesis is that the United States has huge pools of unused labor capacity and industrial capacity that are standing by to absorb increased government spending, increased consumer spending, and increased velocity. The United States also has ample scope for increased investment in infrastructure, manufacturing, housing, and education. In short, the U.S. economy has enormous slack, partly as a result of hyperglobalization and offshoring and partly due to low returns to labor versus capital. This spare capacity can absorb an enormous wave of spending and investment, including debt-financed spending, without creating bottlenecks. This kind of spending, if done wisely, can add to output and increase productivity without causing inflation. Alpert adds that even moderate inflation might not be such a bad thing if it results from higher returns to labor, more purchasing power for households, and is nonaccelerating. That's a fine line to walk, but if it can be achieved it has the added benefit of reducing the real burden of debt, another task the government must face sooner rather than later.

The idea that the United States has a huge pool of potential workers is well founded. The so-called labor shortage affecting the U.S. economy, particularly small- and medium-size businesses, is a misleading artifact. It is true that Help Wanted signs are ubiquitous. Restaurants routinely warn customers their dinners may be delayed because there's a shortage of staff in the kitchen. McDonald's is offering $35,000 starting salaries plus benefits and training for order takers and cashiers. Supermarkets blame empty shelves not on a shortage of goods but on a shortage of clerks to stock shelves. The U.S. unemployment rate fell to 3.5 percent in July 2022 despite the omicron variant of the virus and supply chain impediments. By almost every measure, the labor shortage seemed real.

This data hides a more powerful reality, which is that the United States does not have a shortage of potential workers, it has a shortage of willing workers. Behind the so-called labor shortage is an army of perhaps eight million prime-age potential workers who are simply not looking for work. Part of this cohort has good reason not to pursue jobs, including early retirement, childcare responsibilities, educational opportunities, or health issues. Allowing for that still leaves millions of potential workers not seeking work.

With millions of unfilled jobs and millions of unemployed workers (including those not officially unemployed because they are not seeking jobs), why are the jobs not being filled? The reasons include the inability of employers to pay a market-clearing wage because their own profit margins are squeezed by higher input costs, higher taxes, and reduced demand as a residual effect of the pandemic. This is especially true in the service sector, which has been the hardest hit by lockdowns, quarantines, mask mandates, and social distancing. The goods sector has been more robust to the pandemic than the service sector, yet a large percentage of goods are imported from cheap-labor countries that can manage costs through devaluation of their currencies against the U.S. dollar. In any case, U.S. labor is not a material factor of production in foreign goods. Demand for imports does not exert inflationary pressure in U.S. labor markets. Other causes for the slack in U.S. labor utilization include higher unemployment benefits, extended unemployment benefits, and increased childcare tax credits in the 2021 American Rescue Plan. This made it easier for Americans to stay home, and many remained at home even after benefits ran out. There is extensive research supporting the view that once workers become accustomed to not working, they lose skills and habits that tend to exclude them from the workforce permanently. There is no labor shortage, although there is a dysfunctional labor market. Higher wages, training opportunities, termination of certain government benefits, and expanded private-sector benefits can combine gradually to draw the uncounted millions back to the workforce. It is the case that the huge pool of available labor will ensure that demand-pull inflation will not be a driver of consumer-price inflation for the foreseeable future.

The final element that suggests spending and stimulus will not induce inflation is investment. Spending is not generic; it can be aimed at handouts or long-term investment in productivity, enhancing infrastructure or research and development. When spending is directed to the latter it has two deflationary or disinflationary effects. The first is to absorb the available labor pool into more high-paying jobs with benefits that increase returns to labor and reduce income inequality. That kind of employment is consistent with higher productivity. As long as productivity exceeds wage gains then there is no inflationary impulse. The second effect is that improved infrastructure and research and development forge gains that are spread among society as a whole and not confined to the workers producing them. Again, spending that improves productivity, as the United States experienced in the 1950s and '60s, is noninflationary. In the aggregate, it more than pays for itself.

Any economy can produce deflation with collapsing growth and high unemployment. The challenge is to produce high growth and full employment without producing inflation. This is where decoupling from China complements both disinflation and productivity gains. The attraction of cheap labor is limited to low value-added manufacturing. When high value-added manufacturing is desired, more expensive labor is efficient because it can offer higher productivity. When this process is aided with investment, the result is more jobs, more output, and higher wages without inflation. The inflation is muted both because excess labor is being absorbed and because productivity gains outpace higher input costs, including wages. To the extent some inputs are imported, a stronger U.S. dollar keeps those costs relatively low also. Far from being a drag on growth, higher interest rates are associated with a strong economy and a strong demand for funds. Investment itself creates new capacity, which then absorbs aggregate demand without causing inflation. American policymakers including central bankers have spent so much time chasing low rates, low costs, and low inflation, they have forgotten that higher rates, higher wages, a strong dollar, and modest inflation are all signs of a strong economy. Spare labor, increased capacity through investment, and low foreign input costs through a strong dollar will contain the inflationary potential.

Disinflation and deflation win in every state of the world. If investment is done wisely, added productivity will subdue inflation. If investment is done poorly, the increased debt-to-GDP ratio will also subdue inflation. The difference is that workers and society win in the first case while both lose in the latter. The outcome turns on policy decisions. That's a weak reed in the short run.

Fed Failure Redux

Few factors are easier to forecast than Fed policy. The reason is that the Fed tells you what it is going to do, and it means it. All the forecaster has to do is listen to the Fed, believe it, and then make allowance for its inevitable failure. The forecast will be accurate for a year or more as the Fed stumbles down the wrong path. The challenge is to estimate the point at which even the Fed must bow to reality. For that eventuality you look to market signals, particularly in the bond market and the Eurodollar futures curve. Those and other indicators will validate the fact that the Fed is headed over a cliff. The Fed will be the last to know, yet even it will change course in the end. The only issue is how much damage is done before it wakes up. At that point, the Fed will announce its new policy, and the analyst can repeat the process just described.

As late as the early 1990s, this was not the case. The Fed made policy errors, yet it was both more humble about the fact that errors occur and more circumspect in announcing its policies in the first place. The Fed has always operated through a club of selected banks and securities dealers called primary dealers. The status of primary dealer is not a formal license. Instead, it's a credit approval from the Fed that allows you to deal with the open market desk at the Federal Reserve Bank of New York. The current list of primary dealers includes twenty-four firms, mostly well-known international banks such as Goldman Sachs, Barclays, and Citi, but also some lesser-known specialists such as Amherst Pierpont and Cantor Fitzgerald. The obligation of the primary dealer is to make continuous two-way markets in a variety of U.S. government securities. The primary dealers provide liquidity to Fed operations in a manner not too different from the old-time specialist system on the New York Stock Exchange. What the primary dealer receives in return is the ability to speak directly with Fed traders and take their temperature on scarcity issues, overall liquidity, and any order imbalance. That information is valuable to the dealers in assessing their own risks and offering color to their customers.

Until the late 1990s, another benefit of being a primary dealer was that you were a conduit for changes in Fed policy. The open market desk would typically move to tighten or ease policy in advance of a public announcement. It would make this known to one or two favorite dealers on a rotating basis. It was the ultimate in inside information. Word would leak out through calls with customers or over drinks at Harry's Bar on Hanover Square or other watering holes within walking distance of the New York Fed's fortress-style headquarters on Liberty Street in Lower Manhattan. For a few days, sometimes longer, the favored dealer could make low-risk profits trading ahead of the eventual news. The Fed favored this system because it could test the waters without roiling global markets with headline announcements. If the Fed decided to backtrack, it could do so discreetly. This insider trading was legal because, after all, the government was in on it. It was all in the game.

This cozy yet efficient relationship between the Fed and the primary dealers began to change in February 1994 when the Federal Open Market Committee (FOMC) started to release statements announcing changes in its target for the Fed Funds rate. In February 1995, the FOMC also started releasing transcripts of its meetings, with a five-year lag. In August 1997, the Fed acknowledged that its policy rate was actually targeted and began to announce that target in the form of a directive to the New York Fed. In December 1998, shortly after the Fed's rescue of Long-Term Capital Management, the FOMC started a practice of announcing monetary policy changes immediately; after May 1999 the FOMC issued statements at every meeting, whether there was a policy change or not. These changes continued in baby steps over twelve years, including statements on the balance of risks (1999), announcement of any dissenting votes (2002), the addition of an inflation forecast and the release of FOMC minutes of meetings three weeks after the meeting (2004), the addition of two-year forecasts in monetary reports to Congress (2005), the increasing frequency of forecasts and looking three years ahead instead of two (2007), the addition of long-run forecasts of GDP, unemployment, and inflation (2009), press conferences following FOMC meetings (2011), and publication of FOMC meeting participants' projections for the Fed Funds rate, known popularly as "the dots" (2012). Over eighteen years, from 1994 to 2012, the Fed had gone from nontransparency to full transparency to prognostication. That same span included the Asian financial crisis in 1998, the dot.com market collapse in 2000, the global financial crisis of 2008, and a setup for the pandemic panic of 2020. Every novice statistics student knows correlation is not causation, yet the correlation between efforts at Fed transparency and frequent financial crises is striking. Perhaps a return to the days of a stealthy Fed operating through secrets shared at Harry's Bar is worth consideration.

Nevertheless, transparency rules the day, and the analyst can feast on a steady diet of Fed Funds targets, inflation forecasts, and dots to discern precisely what the Fed will be doing, at least in the short run, and to infer future inflection points based on reasonable estimates of Fed failure. This has important implications for any forecast of inflation or disinflation, even deflation. The Fed has been on a tightening path since August 27, 2021, when Jay Powell presaged a taper of asset purchases before the end of 2021 in his speech at the annual Jackson Hole Economic Symposium. Powell was noncommittal on interest rate hikes following the completion of the taper, but rate hikes were a logical next step. Powell left the timing of the taper's end unclear. The market took the announcement in stride. There was no "taper tantrum" (a sudden rise in rates and fall in bond prices), as happened when former Fed chair Ben Bernanke suggested a similar reduction in asset purchases in May 2013. On November 3, 2021, Powell made the taper announcement official. The FOMC said it would reduce asset purchases by $15 billion per month; at that pace the taper would be completed by July 2022. Just three weeks later, Goldman Sachs told clients that the Fed would double the reduction in asset purchases to $30 billion per month and that the taper would be complete by March 2022. Both the doubling to $30 billion and the March target for ending the taper were confirmed by the FOMC on December 15, 2021. Perhaps Fed leaks to friendly banks still had their place. At the next FOMC meeting, on January 26, 2022, the FOMC confirmed the taper would end in early March and added, "With inflation well above 2 percent and a strong labor market, the Committee expects it will soon be appropriate to raise the target range for the federal funds rate."[3] The Fed did not disappoint. The FOMC raised the Fed Funds target rate to 0.25 percent at its meeting on March 16, 2022, an additional 0.50 percent on May 4, 2022, 0.75 percent on June 15, 2022, and another 0.75 percent on July 27, 2022. By September 2022, the Fed Funds target rate was 2.25 percent and headed higher. The Fed also commenced a new program of quantitative tightening, QT, by reducing its balance sheet by about $100 billion per month.

The reason for this dual tightening through a reduced balance sheet and rate hikes was the inflation scare that Jay Powell suffered in August 2021. As the 2020 base effects ran off in July 2021 and inflation did not prove transitory as Powell expected, he suddenly pivoted to inflation-fighting mode, using the Fed's tightening tools of tapering and rate hikes. The Fed's taper from November 2021 to March 2022 and rate hikes thereafter were right out of the Fed's playbook, devised by Ben Bernanke eight years earlier. This begs the question: Was Bernanke's original playbook successful? And what expectations should market participants have today based on that prior run? The answer points to decidedly unpleasant outcomes for stock market investors.

The current Jay Powell playbook is moving in lockstep with the one created by Bernanke. On May 22, 2013, Bernanke indicated the Fed would begin to reduce asset purchases, a so-called taper. Optimists on Wall Street and financial talking heads thought it was not a big deal; after all, the Fed was still printing money; it was just printing it at a slower rate. Still, the market saw it for what it was. In economics, everything happens at the margin. A taper is a form of monetary tightening. Even if you are still buying securities, the fact that you are buying fewer is enough to cause leveraged investors to get out of carry trades and asset allocators to move back toward the dollar (a strong dollar is another form of tightening). The taper tantrum consisted of investors dumping emerging markets bonds, moving money back into dollars, and reducing leverage across the board. It was not a full-scale financial panic, but it was too close for comfort from Bernanke's perspective. After hinting the taper might begin with the FOMC meeting on September 18, 2013, Bernanke balked at firing the starting gun. The actual taper began on December 18, 2013, and was completed on October 29, 2014.

The market then waited for the "liftoff" consisting of the first increase in interest rates since June 29, 2006. After more than eight years of rate cuts, and zero-interest-rate policy, the countdown to a rate hike had begun. The markets had to wait awhile. The liftoff did not occur until December 16, 2015, under the leadership of new Fed chair Janet Yellen. The global economy had survived two flash crashes in the Chinese yuan in August and December that year, and a U.S. stock market meltdown over the course of August. It was no time to tighten policy, yet the Fed tightened anyway for no better reason than to avoid embarrassment at moving into a third calendar year with no liftoff. It's a good example of the Fed doing the wrong thing at the wrong time merely to live up to its self-inflicted forward guidance. After December 2015, there was a yearlong dry spell before a second rate hike on December 14, 2016. Then the rate hike tempo picked up considerably. There were 0.25 percent increases in March, June, September, and December 2017, and like increases in March, June, September, and December 2018. By December 19, 2018, the Fed Funds target rate was in the range of 2.25 percent to 2.5 percent, the highest it had been since March 2008, during the meltdown of Bear Stearns in the early stages of the global financial crisis. Along the way, Jay Powell became Fed chair on February 5, 2018. It made no difference. The Fed's institutional goals embedded in forward guidance were pursued by Bernanke, Yellen, and Powell in like-minded manner. It was the policy, not the personalities, that mattered. By December 2018, the Fed had practically achieved its long-sought goal of normalized interest rates. While the Fed was hiking rates, it also reduced M0 base money on its balance sheet from a peak of $4.1 trillion in October 2015 (just before the rate liftoff) to $3.2 trillion in September 2019, a 22 percent decline. This shrinkage of the base money supply was complementary to the rate hikes both as a form of monetary tightening and as an effort to normalize rates and money supply after the fire-hose approach to money printing from 2008 to 2015.

There was one enormous problem with the Fed's tightening policy. It ran into a market buzz saw starting in September 2018. After hitting an all-time high of 2,930 on September 20, 2018, the S&P 500 Index plunged to 2,351 by December 24, 2018, the infamous Christmas Eve Massacre. This constituted a 19.8 percent plunge and put the index a hair's breadth from a bear market in less than one hundred days. It's critical to note that the market meltdown progressed even as the Fed continued to raise rates and reduce the money supply. In other words, the Fed was sticking to its forward guidance and its normalization script despite clear market evidence that this was a mistake. Inflation was dropping from 2.5 percent in October 2018 to 2.2 percent in November, 1.9 percent in December, and 1.6 percent in January 2019. The market drop and the inflation drop were clear signs that the Fed was overtightening, but the band played on. The Fed even tightened on December 19, 2018, three months after the market meltdown began. That December rate hike was the last straw. On December 24, 2018, the S&P 500 fell almost 3.0 percent in a single day, the worst Christmas Eve performance ever. The Fed does not particularly care how the stock market is trending (contrary to the views of most Fed critics), but it does care when markets become disorderly. The December 24 performance coming on top of the September–December drawdown qualified as disorderly. The Fed finally got the market message.

The Fed pivot began within days. On January 4, 2019, Jay Powell said, "we will be patient" about further interest rate increases as he sat on a panel alongside Ben Bernanke and Janet Yellen at the American Economics Association annual meeting in Atlanta. Fed watchers know that the word "patient" is code for "we won't raise rates without giving you advance warning so you can square your books." The market loved it. The Dow Jones Industrial Average rose 600 points within minutes of Powell's pivot. Still, Powell's conversion from hawk to dove was only half finished. He still expected to raise rates after a pause for the market to catch its breath. The reduction in base money continued. After an initial bounce, major stock market indices were still at the September 2018 level in October 2019. By late September 2019 the Fed ended net asset sales with the base money supply at $3.2 trillion. The pendulum started to swing. The Fed began a new round of QE and slowly raised M0 to $3.4 trillion by January 2020. The Fed also started to cut rates on July 31, 2019, and continued in 0.25 percent increments the following September and October. Then came COVID. The Fed slashed interest rates by 0.5 percent at an emergency meeting on March 3, 2020. Rates were slashed four more times at emergency meetings on March 15, March 19, March 23, and March 31, 2020. In less than thirty days, rates were back to zero. At the same time, base money exploded to $5.1 trillion in May 2020 before surging again to $6.4 trillion in December 2021. Other measures of money growth spiked even more. The Fed's normalization plan lay in ruins. Rates were back to zero and money supply was at an all-time high. The Fed had failed to escape the room.

What are the lessons of this failure? The first is that the Fed will persist in following its announced policies despite market warnings that it is on the wrong path. It should have been clear by November 2018 that the Fed was tightening into weakness, yet it continued with one last rate hike in December 2018 and triggered a near market collapse. The second is that the Fed does not know how to read the real economy. Its leadership focuses on the unemployment rate (which is misleading because of low labor-force participation), wage increases (which are misleading because of inflation), and a rising stock market (which offers false comfort because of passive index investing). The stock market is a lagging indicator. By the time it turns down, serious damage to the economy has already been done. Much better indicators of success or failure in monetary policy are available in the bond market and Eurodollar futures curve, but the Fed seems not to notice. The third lesson, and the one most pertinent to investors, is that the Fed will fail again, and the result will be disinflation rather than the inflation that is widely expected. Yet there will be important differences between the coming failure and the last.

The best perspective on what the Fed will do next and how it will impact the economy comes from consideration of every step in a complete tightening cycle. The first step is a preview of a taper followed by the start of the taper. This is followed by completion of the taper, then interest rate hikes. Next comes a reduction in base money achieved through asset sales. The goal in each case is to push interest rates to the 2.5 percent range while reducing base money to around $2.5 trillion. As money tightening proceeds, the economy slows because it is dependent on loose monetary policy. Inflationary expectations decline because asset values begin to decline. The Fed persists in monetary tightening despite these signals because it misreads bond market cues and Eurodollar futures curve inversion. The Fed is not troubled by declining stock prices as long as the declines are not disorderly. Finally, a market crash emerges that is disorderly even as a liquidity crisis grows. The Fed quickly stops the rate hikes and base money supply reductions. As the economy and markets weaken further, the Fed pivots to interest rate reductions and base money expansion until rates return to zero and base money reaches new all-time highs. Asset values recover and business conditions improve. At that point, the cycle is complete, and the Fed awaits the next opportunity to taper.

In the case of the cycle commenced by Ben Bernanke and continued by Janet Yellen and Jay Powell, the entire process ran just over eight years from May 2013, when Bernanke signaled a taper, until August 2021, when Jay Powell signaled a new taper. The tightening phase lasted slightly less than six years, from May 2013 to January 2019, when Powell announced no new rate hikes, and the easing cycle lasted fifteen months, from January 2019 to March 2020, when rates hit zero. Because the process is recurring, one could readily demonstrate an earlier easing cycle of fifteen months lasting from September 2007 to December 2008, when rates also hit zero. Obviously, easing cycles run much faster than tightening cycles because they are an emergency response to the disorderly market conditions caused by the tightening.

In this iteration, the tightening cycle will run much faster than the prior six-year process started by Bernanke in 2013. The first reason is that there was only a four-month lag between the start of the Powell taper and his first rate hike, compared with the two-year lag under Bernanke. The second reason is that there was no lag between the end of the taper under Powell and a rate hike, compared with a thirteen-month lag under Bernanke's successor, Janet Yellen. The third reason is that the tempo of rate hikes after the first hike was rapid under Powell, compared with a twelve-month lag between the first and second rate hikes under Yellen. In short, Jay Powell is a man in a hurry. He was surprised by the surge in inflation in late 2021 and wants to make up for lost time in squashing it. He also wants to return to the path of normalizing rates and money supply that he abandoned in January 2019 after the Christmas Eve Massacre. Both purposes are served by rapid rate hikes.

The market has seen this movie before. The tightening process from 2013 to 2018 was initially supported by markets on the view that Fed tightening signaled a stronger economy and a true end to the aftermath of the global financial crisis. If the economy was getting stronger and globalization was producing lower costs and stronger profits, then it made sense to raise interest rates. That's what happens in a normal business cycle. But there was nothing normal about the post-2013 period, least of all a strong business cycle. Average annual growth during the Trump years was almost identical to that of the Obama years, about 2.2 percent from the start of the recovery in 2009 to the arrival of the pandemic in 2020. That was the longest recovery in U.S. history (129 months), yet it was also the weakest. The 2.2 percent average annual growth of the Obama-Trump recovery compares with 4.4 percent average annual growth for all post-1980 recoveries through 2021. The Trump years were adequate but not spectacular, as Trump's apologists continually claimed. The trade war that began in 2018 may have had a strong policy rationale, but it acted as a brake on growth. Quarterly U.S. GDP for 2018 came in at 3.8 percent in the first quarter, 2.7 percent in the second, 2.1 percent in the third, and 1.3 percent in the fourth. Growth fell steadily over 2018 in response to the trade war and as a prelude to the fourth quarter stock market debacle. The Fed tightened into weakness and kept tightening. The stock market responded with a 20 percent drawdown at year end 2018.

Just as Jay Powell has accelerated the tightening timeline, the market will accelerate its response. Powell will likely succeed in stopping runaway inflation, but he will also slow growth and push the economy past the brink of recession, as happened in 2018. At that point, inflation won't be the problem. A market crash will.

Storm Warnings

The shortest path to deflation and the decline of inflationary expectations is a market collapse. That appears to be exactly what's coming in the not-distant future. The precise timing is uncertain; that's the nature of emergent properties in complex dynamic systems. Still, the probability of a crash is quite high based on scaling metrics of the overall system and density functions within the system itself. Policymakers and Wall Street cheerleaders have an understandable aversion to any discussion of crashes. This creates the prospect of an adverse outcome overlooked by everyday investors and institutional asset allocators. Of course, the portfolio implications are enormous. There are ways to make fortunes in crashes; first you have to see them coming. Our immediate purpose is to explain why the crash is coming. From there, the impetus toward deflation is self-evident.

Seasoned investor Jeremy Grantham and his research associates have studied market bubbles using data for the past one hundred years.[4] They define a bubble as a market level that is a 2-sigma deviation from a trend; sigma refers to a standard deviation, a statistical measure. A 2-sigma event occurs about once in forty-four trials using a fair method such as a coin toss. A calendar year can be used as an arbitrary trial period. Markets at a 2-sigma deviation always return to the prebubble trend through the mechanism of a market crash. Because markets are driven by human behavior, which is more irrational than a coin toss, the actual frequency of crashes from 2-sigma deviations is about once every thirty-five years.

Grantham has identified certain deviations he calls superbubbles. These are 3-sigma events, which occur stochastically about once every hundred years, although in marketplaces driven by human behavior the actual frequency is greater, about once every forty years. This increased frequency is also due to the fact that multiple superbubbles can exist in different markets at the same time. Using this methodology, the Grantham team identified the five greatest superbubbles in the past one hundred years: U.S. stocks in 1929 and 2000; U.S. real estate in 2006; Japanese real estate in 1989; and Japanese stocks in 1989. All five of these superbubbles collapsed in spectacular fashion and the price level returned to the prebubble trend. Due to spillover effects and financial contagion, a collapse of one superbubble typically leads to comparable crashes in other markets. For example, the U.S. stock market crash in 1929 led to a collapse in commercial real estate. The U.S. mortgage collapse in 2006 led to a global financial crisis involving stocks, banks, and derivatives. Nowhere was this more true than in the dual real estate and equity collapse in Japan in 1989. Neither market has returned to its 1989 peak in the thirty-three years since.

Grantham posits that the United States and the world are in the midst of four simultaneous superbubbles constituting the most dangerous financial condition ever recorded. These four superbubbles are found in real estate, stocks, bonds, and commodities. Housing prices in the United States today are the highest multiple of family income ever recorded. This level is greater than the multiple that existed just prior to the 2006 real estate collapse. The ratio of market value to family income is even higher in Australia, China, and the UK, making a global collapse a clear possibility. Stock prices are at all-time highs or near highs using multiple metrics, including PE ratios, the ratio of total stock market capitalization to GDP (the Buffett Indicator), and the Shiller CAPE ratio. The stock-to-GDP ratio (using the Wilshire 5000) in February 2022 was 189.8 percent. This compares to a ratio of 105.3 percent prior to the 2008 global financial crisis, and 140.7 percent prior to the 2000 dot.com crash. The Shiller CAPE ratio in February 2022 was 36.17 compared to a 150-year mean ratio of 16.92 and median ratio of 15.87. That ratio is higher than the 1929 peak of 30, and second only to the 2000 dot.com peak of 44.2. The bond market bubble is simply the result of low or zero interest rates. If rates rise for either good reasons (sustained growth) or bad reasons (inflation), bond prices will fall. That's the inescapable math of bond markets. Finally, crashing commodities prices are simply the flip side of the rising commodities prices we see today in food, energy, and metals. Those price increases may persist in the short run, but eventually will raise costs, slow growth, decrease profits, or, in the case of consumers, discretionary income, and cause their own reversal, as happened in the mid-1980s and again after the 2008 global financial crisis.

Grantham is far from the only analyst pointing to these risks. Louis-Vincent Gave of Gavekal Research has devised a unique metric that considers stock valuations in relation to energy prices.[5] The metric is based on the view that economic activity is energy transformed and money is stored energy. This makes sense. To earn money, you expend some form of energy in work, which can be physical, intellectual, or entrepreneurial. Your money stores that energy, which can be released when you spend it for goods or services or invest it in the efforts of others. Energy itself can be measured in the price of oil. Economic efficiency from energy inputs can be measured in stock prices. Therefore, a long-term ratio of stock prices to oil prices produces a baseline for ascertaining whether current stock prices are high or low relative to that trend. Gave's methodology yields an S&P 500/Oil ratio of 487 over 120 years, compared to a current value of 1,080. Gave observes, "Structural bear markets in the US have all started when the S&P 500 was significantly overvalued versus energy (1912, 1929, 1968, and 2000). . . . If energy prices start to rise faster than the system can add value (i.e., faster than the rise in the S&P), the system must raise prices to cover energy costs. In this case, inflation creeps in, demand falls, and a bear market unfolds."[6] This observation fits well with a scenario of the current rise in energy costs followed by a stock market fall and disinflation. It is also consistent with Grantham's view that commodities are as much in a bubble as stocks.

Gave's metrics suggest a stock market fall of about 50 percent in order to return to trend relative to oil. Grantham's metrics suggest a market fall of 47 percent based on February 2022 valuations; that fall will be greater if the bubble expands from there. Other prominent investors and analysts including Stanley Druckenmiller, David Rosenberg, and Jeffrey Gundlach have offered similar dire forecasts of a severe stock market decline. In the face of data demonstrating bubble valuations, and historic market dynamics, Grantham concludes, "If valuations across all of these asset classes return even two-thirds of the way back to historical norms, total wealth losses will be on the order of $35 trillion in the U.S. alone."[7] There are momentous consequences from a crash of this magnitude. We consider some of these consequences in the rest of this book. For now, it's enough to say that inflation will disappear in the face of a market collapse.

Real Money, Real Debt

In addition to labor market slack, productivity-enhancing investment, Fed policy blunders, and superbubbles in multiple markets, there are three other dynamics that lean strongly in the direction of disinflation or deflation, not inflation. These involve market signals, debt levels, and the real role of inflation expectations. We'll examine these in order.

Researcher Jeffrey Snider and his collaborator, Emil Kalinowski, have advanced a thesis that is powerfully supported by hard data yet woefully underappreciated by market participants and policymakers. The difficulty is that their thesis looks under the hood at some of the least understood corners of markets in derivatives and financing tools such as repurchase agreements (repos). While the world is focused on stocks and real estate, Snider and Kalinowski put the bond market under a microscope in the search for predictive analytic clues.[8] They find them galore and sound a warning, yet the subject seems too esoteric for mainstream investment managers and everyday investors. That's their loss. The expert pair have this right.

The starting place is that base money created by the Fed, M0, is almost irrelevant because it is deposited in bank dealer accounts. Those banks then redeposit it with the Fed as excess reserves. That money never enters the real economy and has no impact on inflation, velocity, or the production of goods and services. Money created by U.S. commercial banks or deposited in money market funds, M1 and M2, is more powerful, yet has little impact in global markets due to declining velocity. The real engine of global finance, trade, and investment is a kind of shadow money created by banks outside the purview of central banks and scarcely regulated or even understood by regulators—Eurodollars. These are loans and deposits made by banks to each other and to large corporations, denominated in U.S. dollars but created in London, Frankfurt, Tokyo, and offshore banking centers around the world not subject to direct banking regulation or reporting. Eurodollar deposits can be used to buy high-quality securities, which are then pledged to other banks for more cash used to buy more securities, which are also pledged, and so on until a vast pyramid of unregulated dollars, pledged securities, and extreme leverage exists for the purpose of generating bank fees, banking spreads, trading profits, and greasing the wheels of international trade and direct foreign investment.

As if that pyramid of unregulated dollars and pledged securities were not enough, another even larger pyramid is placed on top of the Eurodollar pile in the form of derivatives, basically side bets on the underlying positions on the bank's books. These derivative side bets are not only unregulated, they are invisible. They exist in opaque financial statement footnotes as aggregate notional values, but do not appear on the financial statements themselves and are not disclosed with more that cursory details. There is no limit on the notional value of derivatives that may be created in relation to a given value in an underlying position. A $1 billion derivative position can be layered on top of a $1 million securities position, bearing in mind the $1 million securities position might be supported by as little as $5,000 in cash, a 0.5 percent so-called haircut, with the remaining $995,000 consisting of pledged securities in the form of repos. If the idea of $1 billion in invisible derivatives supported by only $5,000 in cash equity sounds scary, then you're starting to see what Snider sees every day.

The key to this impossibly leveraged Eurodollar world is collateral. If you're supporting a $1 million position with $5,000 in cash and $995,000 in collateral, then that collateral better be the safest, most liquid security in the world. A minute market move against the leveraged trader will wipe out the cash portion in an instant. The trader will receive a margin call for more collateral that must be met by the end of the trading day, sometimes intraday, depending on market conditions. If the trader defaults on the margin call, the counterparty will terminate the trade and sell the securities collateral to compensate itself for the original loan. Likewise, the much larger derivatives trade has its own variation margin requirements that must be satisfied by the trader with high-quality collateral if the position loses money. From the lender's perspective, it's bad enough if the counterparty is losing money on the trade (hence the collateral call) but matters get worse if the collateral itself loses value, compounding the trading loss and credit default. Given these parameters, there is one and only one type of collateral that satisfies the lender's requirements for liquidity, creditworthiness, and low volatility—short-term U.S. Treasury bills.

From these starting conditions, Snider and Kalinowski postulate the following:

- Short-term U.S. Treasury bills are the preferred safe collateral for the massive pyramid of Eurodollars and leveraged lending and derivatives.
- If short-term U.S. Treasury bills are in short supply, this forces bank dealers to use less desirable forms of collateral. In turn, the riskier collateral forces banks to reduce leverage and shrink balance sheets.
- In extreme cases, the collateral shortage and balance sheet shrinkage can lead to a full-blown liquidity crisis and a general dollar shortage as banks scramble for both dollars and Treasury bills to prop up their lending.
- At the crisis stage, the Federal Reserve will activate dollar swap lines with selected foreign central banks to provide dollars to those central banks so they can bail out their own banks, which can no longer access dollars in interbank markets.

Two corollaries to this sequence of events are that trade and finance contract in ways that kill nascent inflation, and the central banks are always the last to see a dollar crisis coming. This crisis sequence played out like clockwork in 2008 and 2020. The question for investors is, Will it happen again?

Research offers concrete empirical signs that can warn investors if a global dollar shortage and associated Treasury bill shortage are emerging. It is a kind of early warning of another global financial collapse. The first sign is a flattening of the U.S. Treasury yield curve. This is not necessarily a matter of nominal rates declining. It's a matter of short-term and long-term rates converging to the same level. This implies that markets do not see robust growth or inflation ahead; they see the opposite. The extreme form of this is an inverted yield curve, where long-term rates are lower than short-term rates. That's a bright flashing red light almost always associated with a recession or worse.

A closely related warning is the pricing of Eurodollar futures contracts (available from the CME Group, home to the largest exchange-traded derivatives market in the world). These contracts are settled in one- and three-month increments, and are traded in strips out to ten years in advance. Their prices tell you what traders believe short-term Eurodollar rates will be two, three, or more years from today. Prices are discounted against a settlement price set at par value, which means that lower prices indicate higher yields. A normally shaped yield curve would have successively lower prices for each settlement month, since forward rates are higher than rates in the immediate future. Again, any yield curve inversion where rates are lower than some earlier period is a warning sign that markets expect an economic slowdown or worse. A final market signal is the situation in which banks are bidding on new issues of Treasury bills at yields lower than those freely available from the Fed. The Fed will take cash from dealers and pledge securities under reverse repurchase agreements. The Fed pays an interest rate on that cash. Why would a dealer bid for Treasury bills at yields lower than what the Fed offers? The answer is that the banks are desperate to get the bills so they can put them to use as collateral to support leveraged balance sheets.

The Treasury yield curve, the Eurodollar futures curve, and Treasury bill rates are like a thermometer, stethoscope, and EKG applied to a patient. They tell you whether the patient is well or ill. What are markets telling us about the health of the financial system? As of July 22, 2022, the Treasury yield curve is inverted beyond the 1-year maturity. The spread between the yield to maturity on a 1-year Treasury bill (3.029 percent) and a 10-year Treasury note (2.758 percent) is just over 27 basis points (27/100 of 1 percent). This situation where longer-term rates are lower than short-term rates is highly unusual. It is a clear warning sign of recession and disinflation.

The Eurodollar futures prices tell an even more intriguing story. Prices typically go down as you start to move out the curve. That means markets are betting rates will go up; that's to be expected. As of late July 2022, this pattern persists through the first seven contracts through

February 2023. Suddenly prices go higher (rates go lower) in March 2023, and this pattern of lower forward rates persists through eight contracts until June 2025. This is an inverted yield curve. It doesn't happen in normal markets. It signals a slowdown in the economy and a possible recession in early 2023. To be clear, these prices change daily; they will certainly have changed by the time you read this and will change again tomorrow. This distress flare may fade. The fact that the flare was fired at all is serious cause for concern. Recent Treasury bill auctions are also producing yields to maturity that are lower than rates readily available from the Fed. In short, all three indicators—yield-curve spreads, Eurodollar futures, and Treasury bill yields—are flashing red when it comes to the prospects for slow growth, possible recession, and a growing global liquidity crisis. These conditions are consistent with deflation and disinflation, not inflation.

Snider and Kalinowski make two other telling points. The first is that their data comes from actual markets, not from academic models or mere opinion. The information used is from real traders betting real money. The information is updated continually. That doesn't mean the traders are always right. It does mean that updating an a priori expectation of disinflation and recession using Bayesian techniques makes the market forecast more likely to be right than any other. Their second observation is that this forecast varies materially from the Fed's expectation of rate hikes over the next several years. In fact, the Fed's policy is likely the reason markets expect a slowdown or worse. Market participants see the Fed tightening into weakness and infer a slowdown or recession will result. This is consistent with our view that the Fed is almost always wrong and always the last to know.

The next deflationary dynamic comes from the massive level of federal debt. Again, the facts are apparent, and the research supports the view that the United States is headed for a slow-growth, even recessionary, outcome. The U.S. national debt recently passed the $30 trillion mark. More importantly, that amount puts the national debt at 130 percent of U.S. GDP. A growing body of research shows convincingly that national debt levels in excess of 90 percent of GDP shave about 1.2 percentage points off what would otherwise be GDP growth. In advanced economies, average annual GDP growth is about 3.5 percent where debt levels are below 90 percent. Above 90 percent, those growth levels decline to about 2.3 percent. If a 1.2 percentage point decline sounds trivial, it's not. That level of lost growth extrapolated over a twenty-year period of high debt means GDP will be one fourth less than would otherwise be the case. Using today's GDP figures, that level of decline equals $6 trillion in lost wealth. For a real-world example that illustrates this theory, one need look no further than the last U.S. GDP report prior to the pandemic. (The pandemic created an extraordinary decline and recovery that have temporarily skewed GDP averages; a prepandemic report provides a more meaningful baseline.) Average annual GDP growth for all recoveries after 1980 was 3.22 percent. Average annual growth for the long recovery from 2009 to 2019 was 2.1 percent. That decline of 1.1 percentage points from the long-term average to the more recent recovery is almost exactly in line with the projected weak growth and lost wealth based on high-debt models.

The leading scholars in this field are Carmen M. Reinhart and Kenneth S. Rogoff, in collaboration with Vincent R. Reinhart. A paper they coauthored in 2021 focuses on the impact of high debt overhangs on growth since 1800.[9] This study identifies twenty-six episodes of high public debt in advanced economies. High public debt is defined as debt in excess of 90 percent of GDP, and each episode is defined as lasting five years or more to exclude exceptional or anomalous situations. The authors conclude, "We find that the vast majority of high debt episodes—23 of the 26—coincide with substantially slower growth." Importantly, the authors conclude that high-debt/low-growth episodes are not necessarily associated with high interest rates: "We find that countries with a public debt overhang by no means always experience either a sharp rise in real interest rates or difficulties in gaining access to capital markets. Indeed, in 11 of the 26 cases where public debt was above the 90 percent debt/GDP threshold, real interest rates were either lower, or about the same as during the lower debt/GDP years." This finding is entirely consistent with the experience of the United States in the 2009–19 recovery, when debt rose, growth lagged, yet interest rates were at or near zero and the U.S. Treasury had no difficulty funding the debt.

The idea that high debt financed by central bank monetization must inevitably result in hyperinflation is simply untrue. That can happen, but the more likely outcome is a slow descent into a kind of debtor's prison where debt levels rise to 200 percent of GDP or higher and growth gradually slows to zero. To understand this outcome, don't think of Weimar Germany, think instead of Japan since 1989.

There is a practical distinction between those countries that finance in their own currencies and those that finance in foreign currencies, usually the U.S. dollar. Those that finance in dollars but don't print them can devalue their currencies or just default outright and renegotiate the debt. Argentina does not count as an advanced economy in the Reinhart and Rogoff study, but it is a good example of what serial default and debt-induced hyperinflation look like. Countries that issue debt in currencies they print have no need for technical default. They can just print the money and pay the debt. This gives those countries, including the United States, an option to pursue slow, steady inflation that whittles away the real value of the debt without causing panic or changing the behavior of everyday consumers. This policy goes by the name fiscal dominance, meaning that fiscal policy (the debt) dominates monetary policy (the money printing). The United States did this successfully from 1946 to 1980, although inflation did spin out of control after 1976. One key to the success of fiscal dominance is money illusion—the phenomenon that citizens do not recognize low-level inflation even though it steals purchasing power by the day. The danger in a policy of fiscal dominance is that some exogenous event bursts the bubble of money illusion, and behavior shifts suddenly to demand-pull inflation as consumers spend more to beat price increases and workers demand raises to preserve purchasing power. This is what happened in the United States in the late 1970s after the supply shocks of higher oil prices. The money illusion was gone once prices at the pump tripled. That could happen again if modern monetary theory, which supports unlimited deficits and unlimited money printing, lasts much longer.

While long-term inflation cannot be ruled out, short-term disinflation or deflation is far more likely given the dynamics of the debt trap. As described by Reinhart and Rogoff, "This debt-without-drama scenario is reminiscent for us of T. S. Eliot's (1925) lines in 'The Hollow Men': 'This is the way the world ends / Not with a bang but a whimper.'" The high debt case exists in the United States today. The evidence that this will produce slow growth and disinflation is compelling. There will be no inflation in sight for some years to come.

Finally, the proponent of disinflation or deflation must dispose of the argument that inflationary expectations can take on a life of their own and lead to inflationary outcomes through adaptive behavior. It is apparent that consumers will respond to inflation when it's happening in real time. Still, what is the evidence that consumers will change behavior today based on expectations about inflation in the future? It turns out that the empirical evidence to support that proposition is scarce to nonexistent. Federal Reserve Board economist Jeremy B. Rudd has explored this topic in depth in a recent research paper.[10] His summary states, "Many economists view expectations as central to the inflation process; similarly, many central banks consider 'anchoring' or 'managing' the public's inflation expectations to be an important policy goal or instrument. Here I argue that using inflation expectations to explain observed inflation dynamics is unnecessary and unsound: unnecessary because an alternative explanation exists that is equally if not more plausible, and unsound because invoking an expectations channel has no compelling theoretical or empirical basis and could potentially result in serious policy errors."

Rudd readily concedes that if inflation is raging, employees will seek higher wages (either by confronting the boss or by quitting their jobs in search of higher pay), and businesses will raise prices. But that behavior is based on actual inflation, not on expectations. Even if consumers expected inflation next year (something most people probably don't think about at all), it has little or no impact on behavior today. Of course, if today's inflation persists (as outlined in chapter 4), it is possible that the expectation becomes the reality, and behavior begins to change. Still, it can take years (as we saw in 1968–75) before adaptive behavior turns inflation into a self-fulfilling prophecy. The best evidence is that inflationary expectations play no role in causing inflation. If persistent inflation emerges, behavior can change then but not sooner. For now, we have a burst of inflation that will soon be muted by the combined influence of economic slack, new investment, higher productivity, and slower growth under the weight of high debt. Misguided Fed tightening will end inflation before it becomes self-fulfilling. Expectations will not play a role for the foreseeable future. Inflation may prevail in the endgame, yet that is likely years away. For now, disinflation and deflation are dominant and will remain so until confidence in the dollar is lost.

Conclusion

When ideology in places like Castroite Cuba, the old Soviet Union, and Venezuela warped the application of the law, destroyed the role of merit in assessing qualifications, silenced speech, and unequally applied the law, then society unwound. In such ideological dystopias, eventually even the shelves empty, the currency becomes worthless, and the nation regresses into poverty and chaos. Is that the future we await?

—VICTOR DAVIS HANSON
"Why Ideology Is the Ancient Enemy of Civilization" (2022)[1]

A supply chain is a complex system with sources, intermediaries, end users, and multiple way points including warehouses, ports, and factory floors. The connective tissues are the transportation lanes traversed by ships, trucks, planes, and drones. As with any complex system, it can break down when bottlenecks emerge or choke points are clogged. It can also collapse completely as the result of cascades from a single point of failure rippling through the entire system. Such events are not rare, despite expectations to the contrary. Resilience in a supply chain system comes from identifying a breakdown quickly and taking effective remedial measures. Responses of that type are often gamed out in advance, prepared for, and well rehearsed.

The difficulty facing supply chain management today is an order of magnitude greater than the breaking of one link in one chain. There exists what we call a meta supply chain, really a supply chain of supply chains that is global, invisible, and of immeasurable scale. The term "global" may seem obvious after thirty years of hyperglobalization, but it means more than just a lane from Shanghai to Seattle with factories at one end and distribution centers at the other. It means that one supply chain links to another for its supplies, which links to others in a seamless web that touches every country in the world. It's invisible because it's too sweeping and too dense to see whole. One can theorize on it and comprehend the dynamics. Still, no one can apprehend it. And scale is critical. Risk of catastrophic collapse is a superlinear function of scale. When you double the scale, you may increase the risk of collapse by a factor of four. When you increase the scale one million times, the risk of catastrophe is one trillion times greater—in other words, incomprehensible and close to certain. It's just a matter of time.

That's the condition the world faces now. The meta supply chain is collapsing. Data points such as port backlogs, trucker shortages, and bare shelves are symptoms, not the main event.

The tempo of collapse is also a function of scale. An avalanche is an example of systemic collapse. One snowflake triggers a slide that gathers momentum and dislodges an entire snowpack that buries a village below. That can happen in seconds or minutes. Not all systemic collapses proceed that quickly. The collapse of an empire can take decades, as in the case of the British Empire, or even centuries, as happened with the Roman Empire. It should come as no surprise that the collapse of the meta supply chain will take years. What matters most is that the process has begun.

It is possible to pinpoint specific causes, but these are more like catalysts in a volatile mixture rather than simple cause-and-effect elements. The real cause is the scale and complexity of the meta supply chain itself rather than a particular act. Still, something will inevitably set the process in motion. The breakdown began in 2018 with Trump's trade war with China. It was amplified by the pandemic, which closed ports, distribution centers, and transportation lanes. The Bullwhip Effect ran backward from shuttered retail outlets to Chinese factories. Next came the politicized public health response, which included useless masks, pointless lockdowns, and impotent vaccines. Data showed that mandates of these policies did not stop the spread of infection or affect the fatality rates compared to jurisdictions that did nothing so extreme. Still, the public health policies were powerful when it came to destroying the economy. As if a trade war, pandemic, and official fearmongering were not enough, the inevitable civil disobedience in reaction to oppressive public policy emerged around the world in the form of demonstrations, strikes, and most pointedly in the Canadian Freedom Convoys and similar efforts that shut down capital cities from Ottawa to Amsterdam. Critically, the Canadian trucker revolt temporarily closed the Ambassador Bridge, which carries 30 percent of the trade in goods between the United States and Canada, the largest and ninth-largest economies in the world. No one of these might have been enough to break the meta supply chain. In combination, collapse was inevitable.

The problem is now so severe that the practiced remedies won't work. Gradually easing container cargo jams at the Port of Los Angeles won't get goods delivered if the trucker shortage persists. Truckers won't return to ports when they're forming Freedom Convoys. Truckers not in convoys are impeded by those who are. Driverless trucks dissuade young workers from joining the ranks. China's Zero COVID strategy shuts down manufacturing and transportation centers on an unpredictable basis. Russian attacks in Ukraine drive energy prices higher and tighten supplies. Green policies in the United States and Germany shut down coal plants and oil pipelines at a time when wind turbines and solar cannot scale and fill the gap. Blackouts and higher prices are not far behind. Again, these are more symptoms than primary causes. The cause of the supply chain collapse is the scale and complexity of the chain itself.

The remedy is not a patchwork of fixes. The remedy is a reinvented supply chain, or what we call Supply Chain 2.0. This involves bringing commodity inputs and manufacturing back to the United States and allied countries, including Australia, Japan, Taiwan, EU nations, and the UK. New allies can be added to the network guided by democracy and the rule of law, including India, Chile, and Brazil. Aspirants that may still be autocratic or corrupt, such as Turkey, Vietnam, and Nigeria, may be considered for inclusion if they agree to concrete steps in the direction of personal freedom and human rights. Above all, those who abuse human rights, commit genocide, or suppress free speech and freedom of religion must be excluded from global trade networks. The excluded group begins with the obvious cases of China, North Korea, Syria, Cuba, Venezuela, and Iran. Of course, these lists leave a large number of in-between cases from Russia to Argentina. They'll have to decide which team they're on. The United States can help by at least leaving the door open and responding pragmatically, not politically, to overtures. The result will be a new College of Nations dedicated to democracy, human rights, and commerce under a rule of law.

There is more to this reinvention than just compiling membership lists. Supply Chain 2.0 requires concrete steps, including new manufacturing capacity in the collegial states, new trade treaties for liberalizing nations only, infrastructure to facilitate transportation lanes among members, support for direct foreign investment, and respect for intellectual property rights with fair provision for ease of licensing and reasonable royalty arrangements. Major corporations will be told they must onshore production in college members or face bans on sales to their consumers. If Apple wants to manufacture in China and sell to the Chinese that's fine, but they'll be banned from the U.S. market and the markets of college members. This is not as disruptive as it sounds. There are myriad manufacturing competitors waiting in the wings that will thrive using Apple technology that the United States can take under the Fifth Amendment for a modest royalty and donate to the upstarts. The idea is to create the global trading system that liberal states hoped to create when they naively admitted China to the World Trade Organization. China has broken every rule at the WTO and the IMF, and subverted governance at every other multilateral organization it has been allowed to join. The time has come to leave the WTO and IMF behind and create new institutions for the College of Nations. Let China trade with Iran. Let Larry Fink and his ilk party with Chairman Xi in Davos. The turn of the wheel has come; they will be left behind.

This approach is already gaining traction among global elites. In an address to the Atlantic Council on April 13, 2022, U.S. Treasury Secretary Janet Yellen referred to the idea as "friend-shoring" supply chains to include only trusted partners. On May 9, 2022, in a speech to the European Parliament, French President Emmanuel Macron proposed a "European confederation" of democratic nations that would be broader and more flexible than the EU in areas such as investments, infrastructure, and energy. Noted journalist Ambrose Evans-Pritchard referred to Macron's idea as a "constellation of democratic and liberal states" wishing mutually to trade and invest.[2] What these ideas have in common is facilitation of new supply chains while excluding totalitarian states such as China.

While the College of Nations approach is feasible, it will have costs. Labor costs may be higher, although the difference between Chinese and other nations' unit labor costs has already closed considerably. These costs, if they exist, can be mitigated with robotics and AI, while leaving ample room for high-paying jobs in repatriated industries. A fair accounting requires that these visible costs be offset by the invisible costs incurred in today's hyperglobalized world. What is the cost of genocide in China? What is the cost of de facto slavery in the Congo? What is the cost of cartel rule in Mexico? These are some of the many costs of hyperglobalization and indiscriminate supply chain sourcing. A liberal world trade structure by the College of Nations will in time mitigate the visible costs and deny the perpetrators of these hidden costs the resources needed to continue their moral and ethical abominations. Supply Chain 2.0 will be less efficient by some visible measures in the short run, yet more efficient and sustainable when visible and invisible metrics are considered. Only amoral Davos types could object.

The Five Eyes report discussed in chapter 3 is a good blueprint but is only a start for the collegial states. The main idea is to divide the world into a liberal block and the rest. Some states can be collegial adjuncts or admitted on a probationary basis. The collegial system will thrive on open capital accounts, direct foreign investment, relatively free trade, and newly designed supply chains that are efficient and resilient. Those who reject freedom and human rights will be left to themselves. They will fail as such states have always failed.

Neither a reconstituted supply chain nor a College of Nations approach to world trade will succeed without sound money. This does not require a gold standard, although a gold standard could be a good start. The objections to gold are a mix of canards, myths, and noble lies told by monetarists, neo-Keynesians, and central bankers wishing to retain their monetary powers.[3] Ironically, gold enthusiasts should oppose a gold standard since it means the end of dollar profits once the price is fixed. Those who own gold will do best in a world of no gold standard and high inflation, where gold will outperform most asset classes in real and nominal terms.

Inflation is the greatest enemy of sound money. It destroys capital formation, dissuades saving, amplifies capital misallocation, creates asset bubbles that soon burst, and acts as a tax on the poor. Inflation emerged in late 2021 as the result of lingering base effects, supply shocks in energy, supply chain disruption, and profligate federal spending. Whether inflation persists or accelerates has little to do with monetary policy and everything to do with consumer psychology. The danger is that inflation now, as opposed to inflationary expectations, causes behavioral changes, including higher wage demands, job quits in search of higher pay, accelerated purchases of big-ticket durable goods, and increasing leverage. In that world, a feedback loop is created where demand-pull inflation feeds on itself and drives consumer prices higher, faster than central bankers anticipate. Another threat is modern monetary theory, which endorses unlimited spending financed by unlimited monetization by the Fed. Money printing alone does not cause inflation, but if it facilitates prodigal spending it may. That sets the stage for runaway inflation or a policy response that will precipitate a market crash and recession or both. All three inflation scenarios—persistence, acceleration, and crash—are antithetical to the price stability and policy consistency needed to improve supply chains. Apart from broader societal costs, inflation is as much an impediment to supply chain efficiency as the logistical factors described above. The best case is that inflation fades without a monetary policy blunder on the way. That's a slim reed to lean on.

Deflation is another foe of supply chain improvement, albeit one not seen in decades. Despite current inflation, deflation or disinflation will gain the upper hand if inflation does not quickly become self-fulfilling. Forces pushing in this direction include central bank tightening led by the Federal Reserve, slack in labor markets, excessive government debt, persistent declines in money velocity, and the global dollar shortage in Eurodollar markets. Again, if the value of money is unstable, long-term planning is impaired. Credit creation, the real driver of growth, is stunted because the value of debt rises in deflation even as the value of assets declines. Asset allocators prefer to do nothing in a world where cash and government debt become relatively more valuable, even as the values of stocks and real estate melt. Supply chain infrastructure improvements in a deflationary world require government intervention on a par with wartime efforts. That's possible but suboptimal.

This need for monetary stability comes at a time when the idea of money itself is mercurial. The global electronic environment growing since the 1840s has reached a point where developed societies have transformed to a postliterate, nonlinear, acoustic sphere, called the global village by Marshall McLuhan. Those inside the sphere (all of us) are scarcely aware of the preceptual shift despite acquaintance with the gimmicks such as smartphones and Twitter. This has implications far beyond the scope of this book, but as related to money, the idea of money is under siege. The precept of money as gold, then paper notes backed by gold, then paper notes alone, and recently digital credits continues to shape-shift to cryptocurrencies and central bank digital currencies to a point where virtual money can buy virtual land in a virtual world. That's consonant with the notion of an acoustic village, yet inconsistent with 2,500 years of rational thought. Policymakers are concerned about consumer expectations becoming unmoored from price stability and drifting toward inflation. They have scarcely considered ideas of money becoming unmoored from money itself and drifting toward moneyness or quasi money.

This preceptual change may take several paths. The first is toward a benign digital disarray in which government money, private money, and free-floating tokens of moneyness exist in a virtual state space of pulsating values and quantities bumping into each other like ghosts in a large, haunted house. That may work as a medium of exchange. Still, the prospects for saving and investment are problematic at best. Supply chain efficiency may be irrelevant in a world without monetary efficiency or even money as we understand it. Another path is one in which central bank digital currencies are combined with government repression of alternate digital modes, and the rise of total surveillance to promote elite agendas under the banner of the Davos Great Reset. Cutting off money to dissenters will be like cutting off oxygen to patients in intensive care. The result is predictable, at least in the view of the elites. The fact that this will fail does not mean it won't be tried.

With supply chains in disarray and getting worse, inflation here, recession and deflation looming, and a full-scale economic war under way, investors are understandably bewildered. A portfolio that protects against inflation is straightforward to construct. So is a portfolio that protects against deflation. It seems easy to build a portfolio that's robust to inflation with the view that one can easily tilt to a deflationary posture if the time comes. It's not that easy. A deflationary wave may emerge almost overnight if a market crash and recession hit unexpectedly (they're always unexpected). Losses from being on the wrong side of the trade are not easily recouped, even if the transition is made. Worse yet, some positions are not easy to exit. That may be due to lockup periods, gates, exit fees, illiquidity, and other toll booths on the way from one asset allocation to another. Reallocation costs and market losses may wipe out gains from being right in the first place. The attractions of the deflation trade may be gone before you arrive. At best, the costs of reallocation dilute the gains of the original stand.

A better approach is a diversified portfolio robust to uncertainty. This means your initial portfolio will include inflation protection and deflation protection (and cash) at the same time. A portfolio of this sort would include leveraged residential real estate, gold, energy equities, farmland, and museum-quality fine art as inflation protection. It would also include U.S. Treasury notes, utilities, municipal bonds, annuities, and life insurance as deflation defenses. A significant allocation to cash will reduce portfolio volatility and offer optionality to pivot from inflation to deflation protection as needed.

A portfolio set along these lines is not set in stone. There is ample opportunity to unwind inflation hedges, especially leveraged real estate, as deflation emerges. You can add to a Treasury note position as inflation fades. There's ample room to reallocate around the edges. The point is, you don't have to do it on a crash basis. You're already in the deflation trade in some measure. You can afford to wait out inflation trade exit fees. It's a question of balance.

Ordinary asset managers will object to this optimization. They'll claim you're "losing money" on portions of the portfolio when prevailing conditions favor other portions. That critique betrays a failure to understand diversification. Diversification does not mean owning thirty stocks in ten sectors in a bull market. That's not diversification, it's concentration in a single asset class that can be crushed by conditional correlation in a matter of days. True diversification involves a cradle of uncorrelated assets.

Deflation-protection assets will supposedly underperform in an inflationary environment. In fact, the so-called underperformance is an insurance premium you pay for protection in all states of the world. No one wants his home to burn down, but it if happens, you consider the fire insurance premium money well spent.

In truth, the greatest challenge to investors is not asset allocation, it's the demise of sound money. A sound money system is not imposed; it is earned through the trust of system members. Digital money may be a new preceptual mode, but that does not change human nature. Trust is a nice blend of right-hemisphere emotion and left-hemisphere calculation. It exists (or not) in villages and central bank boardrooms. The solution to both supply chain breakdown and monetary disarray is a new College of Nations—like-minded states committed to human rights and republican governance with democratic norms. When efficiency and resilience are pursued with proper accounting for the invisible costs of diminished returns to labor and lost liberty, the latter are eschewed. China and others will be on the outside looking in until they abandon totalistic ideologies. In a decoupled world, the side that values human rights and nurtures trust will rediscover that money takes care of itself.

ACKNOWLEDGMENTS

I am deeply grateful for the encouragement and support of the great team at my publisher Portfolio/Penguin Random House, including Adrian Zackheim, Niki Papadopoulos, Kimberly Meilun, and Jane Cavolina. They are consummate professionals who make the process of writing and publishing a book both harmonious and rewarding. Alongside the publisher team comes my personal team of business manager Ali Rickards and editor Will Rickards. They hold my feet to the fire, and given my proclivity to procrastination, that's a good thing. Rounding out this team of pros is my star literary agent Melissa Flashman. She is the catalyst; nothing happens without her.

Special thanks are owed to Sam Palmisano, chairman of the Center for Global Enterprise and former CEO of IBM. Sam practically invented the twenty-first-century supply chain during his time at IBM and turned IBM itself into a seamless global enterprise held out in academia as the gold standard for globalization and supply chain efficiency. Sam offered priceless insights into how the modern supply chain was built, and why it will take some time to rebuild.

I'm blessed with a dense web of correspondents, colleagues, and friends who provide a stream of sources and insights easily missed in the cascade of information that washes over all of us. This group includes Art Santelli, Frank Giustra, Dave "Davos" Nolan, TraderStef, Velina

Tchakarova, Shae Russell, Larry White, Hans-Joachim Dübel, Dan Amoss, Frank Devechio, Julia Kane, and Terry Rickard. Thank you.

This book could not have been written without the love and support of my large and growing family that now reaches through four generations. That list keeps getting longer yet no less important. Thank you, Scott, Dom, Rob, Ali, Will, Abby, and not least the next generation of Thomas, Sam, James, Pippa, and Remi. When I begin writing I inform everyone that I will be the most asocial person they know until the writing is complete, but I promise to make up for lost time when I'm done. That said, my wife, Ann, does not have the luxury of avoiding me. She's an unfailing source of love, inspiration, and just the right kind of critique. She was the driver, guide, and fun companion on our long road trips to the Andy Warhol Museum in Pittsburgh and the Marcel Duchamp galleries in the Philadelphia Museum of Art during the height of pandemic panic. There was no better way to escape the medical madness and to stay focused than a visit with the artists. The insights gained made this a better book. Thanks. I love you.

And any mistakes in this book are my fault alone.

NOTES

Introduction

1. Reuben E. Slone, J. Paul Dittmann, and John J. Mentzer, *The New Supply Chain Agenda: The 5 Steps That Drive Real Value* (Boston: Harvard Business Press, 2010).

2. John Maynard Keynes, *The Economic Consequences of the Peace* (Las Vegas, NV: IAP Press, 2019), 9.

Chapter One: The Shelves Are Bare

1. Yossi Sheffi, *The Resilient Enterprise: Overcoming Vulnerability for Competitive Advantage* (Cambridge, MA: MIT Press, 2005), 35.

2. Sheffi, *The Resilient Enterprise*, 35.

3. Michael Hugos, *Essentials of Supply Chain Management*, 4th ed. (Hoboken, NJ: John Wiley & Sons, 2018), 21–22.

4. Reuben E. Slone, J. Paul Dittmann, and John J. Mentzer, *The New Supply Chain Agenda: The 5 Steps That Drive Real Value* (Boston: Harvard Business Press, 2010), 172.

5. Lionel Shriver, *The Mandibles: A Family, 2029–2047* (New York: HarperCollins, 2016).

6. Kerry J. Byrne, Steven Vago, and Melissa Klein, "Candy Cane Shortage Fueled by COVID, Weak Peppermint Harvest," *New York Post*, December 18, 2021.

7. Hannah Frishberg, "Cream Cheese Shortage Forces Junior's to Pause Cheesecake Production," *New York Post*, December 9, 2021.

8. Jaewon Kang, "Supermarkets Play Supply-Chain 'Whack-a-Mole' to Keep Products on Shelves," *Wall Street Journal*, October 31, 2021.

9. Jared Malsin, "Turkey's Currency Crisis Slams the Nutella Global Supply Chain," *Wall Street Journal*, December 20, 2021.

10. Patrick Reilly, "Champagne Shortage Ahead of New Year's Eve Due to Supply Chain Issues: Report," *New York Post*, December 30, 2021.

11. Hillary Richard, "A Perfect Storm of Disruptions Will Create a Global Champagne Shortage," *Wine Enthusiast*, December 15, 2021.

12. Matt Stoller, "What the Great Ammunition Shortage Says About Inflation," BIG, Substack, January 5, 2022.

13. Tim Higgins, "Apple Warns of Supply Chain Woes While Amazon Faces Increased Labor Costs," *Wall Street Journal*, October 28, 2021.

14. Francesco Casarotto, "Europe's Fertilizer Crisis Could Become a Food Crisis," Geopolitical Futures, December 14, 2021.

15. "South Korea: CJ Logistics Delivery Workers' Strike to Impact Local Businesses," Stratfor Situation Report, December 28, 2021.

16. Helaine Olen, "American Airlines' Cancellations Are a Window into Why People Are So Upset with the Economy," *Washington Post*, November 2, 2021.

17. Daniel Henninger, "No, Joe Biden Didn't Save Christmas," *Wall Street Journal*, December 29, 2021.

18. Emma Loop, "Black Friday Deals Expected to Be Weaker This Year amid Supply Chain Problems," *Washington Examiner*, November 9, 2021.

19. Stephanie Yang and Jiyoung Sohn, "Global Chip Shortage 'Is Far from Over' as Wait Times Get Longer," *Wall Street Journal*, October 28, 2021.

20. Peter S. Goodman, "A Car a Minute Used to Flow Through Here, but Chaos Now Reigns," *New York Times*, December 2, 2021.

21. Cassie Buchman and Alex Caprariello, "Looters Raid L.A. Cargo Trains, Leaving Tracks Covered in Damaged Packages," KTLA5, Los Angeles, January 14, 2022.

22. Rich Calder, "Supermarkets Face Empty Shelves from Labor Shortages, Shipping Costs," *New York Post*, January 15, 2022.

Chapter Two: Who Broke the Supply Chain?

1. Michael Hugos, *Essentials of Supply Chain Management*, 4th ed. (Hoboken, NJ: John Wiley & Sons, 2018), 89.

2. Lori Ann LaRocco, *Trade War: Containers Don't Lie, Navigating the Bluster* (Stamford, CT: Marine Money, 2019). Much of the shipping

data in the 2018–2019 stage of the trade war in the following pages is derived from this book.

3. LaRocco, *Trade War*, 103.

4. James Rickards, *Currency Wars: The Making of the Next Global Crisis* (New York: Portfolio/Penguin, 2011), 203. The analysis also draws on lectures under the title "Understanding Complexity," delivered in 2009 by Professor Scott E. Page of the University of Michigan.

5. Edward N. Lorenz, "Deterministic Nonperiodic Flow," *Journal of the Atmospheric Sciences* 20 (March 1963).

6. Rickards, *Currency Wars*, 218, as adapted from Eric J. Chaisson, *Cosmic Evolution: The Rise of Complexity in Nature* (Cambridge, MA: Harvard University Press, 2001).

7. Joseph A. Tainter, *The Collapse of Complex Societies* (Cambridge: Cambridge University Press, 1988).

8. Daniel Stanton, *Supply Chain Management for Dummies*, 2nd ed. (Hoboken, NJ: John Wiley & Sons, 2021), 27.

9. See Letter from the Secretary of Transportation and the FAA Administrator to AT&T and Verizon, December 31, 2021; Todd Shields and Alan Levin, "Buttigieg Asks AT&T, Verizon to Delay 5G over Aviation Concerns," *Bloomberg*, December 31, 2021; Drew FitzGerald, "AT&T, Verizon Refuse FAA Request to Delay 5G Launch," *Wall Street Journal*, January 2, 2022; and Andrew Tangel and Drew FitzGerald, "AT&T and Verizon Agree to New Delay of 5G Rollout," *Wall Street Journal*, January 3, 2022.

10. Tina Bellon and Eric M. Johnson, "From Boeing to Mercedes, a U.S. Worker Rebellion Swells over Vaccine Mandates," Thomson Reuters Foundation News, November 2, 2021.

11. Nicole Ogrysko, "Biden Will Now Require Vaccines for All Federal Employees via New Executive Order," Federal News Network, September 9, 2021.

Chapter Three: Why Shortages Will Persist

1. Anthea Nicolas and Nicolas Lamp, *Six Faces of Globalization: Who Wins, Who Loses, and Why It Matters* (Cambridge, MA: Harvard University Press, 2021).

2. Jeff Mordock, "Biden Administration Won't Remove Tariff That Experts Say Could Ease Supply Chain Bottleneck," *Washington Times*, December 3, 2021.

3. Julian Evans-Pritchard, "U.S. China Trade Deal Stalemate Will Drag On," Capital Economics, February 10, 2022.

4. Jeffrey Wilson, "Australia Shows the World What Decoupling from China Looks Like," *Foreign Affairs*, November 9, 2021.

5. Daniel Michaels and Drew Hinshaw, "EU Hits Back at China over Trade Limits, Taking Lithuania Fight Global," *Wall Street Journal*, January 27, 2022.

6. Allysia Finley, "California Is the Supply Chain's Weakest Link," *Wall Street Journal*, November 4, 2021.

7. Madeleine Ngo and Ana Swanson, "The Biggest Kink in America's Supply Chain: Not Enough Truckers," *New York Times*, November 9, 2021.

8. Ngo and Swanson, "The Biggest Kink in America's Supply Chain."

9. Daniel Michaels, "China's Growing Access to Global Shipping Data Worries U.S.," *Wall Street Journal*, December 20, 2021.

10. Interview of Kendra Phillips by Craig Fuller, CEO of FreightWaves, Domestic Supply Chain Summit, December 15, 2021.

11. Thomas V. Inglesby et al., "Disease Mitigation Measures in the Control of Pandemic Influenza," *Biosecurity and Bioterrorism: Biodefense Strategy, Practice, and Science* 4, no. 4 (2006), https://pubmed.ncbi .nlm.nih.gov/17238820/.

12. Chris Bertman, "'Have the Military Run It': CNBC's Jim Cramer Wants Military Enforcement of Vaccine Mandate," *Daily Caller*, November 30, 3021.

13. "Ambassador Bridge Protest: Truckers Block Vital Canada-US Border Crossing," BBC News, February 9, 2022.

14. Liyan Qi and Natasha Khan, "Covid-19 Lockdowns Ripple Across China—'I Wonder How Long I Can Hang On,'" *Wall Street Journal*, November 4, 2021.

15. Data and analysis in this section are mostly taken from Steven E. Koonin, *Unsettled: What Climate Science Tells Us, What It Doesn't, and Why It Matters* (Dallas: BenBella Books, 2021).

16. Edward N. Luttwak, "From Geopolitics to Geo-Economics: Logic of Conflict, Grammar of Commerce," *National Interest*, no. 20 (Summer 1990): 17–23.

17. James Rogers et al., "Breaking the China Supply Chain: How the 'Five Eyes' Can Decouple from Strategic Dependency," Henry Jackson Society, May 2020.

18. Steven Lee Meyers and Alexandra Stevenson, "China's Births Hit Historic Low, a Political Problem for Beijing," *New York Times*, January

17, 2022, quoting Professor Yi Fuxian of the University of Wisconsin–Madison.

19. Darrell Bricker and John Ibbitson, *Empty Planet: The Shock of Global Population Decline* (New York: Broadway Books, 2020), 163.

20. Bricker and Ibbitson, *Empty Planet*, 163.

21. Thomas J. Duesterberg, "Economic Cracks in the Great Wall of China: Is China's Current Economic Model Sustainable?," Hudson Institute, December 2021, 11.

22. Michael Beckley and Hal Brands, "The End of China's Rise," *Foreign Affairs*, October 1, 2015.

23. Daniel H. Rosen, "China's Economic Reckoning," *Foreign Affairs*, July/August 2021.

24. Duesterberg, "Economic Cracks in the Great Wall of China," 40.

25. Thilo Hanemann et al., "Two Way Street—An Outbound Investment Screening Regime for the United States?," Rhodium Group, January 26, 2022.

26. See Beckley and Brands, "The End of China's Rise," and Hal Brands and Michael Beckley, "China Is a Declining Power—and That's the Problem," *Foreign Policy*, September 24, 2021.

27. Jared M. McKinney and Peter Harris, "Broken Nest: Deterring China from Invading Taiwan," *U.S. Army War College Quarterly: Parameters* 51, no. 4, article 4 (November 17, 2021), 23–36.

28. Rogers et al., "Breaking the China Supply Chain," 37.

29. "Background Press Call by Senior Administration Officials on Russia Ukraine Economic Deterrence Measures," White House, January 25, 2022.

Chapter Four: Will Inflation Linger?

1. Frederick Taylor, *The Downfall of Money: Germany's Hyperinflation and the Destruction of the Middle Class* (New York: Bloomsbury Press, 2013), 226.

2. Adam Tooze, as quoted in an interview by Cameron Adabi, "The Fall and Rise of the Russian Ruble," *Foreign Policy*, April 8, 2022.

3. Thomas Barrabi, "Inflation Hits Another 40-Year High as Consumer Prices Surge to 7.5%," *New York Post*, February 10, 2022.

4. This data and the following price-increase data are taken from the U.S. Bureau of Labor Statistics, Consumer Price Index: 2021 in Review, January 14, 2022 (prices not seasonally adjusted), https://www.bls.gov/opub/ted/2022/consumer-price-index-2021-in-review.htm.

5. Consumer Price Index, Federal Reserve Bank of Minneapolis, https://www.minneapolisfed.org/about-us/monetary-policy/inflation-calculator/consumer-price-index-1913-.
6. See Stephanie Kelton, *The Deficit Myth: Modern Monetary Theory and the Birth of the People's Economy* (New York: Public Affairs, 2020).
7. See Darrell Bricker and John Ibbitson, *Empty Planet: The Shock of Global Population Decline* (New York: Broadway Books, 2020); and Charles Goodhart and Manoj Pradhan, *The Great Demographic Reversal: Ageing Societies, Waning Inequality, and an Inflation Revival* (London: Palgrave Macmillan, 2020).
8. Walter Scheidel, *The Great Leveler: Violence and the History of Inequality from the Stone Age to the Twenty-First Century* (Princeton, NJ: Princeton University Press, 2017).
9. Larry H. Summers, "Trump's $2,000 Stimulus Checks Are a Big Mistake," *Bloomberg*, December 27, 2020.

Chapter Five: Is Deflation the Threat?

1. Jeremy Grantham, "Let the Wild Rumpus Begin," GMO Jeremy Grantham Viewpoints, January 20, 2022.
2. Daniel Alpert, "Inflation in the 21st Century," Cornell Research Academy of Development, Law, and Economics, October 2021. Much of the analysis of why conditions today are not supportive of inflation in the U.S. in this section are based on Alpert's work in this paper.
3. Federal Reserve Press Release, January 26, 2022, Board of Governors of the Federal System, https://www.federalreserve.gov/monetarypolicy/files/monetary20220126a1.pdf.
4. Grantham, "Let the Wild Rumpus Begin."
5. Louis-Vincent Gave, "Of Prices, Profits, Energy and Markets," Gavekal Research, January 4, 2022.
6. Gave, "Of Prices, Profits, Energy and Markets," 3.
7. Grantham, "Let the Wild Rumpus Begin," 7.
8. Jeff Snider, "Financial Market Indicators of Global Liquidity Risks," Alhambra Partners, June 15, 2019.
9. Carmen M. Reinhart, Vincent R. Reinhart, and Kenneth S. Rogoff, "Public Debt Overhangs: Advanced Economy Episodes Since 1800," *Journal of Economic Perspectives* 26, no 3 (Summer 2012), 69–86.
10. Jeremy B. Rudd, "Why Do We Think That Inflation Expectations Matter for Inflation? (And Should We?)," Board of Governors of the Federal Reserve System, Series 2021-062, September 23, 2021.

Conclusion

1. Victor Davis Hanson, "Why Ideology Is the Ancient Enemy of Civilization," *Las Vegas Review-Journal*, February 12, 2022.
2. Ambrose Evans-Pritchard, "Emmanuel Macron's 'Confederation' May Be the Perfect Home for Brexit Britain," *The Telegraph*, May 13, 2022.
3. See James Rickards, *The New Case for Gold* (New York: Portfolio/Penguin, 2016).

SELECTED SOURCES

Articles

Acemoglu, Daron. "The Supply-Chain Mess." Project Syndicate, December 2, 2021.

Acemoglu, Daron, Vasco M. Carvalho, Asuman Ozdaglar, and Alireza Tahbaz-Salehi. "The Network Origins of Aggregate Fluctuations," *Econometrica* 80, no. 5 (September 2012): 1977–2016.

Alic, Haris. "Detour Ahead: Biden Infrastructure Package Faces Delays from Workforce Shortage, Supply Chain Snares." *Washington Times*, November 11, 2021.

Alpert, Daniel. "Inflation in the 21st Century." Cornell Research Academy of Development, Law, and Economics, October 2021.

"Ambassador Bridge Protest: Truckers Block Vital Canada-US Border Crossing," BBC News, February 9, 2022.

Anthes, Emily, and Noah Weiland. "As Omicron Spreads, Officials Ponder What It Means to Be 'Fully Vaccinated.'" *New York Times*, December 29, 2021.

Antràs, Pol, and Elhanan Helpman. "Global Sourcing." *Journal of Political Economy* 112, no. 3 (2004): 552–80.

Barrabi, Thomas. "Inflation Hits Another 40-Year High as Consumer Prices Surge to 7.5%." *New York Post*, February 10, 2022.

———. "Walmart Faces Backlash on Chinese Social Media." *New York Post*, December 27, 2021.

Bass, George F. "Oldest Known Shipwreck Reveals Splendors of the Bronze Age." *National Geographic* 172, no. 6 (December 1987): 692–733.

Beckley, Michael, and Hal Brands. "The End of China's Rise." *Foreign Affairs*, October 1, 2021.

Bellon, Tina, and Eric M. Johnson. "From Boeing to Mercedes, a U.S. Worker Rebellion Swells over Vaccine Mandates." Thomson Reuters Foundation News, November 2, 2021.

Bergman, Judith. "China in Latin America—Part 1." Gatestone Institute, December 23, 2021.

Bertman, Chris. "'Have the Military Run It': CNBC's Jim Cramer Wants Military Enforcement of Vaccine Mandate." *Daily Caller*, November 30, 3021.

Blankley, Bethany. "Vaccine Mandate Could Drive Truckers Off the Road, Worsen Supply Chain Crisis, Industry Warns." Just the News, November 8, 2021.

Bobrowsky, Meghan. "Intel to Invest at Least $20 Billion in Ohio Chip-Making Factory." *Wall Street Journal*, January 21, 2022.

Bonifai, Niccolo W., Ifran Nooruddin, and Nita Rudra. "The Hidden Threat to Globalization." *Foreign Affairs*, December 3, 2021.

Bordoff, Jason. "Why This Energy Crisis Is Different." *Foreign Policy*, September 24, 2021.

Borrell, Josep, and Vladis Dombrovskis. "Joint Statement on China's Measures Against Lithuania." EIN Presswire, December 8, 2021.

Bradley Jr., Robert. "The Climate Movement and Its 10 Biggest Failures of 2021." Natural Gas Now, December 29, 2021.

Brands, Hal. "In the Next War, America's Homeland Will Be a Target." *Bloomberg*, December 15, 2021.

———. "The Overstretched Superpower." *Foreign Affairs*, January 18, 2022.

Brands, Hal, and Michael Beckley. "China Is a Declining Power—and That's the Problem." *Foreign Policy*, September 24, 2021.

———. "Washington Is Preparing for the Wrong War with China." *Foreign Affairs*, December 16, 2021.

Buchman, Cassie, and Alex Caprariello. "Looters Raid L.A. Cargo Trains, Leaving Tracks Covered in Damaged Packages." KTLA5 Los Angeles, January 14, 2022.

Byrne, Kerry J., Steven Vago, and Melissa Klein. "Candy Cane Shortage Fueled by COVID, Weak Peppermint Harvest." *New York Post*, December 18, 2021.

Calder, Rich. "Supermarkets Face Empty Shelves from Labor Shortages, Shipping Costs." *New York Post*, January 15, 2022.

Camara, Santiago. "Spillovers of US Interest Rates—Monetary Policy & Information Effects." Arxiv.org, November 17, 2021, arXiv:2111.08631v1.

Casarotto, Francesco. "Europe's Fertilizer Crisis Could Become a Food Crisis." *Geopolitical Futures*, December 14, 2021.

Catenacci, Thomas. "Biden Mulls Shutting Down Pipeline That Supplies Energy to Midwest." *Daily Caller*, November 8, 2021.

"China's Major Port City Under Partial Lockdown to Curb Virus Surge." Global Times, January 4, 2022.

Choi, Joseph. "Top Economist Says Supply Chain Issues Could 'Contaminate' Demand." *The Hill*, November 28, 2021.

Chokshi, Niraj. "Why Christmas Gifts Are Arriving on Time This Year." *New York Times*, December 22, 2021.

Chung, Christine. "Facing a Shortage of Truck Drivers, Pilot Program Turns to Teenagers." *New York Times*, January 9, 2022.

Clark, Joseph. "Cargo Ship Backup Worsens After Biden Attempts to Untangle Supply Chain." *Washington Times*, November 15, 2021.

Cochrane, John M. "The Revenge of Supply." Project Syndicate, October 22, 2021.

Coleman, Justine. "WTO Faces Renewed Scrutiny amid Omicron Threat." *The Hill*, December 5, 2021.

Colias, Mike. "Ford Steps into the Chips Business." *Wall Street Journal*, November 18, 2021.

Colibasanu, Antonia. "Globalization After the Pandemic." Geopolitical Futures, January 3, 2022.

Cookson, Richard. "Shunning Fossil Fuels Too Soon May Be Ruinous." *Bloomberg*, October 21, 2021.

Cox, Jeff. "Wholesale Prices Measure Rises 9.6% in November from a Year Ago, the Fastest Pace on Record." CNBC, December 14, 2021.

Coyle, Diane, et al. "Supply-Shock Therapy." Project Syndicate, October 21, 2021.

Crane, Emily. "Hundreds More Flights Canceled over COVID-Driven Staffing Issues." *New York Post*, December 27, 2021.

Curran, Enda. "The 'Mother of All' Supply Shocks Lurks in China's Covid Crackdowns." *Bloomberg*, January 12, 2022.

Dacey, Elisha. "Crossing Delayed Monday at Manitoba-U.S. Border as Truckers Protest Vaccine Mandate." Global News, January 17, 2022.

Datoc, Christian. "The Supply Chain Crisis Is Exacerbated by Biden's Union Allies." *Washington Examiner*, October 26, 2021.

Daye, Chu. "China Unveils State-Owned Logistics Giant to Improve Competitiveness Globally." Global Times, December 6, 2021.

DeLong, Bradford J. "Why All the Inflation Worries?" Project Syndicate, November 8, 2021.

DePasquale, Ron. "Covid Live Updates: U.S. Daily Record for Cases Is Broken." *New York Times*, December 29, 2011.

Domm, Patti. "Not Since Americans Came Home from World War II Has Inflation Run Through the Economy Like It Is Now." CNBC, November 24, 2021.

Dorsey, James M. "China's Belt and Road Initiative: Slowly Imploding?" The Globalist, December 17, 2021.

Duesterberg, Thomas J. "Economic Cracks in the Great Wall of China: Is China's Current Economic Model Sustainable?" Hudson Institute, December 2021.

Economy, Elizabeth. "Xi Jinping's New World Order." *Foreign Affairs*, January/February 2022.

Evans, Ailan. "Biden Administration Relying on Informants to Enforce Vaccine Mandates." *Daily Caller*, November 10, 2021.

Evans-Pritchard, Ambrose. "Europe's Energy Crisis Is Fast Turning into a Political and Strategic Disaster." *Daily Telegraph*, December 21, 2021.

———. "Omicron Is a Horrible Dilemma for Zero-COVID China." *Daily Telegraph*, December 7, 2021.

Evans-Pritchard, Julian. "U.S. China Trade Deal Stalemate Will Drag On." Capital Economics, February 10, 2022.

Federal Aviation Administration. "Airworthiness Directives; Transport and Commuter Category Airplanes." *Federal Register* 86, no. 234 (December 9, 2021): 69984–87.

Federal Trade Commission. "FTC Launches Inquiry into Supply Chain Disruptions." Press Release, November 29, 2021.

Feuer, Will. "Cargo Thefts Spike as Backlog of Container Ships Continues to Grow." *New York Post*, November 3, 2021.

———. "Inflation Crisis Slamming US Troops, Pentagon Warns of 'Readiness Issue.'" *New York Post*, November 18, 2021.

———. "Plot of Digital Land in the Metaverse Sells for Record $2.43 Million." *New York Post*, November 25, 2021.

Fickenscher, Lisa. "COVID's Labor Market Shakeup: This Is Where the Missing 3.6M Workers Went." *New York Post*, December 17, 2021.

———. "Food Prices Are Reportedly Expected to Rise Again in January." *New York Post*, December 27, 2021.

Fickling, David, Brooke Sutherland, Daniel Moss, and Tom Orlik. "Everything You Need to Know About the Global Supply Chain Crisis." *Bloomberg*, November 26, 2021.

Finley, Allysia. "California Is the Supply Chain's Weakest Link." *Wall Street Journal*, November 4, 2021.

FitzGerald, Drew. "AT&T, Verizon Refuse FAA Request to Delay 5G Launch." *Wall Street Journal*, January 2, 2022.

Flatley, Daniel. "Democrat Blocks Uyghur Forced-Labor Bill over Child Tax Credit." *Bloomberg*, December 15, 2021.

Fosler, Gail. "Awaiting Powell's Next Pivot." GailFosler Group, December 21, 2021.

Fosler, Gail, and Frank Zuroski. "China's Modernization at Risk." GailFosler Group, November 8, 2021.

———. "Fed Asset Purchases Have No Effect on Credit." GailFosler Group, December 20, 2021.

Friedman, George. "The Republic of COVID-19." Geopolitical Futures, December 13, 2021.

Frishberg, Hannah. "Cream Cheese Shortage Forces Junior's to Pause Cheesecake Production." *New York Post,* December 9, 2021.

Galvin, Gabby. "Nearly 1 in 5 Health Care Workers Have Quit Their Jobs During the Pandemic." *Morning Consult*, October 4, 2021.

Gamio, Lazaro, and Peter Goodman. "How the Supply Chain Crisis Unfolded." *New York Times,* December 5, 2021.

Gangitano, Alex. "Rising Omicron Cases, CDC Guidance Threatens Businesses." *The Hill*, December 29, 2021.

Gave, Louis-Vincent. "Of Prices, Profits, Energy and Markets." Gavekal Research, January 4, 2022.

Georgieve, Kristalina, and Ceyla Pazarbasioglu. "The G20 Common Framework for Debt Treatments Must Be Stepped Up." International Monetary Fund IMF Blog, December 2, 2021.

Gertz, Bill. "Global Reach: China Expands Port and Military Base Network to Boost Commerce, Clout." *Washington Times*, January 4, 2022.

Giustra, Frank. "Is the U.S. Purposely Under-Reporting Inflation? It's Hard Not to Wonder When You Look at How It's Calculated." *Toronto Star,* January 11, 2022.

Glenn, Mike. "Aircraft Carrier Moves Closer to Deployment." *Washington Times*, December 24, 2021.

Goodman, Peter S. "A Car a Minute Used to Flow Through Here, but Chaos Now Reigns." *New York Times*, December 2, 2021.

———. "How the Supply Chain Broke, and Why It Won't Be Fixed Anytime Soon." *New York Times*, October 31, 2021.

———. "The Real Reason America Doesn't Have Enough Truck Drivers." *New York Times*, February 9, 2022.

Goodman, Peter S, and Keith Bradsher. "The World Is Still Short of Everything. Get Used to It." *New York Times*, November 14, 2021.

Grande, Peggy. "America's Supply Chain Issues Begin in Our Schools, Not Our Shipyards." *Washington Times*, October 29, 2021.

Grantham, Jeremy. "Let the Wild Rumpus Begin." GMO Jeremy Grantham Viewpoints, January 20, 2022.

Greenfield, Daniel. "Can Feminism Destroy China?" Sultan Knish, December 26, 2021.

Halaschak, Zachary. "Truckers Needed to Help Alleviate Supply Chain Woes Across the Nation." *Washington Examiner*, November 16, 2021.

Hamby, Chris, and Sheryl Gay Stolberg. "Beneath a Covid Vaccine Debacle, 30 Years of Government Culpability." *New York Times*, December 23, 2021.

Hanemann, Thilo, et al. "Two Way Street—An Outbound Investment Screening Regime for the United States?" Rhodium Group, January 26, 2022.

Hanson, Victor Davis. "Hosea's Prophecy for the Democrats." To The Point News, December 28, 2021.

———. "Why Ideology Is the Ancient Enemy of Civilization." *Las Vegas Review-Journal*, February 12, 2022.

———. "Why the Left Always Projects." To The Point News, November 16, 2021.

Hawes, Clarissa. "Exclusive: Central Freight Lines to Begin Closure Proceedings Monday." FreightWaves, December 11, 2021.

Hawley, Sen. Josh. "The Only Way to Solve Our Supply Chain Crisis Is to Rethink Trade." *New York Times*, October 29, 2021.

Hayashi, Yuka. "Retreat from Globalization Adds to Inflation Risks." *Wall Street Journal*, December 5, 2021.

Henninger, Daniel. "No, Joe Biden Didn't Save Christmas." *Wall Street Journal*, December 29, 2021.

Higgins, Tim. "Apple Warns of Supply Chain Woes While Amazon Faces Increased Labor Costs." *Wall Street Journal*, October 28, 2021.

Hille, Kathrin. "Lithuania Shows China's Coercive Trade Tactics Are Hard to Counter." *Financial Times*, December 14, 2021.

Hiller, Jennifer. "Wind Manufacturers Blown Off Course." *Wall Street Journal*, November 6, 2021.

Hiller, Jennifer, and Katherine Blunt. "Wind-Turbine Makers Struggle to Profit from Renewable-Energy Boom." *Wall Street Journal*, August 23, 2021.

Hunt, J. B. "Dwell: How Intermodal Terminal Congestion Impacts Capacity and Service." J. B. Hunt Transport, Inc. White Paper, 2015.

Jiang, Yun, and Jordan Schneider. "The United States Needs More Wine to Stand Up to Chinese Bullying." *Foreign Policy*, December 10, 2021.

Johnson, Keith. "Winter Is Coming, and It's Only a Preview." *Foreign Policy*, October 19, 2021.

Johnson, Stephen, and Dominic Giannini. "Unemployed Australians Could Be Forced to Work for Their Centrelink Benefits to Solve Supply Chain Crisis Leaving Supermarket Shelves Bare." *Daily Mail*, January 12, 2022.

Kang, Jaewon. "Supermarkets Play Supply-Chain 'Whack-a-Mole' to Keep Products on Shelves." *Wall Street Journal*, October 31, 2021.

Kelley, Alexandra. "FTC Investigating Major Retailers over Supply Chain Backlog." Nextgov, November 30, 2021.

Kelly, Laura, and Brett Samuels. "Biden Sparks Confusion, Cleanup on Russia-Ukraine Remarks." *The Hill*, January 1, 2022.

Klatzkin, Shmuel. "Lockdowns Have Continuing Tragic Consequences." *American Spectator*, November 19, 2021.

Kofman, Michael. "Putin's Wager in Russia's Standoff with the West." War on the Rocks, January 24, 2022.

Kofman, Michael, and Andrea Kendall-Taylor. "The Myth of Russian Decline." *Foreign Affairs*, November/December 2021.

Kolmar, Chris. "17 Stunning Supply Chain Statistics [2021]: Facts, Figures, and Trends." Zippia, September 28, 2021.

Kuo, Simon. "Progress in Importation of US Equipment Dispels Doubts on SMIC's Capacity Expansion for Mature Notes for Now, Says TrendForce." TrendForce Press Center, March 5, 2021.

Lane, Sylvan. "Consumer Prices Rise 0.9 Percent in October, 6.2 Percent in Past Year." *The Hill*, November 10, 2021.

LaRocco, Lori Ann. "HIDA: Millions of Critical Medical Supplies Delayed at Congested Ports." FreightWaves, December 17, 2021.

Lee, Hau, V. Padmanabhan, and Seungjin Whang. "The Bullwhip Effect in Supply Chains." *MIT Sloan Management Review*, Spring 1997.

Lee, Julian. "Saudis Are Right to Warn of a Collapse in Oil Supply." *Bloomberg*, December 19, 2021.

Lee, Yen Nee. "2 Charts Show How Much the World Depends on Taiwan for Semiconductors." CNBC, March 15, 2021.

Lee, Yimou, Norihiko Shirouzu, and David Lague. "T-Day, The Battle for Taiwan." Reuters, December 27, 2021.

Letter from the Secretary of Transportation and the FAA Administrator to AT&T and Verizon, December 31, 2021.

Lichtenstein, Sam. "What Unrest Provoked by Inflation Could Look Like in 2022." Stratfor, December 27, 2021.

Lighthizer, Robert. "The Era of Offshoring U.S. Jobs Is Over." *New York Times*, May 11, 2020.

Lim, Naomi. "Biden Supply Chain Spin Adds Political Kinks to Policy Response." *Washington Examiner*, December 14, 2021.

Lincicome, Scott. "America's Broken Supply Chain." *Washington Examiner*, October 19, 2021.

Liu, Jiangwei, and Xiaohong Huang. "Forecasting Crude Oil Price Using Event Extraction." IEEE Access 9 (2021): 149067–76.

Liu, Melinda. "China's Energy Conundrum." *Foreign Policy*, November 5, 2021.

Loop, Emma. "Black Friday Deals Expected to Be Weaker This Year amid Supply Chain Problems." *Washington Examiner*, November 9, 2021.

Lorenz, Edward N. "Deterministic Nonperiodic Flow." *Journal of the Atmospheric Sciences* 20 (March 1963).

Lott, Jeremy. "The Administration's 'Mission Accomplished' on Container Bottleneck Didn't Hold Up." *Washington Examiner*, November 2, 2021.

———. "Rail Freight Is at the Center of the Supply Chain Crisis." *Washington Examiner*, October 26, 2021.

———. "Shortage of Electronic Parts Making Car Repairs More Expensive." *Washington Examiner*, December 7, 2021.

———. "The Supply Chain Crisis Puts Pete Buttigieg in an Unfriendly Spotlight." *Washington Examiner*, December 14, 2021.

Luttwak, Edward N. "From Geopolitics to Geo-Economics: Logic of Conflict, Grammar of Commerce." *National Interest* 20, no. 20 (Summer 1990): 17–23.

Maheshwari, Sapna, and Michael Corkery. "Retailers Scramble to Attract Workers Ahead of the Holidays." *New York Times*, November 8, 2021.

Mahtani, Shibani. "Hong Kong Bans All Flights from U.S. and Seven Other Countries as Omicron Spreads." *Washington Post*, January 5, 2021.

Makarov, Igor, and Antoinette Schoar. "Blockchain Analysis of the Bitcoin Market." SSRN Abstract 3942181, October 13, 2021.

Malsin, Jared. "Turkey's Currency Crisis Slams the Nutella Global Supply Chain." *Wall Street Journal*, December 20, 2021.

McCabe, Caitlin. "Day Traders as 'Dumb Money'? The Pros Are Now Paying Attention." *Wall Street Journal*, January 16, 2022.

McKinney, Jared M., and Peter Harris. "Broken Nest: Deterring China from Invading Taiwan." *U.S. Army War College Quarterly: Parameters* 51, no. 4, article 4 (November 17, 2021): 23–36.

Menge, Margaret. "Indiana Life Insurance CEO Says Deaths Are Up 40% Among People Ages 18–64." Center Square Contributor, January 1, 2022.

Metcalf, Tom, and Alex Morales. "Carney Unveils $130 Trillion in Climate Finance Commitments." *Bloomberg*, November 3, 2021.

Meyers, Steven Lee, and Alexandra Stevenson. "China's Births Hit Historic Low, a Political Problem for Beijing." *New York Times*, January 17, 2022.

Michaels, Daniel. "China's Growing Access to Global Shipping Data Worries U.S." *Wall Street Journal*, December 20, 2021.

Michaels, Daniel, and Drew Hinshaw. "EU Hits Back at China over Trade Limits, Taking Lithuania Fight Global." *Wall Street Journal*, January 27, 2022.

Michta, Andrew A. "Russia and China's Dangerous Decline." *Wall Street Journal*, December 14, 2021.

Miller, Greg. "It's Official: 96 Container Ships Are Waiting to Dock at So-Cal Ports," FreightWaves, December 5, 2021.

———. "Ships in California Logjam Now Stuck Off Mexico, Taiwan and Japan." FreightWaves, December 5, 2021.

Moore, Mark. "Top Economist Warns Conditions Are Ripe for 1970s-Style 'Stagflation.'" *New York Post*, November 28, 2021.

Moran, Rick. "Report: Russia Is Planning a Military Offensive Against Ukraine in Early 2022." PJ Media, December 4, 2021.

Mordock, Jeff. "Biden Administration Won't Remove Tariff That Experts Say Could Ease Supply Chain Bottleneck." *Washington Times*, December 3, 2021.

Moynihan, Lydia. "Wall Street's Smartest Hedge Funds Are Now Getting Smacked by Inflation." *New York Post*, November 3, 2021.

Murphy, Colin. "Covid Zero Challenge Spells Trouble for Xi." *Bloomberg*, January 7, 2022.

Myllyvirta, Lauri. "The Real Reasons Behind China's Energy Crisis." *Foreign Policy*, October 7, 2021.

Nakashima, Ellen, and Jeanne Whalen. "U.S. Threatens Use of Novel Export Control to Damage Russia's Strategic Industries If Moscow Invades Ukraine." *Washington Post*, January 23, 2022.

Newman, Kesse, and Jaewon Kang. "U.S. Food Supply Is Under Pressure, from Plants to Store Shelves." *Wall Street Journal*, January 23, 2022.

Ngo, Madeleine, and Ana Swanson. "The Biggest Kink in America's Supply Chain: Not Enough Truckers." *New York Times*, November 9, 2021.

Ogrysko, Nicole. "Biden Will Now Require Vaccines for All Federal Employees via New Executive Order." Federal News Network, September 9, 2021.

Olen, Helaine. "American Airlines' Cancellations Are a Window into Why People Are So Upset with the Economy." *Washington Post*, November 2, 2021.

O'Neil, Shannon K. "Why the Supply Chain Slowdown Will Persist." *Foreign Policy*, December 21, 2021.

O'Neill, Jesse. "Hundreds of More Flights Canceled as Omicron Surge Wreaks Havoc on Christmas Travel." *New York Post*, December 26, 2021.

Orr, Michael. "Four Scenarios for Rising Russia-Ukraine Tensions." Stratfor, December 23, 2021.

Ortiz, Alfredo. "Bideninflation Is the Next Pandemic." RealClearPolitics, November 12, 2021.

Palacio, Ana. "Five Visions for a New International Order." Project Syndicate, October 13, 2021.

Petrova, Magdalena. "We Traced What It Takes to Make an iPhone, from Its Initial Design to the Components and Raw Materials Needed to Make It a Reality." CNBC, December 14, 2018.

Philipp, Joshua. "'I'm the Big Problem': COVID-19 Whistleblower on Why She Won't Be Silent Despite Threats to Her Life." Epoch Times, December 21, 2021.

Porter, Jack. "Viewpoint: 'As I See It' from the Trucking Activist—To Vax or Not to Vax." FreightWaves, November 17, 2021.

Puzder, Andy, and Will Coggin. "Meatpackers Are Biden's Latest Inflation Scapegoat." *Wall Street Journal*, January 9, 2022.

Qi, Liyan, and Natasha Khan. "Covid-19 Lockdowns Ripple Across China—'I Wonder How Long I Can Hang On.'" *Wall Street Journal*, November 4, 2021.

Rasmussen Reports. "Americans Concerned About Supply Chain Crisis, Expect Federal Action," October 14, 2021.

———. "82% Worry Supply-Chain Problems Could Cause Shortages," November 12, 2021.

Rasoolinejad, Mohammad. "Universal Basic Income: The Last Bullet in the Darkness." Arxiv.org, arXiv:1910:05658v2, November 24, 2021.

Rees, Daniel, and Phurichai Rungcharoenkitkul. "Bottlenecks: Causes and Macroeconomic Implications." Bank for International Settlements, BIS Bulletin 48, November 11, 2021.

Reilly, Patrick. "Champagne Shortage Ahead of New Year's Eve Due to Supply Chain Issues: Report." *New York Post*, December 30, 2021.

Reinhart, Carmen M., and Clemens Graf von Luckner. "The Return of Global Inflation." Project Syndicate, February 11, 2022.

Reinhart, Carmen M., Vincent R. Reinhart, and Kenneth S. Rogoff. "Public Debt Overhangs: Advanced Economy Episodes Since 1800." *Journal of Economic Perspectives* 26, no. 3 (Summer 2012): 69–86.

Reuters. "Chinese Manufacturing Hub Fights Its First 2021 COVID-19 Outbreak," December 13, 2021.

———. "Delta, Alaska Air Cancel Hundreds of Flights Due to Bad Weather, Omicron Cases," December 29, 2021.

Richard, Hillary. "A Perfect Storm of Disruptions Will Create a Global Champagne Shortage." *Wine Enthusiast*, December 15, 2021.

Rogers, James, et al. "Breaking the China Supply Chain: How the 'Five Eyes' Can Decouple from Strategic Dependency." Henry Jackson Society, May 2020.

Rogoff, Kenneth. "Why Is the IMF Trying to Be an Aid Agency." Project Syndicate, January 3, 2021.

Roos, Michael, and Matthias Reccius. "Narratives in Economics." Arxiv.org, arXiv:2109.02331, September 6, 2021.

Rosen, Daniel H. "China's Economic Reckoning." *Foreign Affairs*, July/August 2021.

Rudd, Jeremy B. "Why Do We Think That Inflation Expectations Matter for Inflation? (And Should We?)." Board of Governors of the Federal Reserve System, Series 2021-062, September 23, 2021.

Salai, Sean. "Pandemic, Supply Shortages Transform Black Friday into Monthlong Event." *Washington Times*, November 11, 2021.

Scheer, Steven. "IMF, 10 Countries Simulate Cyber Attack on Global Financial System." NASDAQ, December 9, 2021.

Schnell, Mychael. "Biden Adviser Points to Spending Package as Solution to Inflation." *The Hill*, November 14, 2021.

Scott, Heather. "IMF Warns of 'Economic Collapse' Unless G20 Extends Debt Relief." Agence France-Presse, December 2, 2021.

"SCRLC Emerging Risks in the Supply Chain 2013." Supply Chain Risk Leadership Council White Paper, 2013.

Seneff, Stephanie, and Greg Nigh. "Worse Than the Disease? Reviewing Some Possible Unintended Consequences of the mRNA Vaccines Against COVID-19." *International Journal of Vaccine Theory, Practice, and Research* 2, no. 1 (May 10, 2021): 38–79.

Shaffer, Brenda. "Is Europe's Energy Crisis a Preview of America's?" *Foreign Policy*, October 5, 2021.

Shan, Shi, and Anne Zhang. "US and China Race to Control the Future Through Artificial Intelligence." Epoch Times, November 27, 2021.

Shepardson, David. "Biden Holding Meeting on Supply Chain Issues." Reuters, December 22, 2021.

Shields, Todd, and Alan Levin. "Buttigieg Asks AT&T, Verizon to Delay 5G over Aviation Concerns." *Bloomberg*, December 31, 2021.

Smialek, Jeanna. "Consumer Prices Popped Again in December as Policymakers Await an Elusive Peak." *New York Times*, January 12, 2022.

Smialek, Jeanna, Sara Chodosh, and Ben Casselman. "Millennials Confront High Inflation for the First Time." *New York Times*, November 28, 2021.

Smith, Adam M. "SWIFT and Certain Punishment for Russia?" *Foreign Affairs*, January 4, 2022.

Smith, Brandon. "Here's Why U.S. Supply Chain Problems Will Only Get Worse." Alt-Market.us, November 6, 2021.

Smith, Jennifer, Paul Berger, and Lydia O'Neal. "Shipping and Logistics Costs Are Expected to Keep Rising in 2022." *Wall Street Journal*, December 19, 2021.

Sneider, Jeff. "Financial Market Indicators of Global Liquidity Risks." Alhambra Partners, June 15, 2019.

Sohn, Jiyoung. "Samsung to Choose Taylor, Texas, for $17 Billion Chipmaking Factory." *Wall Street Journal*, November 22, 2021.

Soper, Spencer, Michael Tobin, and Michael Smith. "Amazon Driver Texts Reveal Chaos as Illinois Tornado Bore Down." *Bloomberg*, December 16, 2021.

Spence, Michael. "Regime Change in the Global Economy." Project Syndicate, January 14, 2022.

———. "Why Are Supply Chains Blocked?" Project Syndicate, November 3, 2021.

Stock, James H., and Mark W. Watson. "Has the Business Cycle Changed and Why?" National Bureau of Economic Research, Working Paper 9127, September 2002.

Stoller, Matt. "What the Great Ammunition Shortage Says About Inflation." BIG, Substack, January 5, 2022.

Stratfor. "South Korea: CJ Logistics Delivery Workers' Strike to Impact Local Businesses," December 28, 2021.

Summers, Lawrence H. "The Fed's Words Still Don't Measure Up to the Challenge of Inflation." *Washington Post*, December 17, 2021.

———. "On Inflation, It's Past Time for Team 'Transitory' to Stand Down." *Washington Post*, November 16, 2021.

———. "Trump's $2,000 Stimulus Checks Are a Big Mistake." *Bloomberg*, December 27, 2020.

"Supply Chain Risk Management: A Compilation of Best Practices." Supply Chain Risk Leadership Council, August 2011.

Swanson, Ana, and Keith Bradsher. "Supply Chain Woes Could Worsen as China Imposes New Covid Lockdowns." *New York Times*, January 16, 2022.

Tan, Huileng. "China Is Imposing Quarantines of Up to 7 Weeks for Cargo Ship Crew, and It's Bad News for the Supply Chain." *Bloomberg*, November 26, 2021.

Tangel, Andrew, and Drew FitzGerald. "AT&T and Verizon Agree to New Delay of 5G Rollout." *Wall Street Journal*, January 3, 2022.

Tankersley, Jim, and Alan Rappeport. "As Prices Rise, Biden Turns to Antitrust Enforcers." *New York Times*, December 25, 2021.

Timiraos, Nick, and Gwynn Guilford. "How Do You Feel About Inflation? The Answer Will Help Determine Its Longevity." *Wall Street Journal*, December 12, 2021.

Tita, Bob, and Austen Hufford. "Workers Sick with Omicron Add to Manufacturing Woes. 'The Hope Was That 2022 Would Get Better.'" *Wall Street Journal*, January 10, 2022.

Tracinski, Robert. "The Left's Magical Thinking." *Washington Examiner*, November 23–30, 2021.

Tracy, Marc, Daniel Victor, Adeel Hassan, and Ana Ley. "Flight Disruptions Continue with Thousands More Cancellations as Omicron Thins Airline Crews." *New York Times*, December 27, 2021.

"Vax Mandates Will Disrupt Supply Chains Further, Truckers Warn." Newsmax, December 3, 2021.

Vigna, Paul. "Bitcoin's 'One Percent' Controls Lion's Share of the Crypto-currency's Wealth." *Wall Street Journal*, December 20, 2021.

Wang, Orange. "Xi Jinping Says China Must Be 'Self-Sufficient' in Energy, Food and Minerals amid Global Challenges." *South China Morning Post*, December 14, 2021.

Weise, Karen, and Glenn Thrush. "As Omicron Overshadows Christmas, Thousands of Flights Are Cancelled." *New York Times*, December 24, 2021.

Welling, Kate. "Disinflation Isn't Dead." Welling on Wall Street 11, no. 15, November 19, 2021.

White House. "Background Press Call by Senior Administration Officials on Russia Ukraine Economic Deterrence Measures." January 25, 2022.

White House. "Building Resilient Supply Chains, Revitalizing American Manufacturing, and Fostering Broad-Based Growth." June 14, 2021.

Williams, Jordan, and Laura Kelly. "Five Things to Know About Russia's Troop Buildup Near Ukraine." *The Hill*, December 6, 2021.

Wilmerding, Harry. "Republican Leaders Slam Biden as 'Inflation Contagion' Plagues the Nation." *Daily Caller*, December 10, 2021.

Wilson, Jeffrey. "Australia Shows the World What Decoupling from China Looks Like." *Foreign Affairs*, November 9, 2021.

Wood, Molly. "Video Games Went from Virtual Currency to Real Money, and It Changed the Business." Marketplace Tech, June 11, 2009.

Xi, Yu. "Birth Rates in 10 Provincial-Level Regions Fall Below 1% in 2020." Global Times, January 4, 2022.

Yang, Stephanie, and Jiyoung Sohn. "Global Chip Shortage 'Is Far from Over' as Wait Times Get Longer." *Wall Street Journal*, October 28, 2021.

Yergin, Daniel. "Oil and War: Why Japan Attacked Pearl Harbor." danielyergin.com, December 2021.

Zhu, Charlie, et al. "China's Property Developers Struggle to Find Buyers for Billions in Assets." *Bloomberg*, November 2, 2021.

Ziobro, Paul, and Tarini Parti. "FTC Asks Amazon, Walmart for Information About Supply-Chain Issues." *Wall Street Journal*, November 29, 2021.

Zumbrun, Josh. "Biden's China and Climate Goals Clash over Solar Panels." *Wall Street Journal*, December 20, 2021.

Books

Allison, Graham. *Destined for War: Can America and China Escape Thucydides' Trap?* Boston: Mariner Books, 2018.

Alpert, Daniel. *The Age of Oversupply: Overcoming the Greatest Challenge to the Global Economy.* New York: Portfolio/Penguin, 2015.

Anton, Michael. *The Stakes: America at the Point of No Return.* Washington, DC: Regnery Publishing, 2020.

Ayers, James B. *Handbook of Supply Chain Management*, 2nd ed. Boca Raton, FL: Auerbach Publication, 2006.

Bricker, Darrell, and John Ibbitson. *Empty Planet: The Shock of Global Population Decline.* New York: Broadway Books, 2020.

Brunnermeier, Markus K. *The Resilient Society.* Colorado Springs: Endeavor Literary Press, 2021.

Carroll, Lewis. *Alice's Adventures in Wonderland.* Vancouver: Royal Classics, 2020.

———. *Through the Looking-Glass.* Vancouver: Royal Classics, 2021.

Chaisson, Eric J. *Cosmic Evolution: The Rise of Complexity in Nature.* Cambridge, MA: Harvard University Press, 2001.

Chopra, Sunil, and Peter Meindl. *Supply Chain Management: Strategy, Planning, and Operation*, 6th ed. Harlow, Essex, UK: Pearson, 2016.

Flynn, Stephen. *America the Vulnerable: How Our Government Is Failing to Protect Us from Terrorism.* New York: HarperCollins, 2004.

Gattorna, John. *Dynamic Supply Chains: Delivering Value Through People*, 2nd ed. Harlow, Essex, UK: Prentice Hall, 2010.

Goldratt, Eliyahu M., and Jeff Cox. *The Goal: A Process of Ongoing Improvement.* Great Barrington, MA: North River Press, 2014.

Goodhart, Charles, and Manoj Pradhan. *The Great Demographic Reversal: Ageing Societies, Waning Inequality, and an Inflation Revival.* London: Palgrave Macmillan, 2020.

Gurri, Martin. *The Revolt of the Public and the Crisis of Authority in the New Millennium.* San Francisco: Stripe Press, 2018.

Hemingway, Ernest. *The Sun Also Rises.* New York: Scribner, 2016.

Hugos, Michael. *Essentials of Supply Chain Management*, 4th ed. Hoboken, NJ: John Wiley & Sons, 2018.

Kelton, Stephanie. *The Deficit Myth: Modern Monetary Theory and the Birth of the People's Economy.* New York: Public Affairs, 2020.

Keynes, John Maynard. *The Economic Consequences of the Peace*, Las Vegas: IAP Press, 2019.

———. *The General Theory of Employment, Interest, and Money.* New York: Harcourt, Brace, Jovanovich, 1964.

Kissinger, Henry, Eric Schmidt, and Daniel Huttenlocher. *The Age of AI: And Our Human Future.* New York: Little, Brown and Company, 2021.

Knapp, Georg Friedrich. *The State Theory of Money*. Eastford, CT: Martino Fine Books, 2013.

Koonin, Steven E. *Unsettled—What Climate Science Tells Us, What It Doesn't, and Why It Matters*. Dallas: BenBella Books, 2021.

LaRocco, Lori Ann. *Trade War: Containers Don't Lie, Navigating the Bluster*. Stamford, CT: Marine Money, 2019.

Leonard, Mark. *The Age of Unpeace: How Connectivity Causes Conflict*. London: Bantam Press, 2021.

Mackinder, Halford. *Democratic Ideals and Reality: The Geographical Pivot of History*. Singapore: Origami Books, 2018.

McDonough, Ashley. *Operations and Supply Chain Management: Essentials You Always Wanted to Know*. Broomfield, CO: Vibrant Publishers, 2020.

McLuhan, Marshall. *The Gutenberg Galaxy: The Making of Typographic Man*. Toronto: University of Toronto Press, 2011.

———. *The Medium and the Light: Reflections on Religion*. Eugene, OR: Wipf & Stock, 1999.

———. *Understanding Me: Lectures and Interviews*. Cambridge, MA: MIT Press, 2003.

———. *Understanding Media: The Extensions of Man*. Cambridge, MA: MIT Press, 1994.

McLuhan, Marshall, and Quentin Fiore. T*he Medium Is the Massage: An Inventory of Effects*. Berkeley, CA: Gingko Press, 1996.

McLuhan, Marshall, and Eric McLuhan. *Laws of Media: The New Science*. Toronto: University of Toronto Press, 1988.

McLuhan, Marshall, and Bruce Powers. *The Global Village: Transformations in World Life and Media in the 21st Century*. Oxford: Oxford University Press, 1992.

Ong, Walter J. *The Presence of the Word: Some Prolegomena for Cultural and Religious History*. Albany: State University of New York Press, 2000.

Prasad, Eswar S. *The Future of Money: How the Digital Revolution Is Transforming Currencies and Finance*. Cambridge, MA: Belknap Press, 2021.

Reinhart, Carmen M., and Kenneth S. Rogoff. *This Time Is Different— Eight Centuries of Financial Follies*. Princeton, NJ: Princeton University Press, 2009.

Rickards, James. *Aftermath: Seven Secrets of Wealth Preservation in the Coming Chaos*. New York: Portfolio/Penguin, 2019.

———. *Currency Wars: The Making of the Next Global Crisis*. New York: Portfolio/Penguin, 2011.

———. *The New Case for Gold*. New York: Portfolio/Penguin, 2016.

———. *The New Great Depression: Winners and Losers in a Post-Pandemic World*. New York: Portfolio/Penguin, 2021.

Roberts, Anthea, and Nicolas Lamp. *Six Faces of Globalization: Who Wins, Who Loses, and Why It Matters*. Cambridge, MA: Harvard University Press, 2021.

Rogoff, Kenneth S. *The Curse of Cash*. Princeton, NJ: Princeton University Press, 2016.

Russell, Stuart. *Human Compatible: Artificial Intelligence and the Problem of Control*. New York: Penguin Books, 2020.

Sarkar, Suman. *The Supply Chain Revolution: Innovative Sourcing and Logistics for a Fiercely Competitive World*. New York: AMACON, 2017.

Sassen, Saskia. *The Global City: New York, London, Tokyo*, 2nd ed. Princeton, NJ: Princeton University Press, 2001.

Scheidel, Walter. *The Great Leveler: Violence and the History of Inequality from the Stone Age to the Twenty-First Century*. Princeton, NJ: Princeton University Press, 2017.

Schreiber, Zvi. *Importing from China: The Experts Guide*. Hong Kong: Freightos, 2021.

Schwab, Klaus, and Thierry Malleret. *COVID-19: The Great Reset*. Geneva: Forum Publishing, 2020.

Schweizer, Peter. *Red-Handed: How American Elites Get Rich Helping China Win*. New York: HarperCollins, 2022.

Sheffi, Yossi. *The Resilient Enterprise: Overcoming Vulnerability for Competitive Advantage*. Cambridge, MA: MIT Press, 2005.

Shiller, Robert J. *Narrative Economics: How Stories Go Viral & Drive Major Economic Events*. Princeton, NJ: Princeton University Press, 2019.

Shlaes, Amity. *Coolidge*. New York: HarperCollins, 2013.

———. *The Forgotten Man: A New History of the Great Depression*. New York: HarperPerennial, 2008.

———. *Great Society: A New History*. New York: HarperCollins, 2019.

Shriver, Lionel. *The Mandibles: A Family, 2029–2047*. New York: HarperCollins, 2016.

Shum, Desmond. *Red Roulette: An Insider's Story of Wealth, Power, Corruption and Vengeance in Today's China*. London: Simon & Schuster, 2021.

Slone, Reuben E., J. Paul Dittmann, and John J. Mentzer. *The New Supply Chain Agenda: The 5 Steps That Drive Real Value*. Boston, MA: Harvard Business Press, 2010.

Somary, Felix. *The Raven of Zürich: The Memoirs of Felix Somary*. New York: St. Martin's Press, 1986.

Stanton, Daniel. *Supply Chain Management for Dummies*, 2nd ed. Hoboken, NJ: John Wiley & Sons, 2021.

Tainter, Joseph A. *The Collapse of Complex Societies*. Cambridge: Cambridge University Press, 1988.

Taylor, Frederick. *The Downfall of Money: Germany's Hyperinflation and the Destruction of the Middle Class*. New York: Bloomsbury Press, 2013.

Tooze, Adam. *Shutdown: How Covid Shook the World's Economy*. New York: Viking Press, 2021.

Wells, H. G. *The New World Order*. New York: Orkos Press, 2014.

———. *The Open Conspiracy: Blue Prints for a World Revolution*. Naples, FL: Albatross Publishers, 2017.

INDEX

Note: Italicized page numbers indicate material in tables or illustrations.

Japan
  birthrates in, *150*
  China's potential invasion
    of, 111
  debt-to-GDP ratio of, 148
  and geoeconomics, 96
  market collapse (1989), 185, 194
  population decline in, 151
  and strategical dependence on
    China, 100
  and Supply Chain 2.0, 200
J.B. Hunt, 79
Jiang Zemin, 98
just-in-time inventory, xix, 48, 60

Kalinowski, Emil, 188–92
Kelton, Stephanie, 148
Keynes, John Maynard, xvi
Keynesian economics, 169
Keystone XL Pipeline, 36, 94
Kissinger, Henry, 109, 125
Klain, Ron, 66
Koonin, Steven E., 86
Korean War, 116
Kuznetsova, Inna, 78

labor
  cheap, xix, 60
  costs of, in Supply Chain 2.0, 201
  and COVID pandemic, 79–80
  demands for higher wages,
    194–96, 202
  and school closings, 82
  and slack in labor utilization, xxi,
    172–73, 203
  strikes/disputes, 18
  See also labor shortages;
    unemployed population
Labor Force Participation Rate
  (LFPR), 160–61
labor shortages
  and aging societies, 153
  and Black Death, 153
  causes of, 36, 66, 173

COVID-related, 25, 36, 80, 161
  and demographic collapse, 164
  and extreme cold weather, 35
  impact on inflation, 160–61
  and linen delays in restaurant
    industry, 15–16
  and non-work subsidized by
    government, 36
  and slack in labor utilization, xxi,
    172–73
  and vaccine requirements, 66
  at Vietnamese parts
    manufacturers, 19
Lamp, Nicolas, 71
LaRocco, Lori Ann, 42, 44
Lean, 47–48
learning/adaptation, 55–56
Lebanon, 148
"Let the Wild Rumpus Begin"
  (Grantham), 167
Lighthizer, Robert, 40
linen delays in restaurant industry,
  15–16
Lithuania, 74, 110, 114
Lomborg, Bjorn, 86
Lorenz, Edward, 56–57, 61
Luttwak, Edward N., 96–97, 111,
  116–17

Ma, Jack, 85
Ma, Pony, 85
Macron, Emmanuel, 201
Malaysia, 25, 108
Manchuria, 37
The Mandibles (Shriver), 12
manufacturing inputs, sourcing
  for, 10
Mao Zedong, 98, 106, 109
Marine Exchange of Southern
  California, 32–33
Maritime and Port Authority of
  Singapore, 18
market collapse, risk of, 184–87
Master Scheduling, 49–50

PENGUIN PARTNERSHIPS

Penguin Partnerships is the Creative Sales and Promotions team at Penguin Random House. We have a long history of working with clients on a wide variety of briefs, specializing in brand promotions, bespoke publishing and retail exclusives, plus corporate, entertainment and media partnerships.

We can respond quickly to briefs and specialize in repurposing books and content for sales promotions, for use as incentives and retail exclusives as well as creating content for new books in collaboration with our partners as part of branded book relationships.

Equally if you'd simply like to buy a bulk quantity of one of our existing books at a special discount, we can help with that too. Our books can make excellent corporate or employee gifts.

Special editions, including personalized covers, excerpts of existing books or books with corporate logos can be created in large quantities for special needs.

We can work within your budget to deliver whatever you want, however you want it.

For more information, please contact
salesenquiries@penguinrandomhouse.co.uk